WHISTLEPUNKS &

GEODUCKS

ALSO BY RON STRICKLAND:

Shank's Mare: A Compendium of Remarkable Walks
River Pigs and Cayuses: Oral Histories from the Pacific Northwest
Vermonters: Oral Histories from Down Country to the Northeast
  Kingdom
Pacific Northwest Trail Guide

and forthcoming from Paragon House

Texans
Cajuns, Crackers, & Tarheels: Oral Histories from the South

WHISTLE

Oral

Histories

from the

Pacific

Northwest

PUNKS & GEODUCKS

RON STRICKLAND

PARAGON HOUSE
NEW YORK

FIRST EDITION, 1990

PUBLISHED IN THE UNITED STATES BY
PARAGON HOUSE
90 FIFTH AVENUE
NEW YORK, NY 10011

DESIGNED BY KATHY KIKKERT

10 9 8 7 6 5 4 3

LIBRARY OF CONGRESS CATALOGING-IN-PUBLICATION DATA
WHISTLEPUNKS AND GEODUCKS : ORAL HISTORIES FROM THE PACIFIC
   NORTHWEST / [EDITED] BY RON STRICKLAND.—1ST ED.
    P. CM.
    ISBN 1-55778-183-4—ISBN 1-55778-316-0 (PBK.)
    1. WASHINGTON (STATE)—SOCIAL LIFE AND CUSTOMS.
    2. WASHINGTON (STATE)—BIOGRAPHY. 3. ORAL HISTORY.
    I. STRICKLAND, RON.
F895.W45 1990
979.7—DC20   89-29737

MANUFACTURED IN THE UNITED STATES OF AMERICA
THIS BOOK IS PRINTED ON ACID-FREE PAPER.

To my cousin Heather Gordon (1941–1986)
To my friend Tom Cole, Himalayan Guide

CONTENTS

ACKNOWLEDGMENTS

I am often asked how I find the interviewees who appear in my books. The answer is actually very simple. In researching *Whistlepunks and Geoducks* I asked everyone I met if he or she knew anyone whose personal story would be somehow typical of an aspect of Washington state. The successes and failures of my initial list led to more lists. My travels led to new names and more travels.

I hope that it is obvious that *Whistlepunks and Geoducks* is the work of many good people. First, I am forever indebted to the interviewees themselves. If my personal pleasure in meeting them is in some small part transmitted to you the reader, I will consider my work a success.

Second, this book would not have been possible without the help of many Washingtonians who steered me toward their favorite friends, relatives, teachers, and neighbors. The following is a partial list of my informants:

Greg Arnold, Director, Makah Cultural and Research Center, Neah Bay, WA (about Neah Bay folks); Robert Bennett (recommended Dwelley Jones); Galen Biery (tape of the Bellingham coal miner Ed Morray); Don and Darcia Fleury (for hospitality in Ferry County); Bill and Diana Hottell (about Bill Hottell, Sr., Dr. Bill Henry, and many Methow folks); John Hughes, Editor, *Aberdeen Daily World;* Joe Krupa (about Judge John Langenbach); John Kvasnosky (about Tiny Struble); Pauline La Marsh, Pauline's Fur and Leather Alterations, Seattle; Mary Jane Lewis, *Tri-City Herald,* Kennewick, WA (about Fred Harris); Paul Louden, (about Vic Barnes); Gayle Luedke, Border patrolwoman at Lynden, WA (about her

and Walter Olsen, (about Fred Harris); Dr. Robert Ruby, (photo
of Isabelle Arcasa); Helen and Dick Slagle, (about Dutch Monaghan); Jack Slagle (about Gordon Poston); Sylvia Schonberg (about
Laugi Thorstenson); Josephine Storment (about Fred Harris); Jack
Walters; Jane Ward (recommended Babe Russell); Hod Wood
(about Bow Hill); Ollie Mae Wilson (about Konrad Hartbauer).

INTRODUCTION

This book is a sequel to *River Pigs and Cayuses: Oral Histories from the Pacific Northwest,* a collection of interviews I completed in 1979. *River Pigs* portrayed the region through first-person narratives by rural old-timers, who talked about their experiences as log drive river runners (river pigs), wranglers of wild horses (cayuses), and many other folksy, nostalgic occupations. I believed then that *River Pigs* was the most evocative portrait I could ever paint of *my* Pacific Northwest. The experiences of its ranchers, prospectors, blacksmiths, fishermen, gamblers, cowboys, and others *were* the region for me. I had done it. I had told that story, crossed its t's and dotted its i's.

Well, not quite. I soon wrote *Pacific Northwest Trail Guide,* a guidebook to a foot-and-horse trail my friends and I had pioneered between the Rockies and the Pacific. In 1983 I hiked that trail's eleven hundred miles.

Clearly I had a tiger by the tail. Certainly there were many more great stories out there if only I would seek them out.

During most of the 1980s I was busy writing and publishing oral histories about other regions of the United States. The experience I gained in writing those books made me realize that I had some unfinished business in my own delightful region. I had to return to finish the story begun in *River Pigs and Cayuses.* The 1989 Washington state centennial provided the justification for *Whistlepunks and Geoducks.*

I decided on an extensive tour of Washington similar to ones I had made in Texas and California. My goal was to find people whose stories and experiences would add up to a portrait of the Evergreen state.

If you are a Washingtonian, you may feel slighted because I have not included your favorite story, place, or person. I can only invite you to find and record your own Washingtonians to fill in the gaps I have left.

If you are a newcomer to Washington, I hope that you will be caught up in the thrill of discovery as I was so long ago and happily still am. As an Easterner I love the differences which make Washington unique. In northeastern Washington I have encountered the custom whereby a bride and groom's friends will play tricks on them and make a huge hullabaloo after the wedding. On the Strait of Juan de Fuca I have hunted the gargantuan clams called geoducks. In the Methow I have heard old-timers conversing in Chinook, our state's once universal *lingua franca*. Everywhere I have revelled in the pleasure of studying local flora and fauna. Take pine trees, for instance. I like the humble lodgepole, especially for its name, so reminiscent of the tree's use in building tepees (which themselves have provided me with fine adventures among the Hill People). A stand of ponderosa pines cries out to me of openness and freedom. Just thinking of whitebark pines transports me to the alpine delights of windswept ridges and distant views.

Washington at its best has always meant Nature to me, and I believe that most ordinary Washingtonians are more Nature-oriented than the citizens of places less blessed by natural beauty.

Only a short time ago the human population was still secondary here to the fish, oysters, deer, elk, bear, and fowl. Even today sea lions routinely gormandize on salmon at Seattle's Ballard locks fish ladder. And just a couple of years ago a cougar was found living in Seattle's Discovery Park.

Love of Nature is such a strong part of our character that I want to share with you a Home Valley, Washington story told to me by ninety-one-year-old Phoebe Yeo.

In 1907 the family by the name of Hadley that lived at Collins got a big Newfoundland dog. We had never seen a Newfoundland and we wanted to pet it.

One day we happened to see the Newfoundland on the road as we were walking the two miles home from school. Well, that silly thing led us right down the road and to the trail that led on up to the woods. We followed it and it would let us get just so close to it. Then it would turn and trot on away from us. It had a long, long tail.

We got tired of following the silly thing. We told it to go on and we'd continue on our way home.

We did not know that that Newfoundland dog was a cougar, because we had never seen a mountain lion or a Newfoundland before.

My mother went out to the root cellar to get something for dinner that night. When she was coming back, the cougar went across the field in front of our house after following us children home. Mama knew what it was. So she kept us inside the house.

The mailman, Mr. Sholin, carried the mail on foot. Up beyond our house and beyond Collins, where the schoolhouse was later, there was an old pine tree. There was a saloon there at that time run by a man named George Raymond. He and his wife raised those nasty pit bulls. I hate those dogs! The pit bulls were out in this field barking up this tree. They had fifteen of them and they were all out there beneath this tree. Mr. Sholin saw it was a cougar. The dogs had treed it.

He went to the saloon a short ways away and told Mr. Raymond that his dogs had treed a cougar and that he should take his rifle out there and shoot it.

So that's what Mr. Raymond did. He put twelve shots into that animal before it fell out of that tree.

It measured nine feet in length. He skinned it out real carefully and had it mounted into a rug which practically covered their living room floor.

Cougars mate for life, and every year after that the mate would come and scream around, hunting for her mate.

Every day my two older sisters, my brother Bruce and I, and our dog Queen would walk two miles up to Porter's mill to school. We'd see that animal. We knew what it was then. But it never bothered us and Queen was with us anyway.

We'd see it when we went by. It would be down in a gully lying *on a log. It would look up at us and wag and thump its tail and we'd just go on to school and never pay any attention to it. I am sure that it never meant any harm to us children because it had ample time to have killed us all. She was so friendly, making little purring noises and wagging that long tail.*

We were never afraid of her. But, do you know, people hunted that thing!

They never got it. When they didn't have a gun, they would see it. And when they hunted it, they'd never see it.

I didn't want them to catch it. I wanted it to go free.

My Washington is a bit like that cougar. I want it to go free. The Washington which I first experienced in 1968 has been slipping inexorably away. The Washington I have known in several decades of rural roaming has changed, developed, and changed some more.

I am not advocating a static society or a declining economy. Revitalization and progress *are* necessary. But our special Northwest heritage should be appreciated and cherished like that cougar.

Some changes, of course, have been for the better. I am thinking of the improved status of women and minorities in Washington. But consider the following lament from Isabelle Arcasa (born 1889), who complained that at Fourth of July bucking horse contests, "They never had ladies ride or I would have got into it." I asked her about women's liberation. "I think it's great," she said. "If I was young, I'd probably be in amongst them. Couldn't even ride a broomstick now though."

I know that you will enjoy Isabelle Arcasa's story of her parents' marriage. Her mother was a pre-pioneer, an Entiat band Indian, her father a soldier-immigrant from the Middle West. How I wish that I could have talked with them!

However, the richness of Washington folklife has been greatly blessed for me with both Native Americans and genuine pioneers. I wish I could introduce you to prospector Felix Lasota. Eight decades ago, Felix Lasota had tramped through, looking for pay-dirt.

When I came in 1903, there was only one cabin in Metaline Falls. There was nothing but a blazed trail between Ione and Metaline Falls.

This was a gold mine strike on this (Pend Oreille) River here. They had less than a dozen cabins and one little store across the river over at Metaline.

And there were prospectors all down the Pend Oreille River placer mining. At one time there were over fifty Chinamen here working the river, too.

There was nothing in Metaline Falls until 1910 when the railroad came in.

My emphasis in *River Pigs and Cayuses* was on such old-timers. But as one of them, Deke Smith, told me recently, "Dying is just the natural course of Nature. You're born to die. Oh, I feel sad about young people going. Me, I'm just fading out. Like a rock rolling down the hill, he don't roll fast at first. Then he speeds up. I'm rolling faster now than I would like."

My interviewing has evolved in the last decade to be representative of today as well as of yesterday. After all, as people like Deke Smith round their "last switchback," I don't want to work myself out of a wonderful job.

And what is my job, you ask? Besides choosing interesting people who are relevant to the regional portrait I am trying to paint, my art as a folklorist is to bring out the best in someone. The best stories. The most honest and/or deeply felt recollections. Such interviews are difficult, not only because the subject is likely to be foreign to the interviewer, but also because the goal of the hunt may not be known at the beginning of the chase.

Beyond that, the question arises of how authentic the edited version is compared to what an interviewee actually said into the microphone. My approach is to edit a person's speech very carefully to retain his actual words and characteristic expressions, but to make the story flow smoothly as a first-person account. I then test the edited version on the interviewee. I become in effect a ghostwriter of short autobiographies.

I have always thought that the possibilities of this format are particularly appropriate for a state such as Washington where people are so divided by vast gulfs of distance and culture. How many of us have had the opportunity to meet a salmon-smoking Makah from Neah Bay, or a gold miner from Ferry County, or a wheat rancher from Walla Walla? Do they speak the stereotypes we might expect of them? Or do their experiences open up new worlds for us?

That brings me to the subject of mentors, heroes, and teachers, the people who at some formative moment in our lives open up new possibilities for us. This theme has fascinated me so much that it is a common thread throughout all of my oral history books.

I ask the people I interview to tell me about their heroes or mentors, because the answers are likely to reveal a great deal about both the person and his or her enthusiasm. For instance, the late Guy Anderson, one of the artists in our "Northwest School" of Puget Sound painting, once told me that, "You can have strong primitive urges but not be naive." He meant that, just as the Northwest coastal Indians had used "heavy, rich designs and color," he and other Northwest artists, such as Mark Tobey and Morris Graves, used the visual language of the Northwest in a sophisticated way. Guy said that he had been inspired in this direction at an early age by one of his high school teachers in Edmonds who had been to the Orient.

Guy Anderson had strong opinions about how we are influenced by our teachers and mentors (my favorite question in this book). He said that any art teacher who did not expose students to ten thousand years of art was "criminal." "Students need such a broad background," he said, "to make a great creative contribution. They'll find their own way if they are honest."

The question of heroes and mentors gets to the heart of the human condition. *Whistlepunks and Geoducks* is not designed to be parochial reading. I have sought universal significance in the particular. What were the influences which led a Guy Anderson in *his* chosen direction; what influences are likely to affect *us?*

I was born north of Seattle and raised here. We spent a lot of time hiking the mountain trails in the Cascades and Olympics. So there is something distinctly characteristic of the region in my work. Rich colors, etc. We do have that feeling of relationship. We

*always felt the California School was very different. They've always
used much brighter and sunnier colors. Everything looks darker
and richer in heavy rains. The Japanese painted in rich, somber
colors. Rock formations. Mossy vegetation. I've found that many
times on Mount Pilchuck.*

I am always looking to see how the twig was bent. I am always
hoping to find stories that are like treasures out in plain sight. But
do not be fooled by me into thinking that this search is easy. Many
a tale has escaped as I have roamed from the Palouse to Puget
Sound. The most frustrating cases were people who simply did not
want to talk; the saddest were when someone had died who was an
irreplaceable part of Washington.

For instance, Mary Wurth was ninety-two when she spoke with
me on the phone from her home in Spokane. A blizzard prevented
me from visiting her immediately. Then—suddenly it was too late.

Until her death Mary Wurth had been a stalwart member of
Spokane's chapter (organized in 1883) of the Women's Christian
Temperance Union, the antialcohol crusade of legendary saloon-
smasher Carrie Nation. As a child Mary Wurth had met her heroine
and now owned a genuine Carrie Nation hatchet.

How I wanted to see that hatchet and to sense the old fires
glowing in Mary Wurth! Just before her death, the WCTU's Spokane chapter had voted to change its motto from "agitate, educate
and legislate" to "educate, legislate and energize."

"I didn't like it one bit," said the woman whose mentor was
Carrie Nation. "I didn't want to drop *agitate* from our stationery
and I don't think we should stop [agitating]. I think we ought to
get out there today and do a little more agitating."

Each time someone dies, an irreplaceable world disappears.

The Northwest, as historian Robert Cantwell explained in *The
Hidden Northwest,* is such a new region that it has produced less a
body of literature than a mass of personal experience from those
who sailed, traded, farmed, trapped, invented, preached, and
fought their way into what had been the Oregon Territory.

Whistlepunks and Geoducks is my latest effort to record that experience. It grew out of my own 1970 goal to walk from the Idaho
border to the Pacific Ocean. By 1977, with many Pacific Northwest

Trail treks behind me, I became a permanent resident, moving out from that other Washington on the Potomac. But somehow I was never content just to be *in* Washington state. I was always trying to explain it to myself and to others.

Today, more than twenty years after my first adventures here, I still get excited when I return from afar and cross our state's border. When I arrive by plane, the first whiff of our air always invigorates me. Arriving by car, I am thrilled by the sight of so many Washington license plates on the road. If I arrive on foot, the day suddenly glows with new pleasure as soon as I realize that I am home.

Washington is not easily summed up, even by someone like me who has literally walked every foot of the way across the state to see the sun set over the Pacific Ocean. As painter Guy Anderson told me a decade ago, "I'd like the south of France for two or three years, but then I'd return to La Conner. Not even if I were terribly rich, would I leave here permanently."

ISABELLE ARCASA:
AN INDIAN WIDOW
SCORNS A CHIEF
Nespelem, WA
Born: 1889

At first glance I thought that the most amazing thing about diminutive Isabelle Arcasa was that her life had spanned the end of the Old West to the high-tech fadeout of the twentieth century. Growing up at the Colville Reservation, she participated on horseback in what she calls the true "Western days." A favorite activity was rounding up her uncle's wild horses at Kartar Valley near Omak. "I was never thrown from a wild horse," she says. "Only gentle horses, because they'd stumble."

But the more I listened to Isabelle Arcasa the more I realized that her life had seen remarkable progress in the role of women in Washington state. In the story below, her mother had originally been treated practically as a chattel. She had escaped from that by marrying a white soldier, Herman Joseph "Frank" Friedlander. He had come from a well-to-do Cincinnati, Ohio family and had a brother with a jewelry store in Seattle. The Friedlander family had disowned Frank, says his daughter, because, "They said it was a disgrace marrying an Indian woman."

The Indian woman, Elizabeth (Squin-Malx before her Catholic baptism), knew no English when she married soldier Friedlander but she became well-known as a comedian. "Everyone would be laughing at things she'd say at a gathering," says Isabelle. "She'd be telling funny Indian stories and fairy tales."

In the photo, Isabelle is on the left and her stern-faced but well-loved mother on the right. Here is Isabelle's account of how the photo came to be taken in 1907.

I was eighteen when I had that photo taken. I was single.

My grandmother (my mother's mother) never had any pictures of herself. She didn't seem to care much for the whites. She was really an old-fashioned, old Indian.

One day I said to her, "Hey, let's go to Wilbur and have a picture of you."

She said, "Oh, no!"

I said, "Grandmother, if you die, we'll never have any pictures of you. We'd like to have one to look at."

Her sister Agatha and my mother, we were going. So grandmother said, "All right, I'll go and have my picture."

She and my aunt took their Indian outfits to Wilbur.

We were all walking down the sidewalk, going for the picture. In them days in Wilbur they didn't have no concrete sidewalks. They had boardwalks.

My aunt was the cause of my grandmother changing her mind about the picture. My aunt turned around and said, "Oh Mom, some of these days we'll find your picture around a canned salmon."

That was slapping grandmother in the face. She turned right around and left.

So my mother says to me, "You'd better put her outfit on."

So I put my grandmother's outfit on.

Mother, she dressed up. Her earrings are made of shells and around her neck she has those wampum beads. I used to do the beadwork.

She has that beaver round her hair. They cut it into strips like ribbon and they wrap their hair with it.

Mother's hair was long. Oh, she had long hair!

Look how thick my hair is! It used to be four inches above my knees.

I wish that I had a photograph of young Isabelle Arcasa on a wild range horse. She complained to me that at bucking horse contests at Fourth of July celebrations, "They never had ladies ride or I would have got into it."

I wondered what Isabelle Arcasa would say about womens' liberation. "I think it's great," she said fervently. "If I was young, I'd probably be in amongst them. But I couldn't even ride a broomstick now!"

Isabelle Arcasa and her mother Elizabeth Friedlander. Photograph courtesy of Robert H. Ruby

My mother was a full-blood (Indian) and my dad was a white. In those days (late nineteenth century), there were very few Indians who could talk English. She didn't know how to speak a word of English when she married my dad.

She was married first to Chief Moses's younger brother, Gherman-choot, and had three little girls from him. Two of them died and one grew up. In the Indian days, a long time ago, a man whose wife died was expected to marry her sister or her cousin, the nearest relative. That's the way the Indians do. So when my mother's first husband died, Chief Moses, who was his brother, thought in the Indian way that he should come over and take her up. She couldn't say no.

Her first husband had quite a few head of horses when he died. They lived way down by Bandish with her in-laws. It was in late October when he died and old Chief Moses came over and took everything his brother owned, horses and everything. My sister Mary had a little Shetland pony, a little tiny horse. He even took that—his niece's horse. He took them all away, and my mother couldn't say anything. He took everything and left her stranded there. She stayed at her in-laws all winter near Vantage, and in the springtime one old lady said, "Would you like to go back home to your parents?"

She said, "I sure would like that!"

So this lady gave Mother a horse and the little girl a horse, like a packhorse, and they started back up to Entiat where her father and mother lived.

My dad was then a soldier at Chelan Falls across from Chelan, where they had great big soldier tents of white, square canvas. And he had a store and a saloon.

One day my mother and her brother and her young sister wanted to do some shopping, so they went up to Chelan from Entiat by horseback. Her uncle went with her. They shopped and when they got through, the store owner, Frank Friedlander, said to my uncle about my mother, "Such a beautiful lady. I sure would like her for my wife."

Of course, her brother never told her anything then, but on the way back to Entiat he said, "You know that man that owns the store? They call him Frank. He said, 'Gee, you sure are a nice-looking woman.' He sure would like to have you for a wife."

My mother never said a word.

Well, in the meantime, while they were shopping up there at Chelan, old Chief Moses came to her dad and mother and he said, "I came over to get my little niece and my sister-in-law." He was going to marry his sister-in-law the way Indians used to do, not by the justice of the peace or anything, but just the Indian way.

When she got back home, her dad, Stilcusasts, told her, "Your brother-in-law was here, Chief Moses, and he said next week he's coming back after you."

In those days, instead of giving presents to a married couple, the woman's parents would receive presents. So her dad says, "Chief Moses says he's going to bring me some horses and saddles."

My mother said, "I would never marry that man, not if he was the last man on earth. I'd rather go to hell than marry that man! The way he treated us! Took his little niece's horse and left us stranded. If it wasn't for those good old people there, we'd have nothing. Took everything with him. He didn't think about his little niece then. Never. I'd never!"

So she turned around and said to her uncle, "Take me back to that white man. I'd rather marry him than Moses."

So then her uncle took her and she told my dad the story of what Chief Moses had done. They talked together in the Chinook jargon. There was a justice of the peace among the soldiers, so they got married.

The next weekend, here comes Chief Moses with his horses. So my grandfather went out and told him, "I'm sorry," he says, "she married Frank." Everyone knew my dad. "She's married now."

And it made Moses mad. He got on his pony. "I'm going to kill that man," he said. "She's supposed to be *my* wife."

When he approached, Mother said, "There he is! Old Moses is coming!"

So Dad took his rifle and put it by the door. "Frank," Moses hollered. "Frank, come out. I'm going to kill you. You took my wife!"

My dad says, "She's not your wife. I'm married to her. Married by the justice of the peace."

"Not in the Indian way! She's *my* wife. I'm going to kill you!" He was getting out his gun.

"Go ahead. Shoot me!" my dad said. He had *his* gun. "Go ahead and shoot."

Instead of that, Moses just turned around with all of his ponies and left. He was so mad! But there wasn't anything he could do.

That's how my mother married my dad.

[Isabelle Arcasa's daughter, Maybelle Gendron of Spokane, remembers this about Isabelle's mother:]

My grandparents were both very joyful people with a tremendous sense of humor. They were the life of the party. This was passed on to their children at any gathering, powwow, or feast. Laughter would ring out wherever they were. Humorous stories and pranks could continue until morning.

I lived with my grandmother a greater part of my early life. Though she could speak a good deal of English, she and my grandfather still spoke Chinook.

My grandmother preferred living on the reservation, so grandpa built her a home there. He hired a young lady to help grandma with the children and a Chinese to cook. Grandpa built himself a large house in Wilbur, where he owned a store. He spent his time between the reservation and Wilbur. Grandma made few trips to Wilbur, but they spent many happy days together.

My grandmother was a gentle but feisty person. One day a year before she passed away, she had me saddle up the two horses so we could go huckleberry picking. I'll never forget that when grandma mounted, her horse got a sudden surge of energy and decided to buck.

This irritated my grandmother and she immediately asked for her quirt and proceeded to make her horse buck until he had no thought of rebellion again. Grandma's many flannel underskirts and dresses and shawls flapped and flopped as she was giving her last bucking horse performance.

DAVE BECK:

TEAMSTER

Seattle, WA

Born: 1894

Although Washington has rarely been front and center on the stage of American life, its labor relations history is one of national prominence. That history could have turned in a radically different direction had Dave Beck not been on the Seattle scene.

Early in the century we were often referred to as the Soviet of Washington because of our widely-publicized International Workers of the World (Wobblies). Today labor relations has become a ho-hum subject of diminished popular interest because union membership nationally has declined from twenty-nine percent of all workers in 1975 to an estimated ten percent by the year 2000. Who today remembers violent I.W.W. confrontations, such as the Centralia Massacre (1919) and the Everett Massacre (1916)? Such events seem as quaint to us as the "Pig War" of the San Juan Islands.

But not to Dave Beck. He lived through the rough and tumble world of the early twentieth century American labor movement. His phenomenal organizing skill helped make the Pacific Northwest and then the West Coast the most thoroughly organized part of the United States. And at the crucial period in the state's history when the Communist-leaning Wobblies were taking timber industry workers far to the left, Dave Beck became the leading advocate for a non-Communist course for Northwest labor.

As president of the International Brotherhood of Teamsters from 1952 to 1957, Dave Beck was the first Washingtonian in the labor movement to achieve national prominence. Or notoriety, if you wish. His strong-arm methods of organizing delighted the news media much the same way that Governor Dixie Lee Ray's actions did years later. In the late 1950s U.S. attorney general Bobby Kennedy landed the old laundry truck driver in the federal prison at McNeil Island for routinely filing an unsigned "fraudulent United States Annual Return of Organization" with the secretary of labor.

Dave Beck still forcefully maintains his innocence. But that very public Washington, D.C. part of his life is less interesting to me than his formative years in Seattle. I discussed many subjects with the legendary teamster, such as his successful organizing of Carnation Milk Company drivers in Los Angeles and of brewery workers in Seattle (1932) and then in the entire United States. His 1930s region- and industry-wide organizing was an ingenious innovation. But that story is well-known. What interests me most is how he came to be the person he was, the tenth-grade dropout who became president of the Board of Regents of the University of Washington, an honor as close to knighthood as this state can bestow.

Dave Beck came across to me as an old-time buccaneering American businessman. His product was work. "I ran the Teamsters international union strictly as a business," he told me. "The people I represented had only one thing to sell. Their labor. They didn't own department stores or laundries or dairies. We were selling under open competition just as the Bon Marche and Frederick and Nelson were doing with their merchandise. I was running a union based on the principle to get the very best price for the product we were selling."

If he had not been a businessman labor-broker, he would certainly have been a real estate broker. In fact, he made a fortune in real estate both for his own account and for that of his union. Today his reminiscences are full of contracts, buildings, and dollars and cents.

Communism, once so attractive in the woods of Washington, was the evil which Dave Beck thought would destroy *both* capital and labor. And it was the free enterprise system which gave the impoverished kid named Beck his chance. "It's just like you were building a tremendous business and making progress," he told me happily. "First thing you knew, business was your whole life."

Whatever he went into, says Dave Beck, he "worked like hell to become efficient and qualified to go to the top of it." From thirteenth or fourteenth in membership, the Teamsters became number one. "I loved every minute of it because I was making progress."

In 1957, at the height of his power, Dave Beck left the Teamsters presidency to look after his first wife, Dorothy, who was dying of cancer. When she died in 1959, they had been married for forty-one years.

Dave Beck and his mother October 1, 1958. (Credit: Museum of History and Industry, Seattle, WA)

"Dorothy was living with my friend Paul's aunt in the one hundred block on Eastlake Avenue between Denny Way and John. Her father and mother lived over on a farm on Bainbridge Island at Fletcher Bay. I don't recall where we met, but we fell in love with each other and were going to be married when the First World War broke out. I immediately said, 'No marriage! Because I may never come back from the war. I'm going to enlist.' "

Our father, Lemuel Beck, was born around Knoxville, Tennessee, probably of German extraction. He died in 1924 when I was about thirty. My mother, Mary Tierney, was born in San Francisco and her mother had been born in Ireland.

After my parents married, they lived in San Francisco, but I was born in Stockton, California when my parents visited my father's dad there. I was born on June 16, 1894, followed by my sister Reta in San Francisco sixteen months later.

When I was about two, my father went up to Seattle to establish a business. Mom, Reta, and I joined him two years later.

We journeyed from California on the Walla Walla in steerage way down in the bowels of the ship. There was little money and we were forced to travel under the most rigid of conditions. The Walla Walla was one of the steamboats with the Umatilla and the Pueblo that were the main artery of traffic between Seattle, San Francisco, and Los Angeles.

Father was operating a carpet shop on Third Avenue between Seneca and Spring. Laying carpets, repairing them, fixing furniture, that sort of thing. He was a hard worker. A robust, aggressive man who stood five ten and weighed two hundred forty pounds. Terribly overweight. I resemble my dad in a lot of ways, even to an identical baldness.

The exception was business judgment. We were always poor. Very, very poor. If it hadn't been for mother handling what money there was, our family would have starved.

But Dad was a wonderful man in other ways. They say that the best headstart a boy can get in life is a father he can respect and care for. Once an auctioneer, he was a very fine speaker and a sound thinker. He handled himself aptly in front of an audience. He had a good speaking voice and a grasp for words. He was an inveterate reader and encouraged me to read books.

Our first home in Seattle was in the Belltown district, which was mostly small boarding houses. I was nine years old when we moved from Belltown to 815 Pike Street, where we lived in the back of Dad's carpet shop. It was cheaper, combining the working and living quarters. We simply partitioned the two sections with a curtain.

At Christmas our family was too poor to give gifts, and Thanksgiving was a day without the traditional family dinner if turkey was over sixteen cents a pound. If it was under sixteen cents, we were able to have it. We always worked during summer vacations and there was no time for a real vacation at all.

We were poor as hell. Sometimes my father and I fished in Lake Union for something to eat that day. I caught thousands of perch and bass in Lake Union and sold them illegally to some of the finest restaurants, like Mancas at 115 Cherry Street and Gerald's Cafe at First and Madison. Also, we used to go up to where the University of Washington is now and catch minnows near the log chute.

Along with Ervie Bowen[1] I sold Christmas trees that we cut from the second and third growth forest adjacent to Lake Union, north clear to the University. As each year went by we had to go farther and farther out to get Christmas trees because the forest was disappearing.

Sometimes to make a little money I borrowed a .22 and shot rats under the wharves along Lake Union. In those days, Seattle was on guard against signs of the bubonic plague brought in by rats from ships out of the Orient. When I got a sackful of rats, I'd take them up to the Health Department. They would nail them on wooden slabs and cut them open. For every rat that showed signs of the plague, I got five dollars.

If my mother had ever found out I was carrying around sacks of dead rats, she would have slapped me good. So I told her I made money running errands or helping out an old Mississippi River boatman, Captain Allerbach. Sometimes I really did help Captain Allerbach and he'd give me a quarter if he was feeling good.

My mother was my heroine until she died at age ninety-four. I will never forget how hard my mother worked to keep the family together. She had a job in a laundry at 8th and Olive. There were no regular hours except that she had to be at work at seven in the morning. She worked in the flatwork department, sheets, pillowcases, and table covers, until the day's load had been done. My sister and I would go up to the laundry nights and wait outside until she was through. It was seven or eight o'clock before she was done, and there wasn't any overtime pay.

I had heard something about unions and believe me, it was then and there that I decided they were all to the good! I can still see

---

[1]Later I put him on as an organizer under me in the Laundry and Dye Workers Union when I was secretary. He was a damn good organizer. Later he organized every cab driver in Seattle. He took in the Yellow Cab and all the rest of them.

myself and my little sister sitting on the curb outside that laundry while our mother drudged on into the night behind those sweaty windows. And off in the distance lived the rich in their ornate houses on Capitol Hill. I resolved to be as good as any of them.

Ironically, the first full-time job I ever had (in 1914) was running a washroom wringer. Like mother, like son.

Mom, Reta, and I ate out once a week on her payday. It was a six-day week and the laundries all paid in cash. After twelve, thirteen hours on her feet, Mother was just too tired to rush home and prepare supper. So the three of us would go to this little Chinese restaurant around the corner at First Avenue between Pine and Pike and order a big bowl of noodles with a little meat in them. We knew the cook, a Chinaman, and he would furnish us with three little empty bowls so we could divide them up. Our total bill was thirty-five cents.

I first started selling newspapers when we lived at 815 Pike Street and I was attending Cascade School. I was eight or nine years old then. As I remember, newspapers sold for three cents, half of which went to me. My profit was based on how many papers I could sell. You had to be a hustler to make it pay.

From the age of twelve to the age of fourteen or fifteen, I had a *P-I* route delivering papers in a district where the elite lived. I had about three hundred fifty customers, the biggest route in the *P-I*'s chain, and I worked seven days a week. The route extended from Pine to Madison and from Terry to Broadway.

It was impossible to carry three hundred fifty papers at once. So I broke them up into two packs. The streetcar went up Pike Street and dropped off half my load at the corner of Boren Avenue. I picked up the second load, left there by the streetcar, at old Seattle High School at Pine and Broadway, and finished my route.

I continued to carry papers through my first year of high school. As I grew, I carried both the *P-I* and the *Times.* That meant getting up at five A.M. for the *P-I* and working after school for the *Times.* Those were long days. I got twelve dollars a month from the *Times* and three dollars and fifteen cents a week from the *P-I.*

Sound like hard work? It was. But it was nothing compared to those times when I first broke in selling papers. I didn't have a standard delivery route originally. Only street corners. And we had

to fight for the good corners. We'd get our papers, station ourselves on a corner, and then hold it for as long as we could, until
a bigger kid came along and muscled us out. I had many a fight but
I was too goddamned small to win 'em in most instances.

If it was an especially good corner, you just put down your
papers and fought the guy. The winner kept the corner.

The fighting got so bad that Seattle judges were forced to step
in and decide which of us got which corners. Those decisions were
backed up by the newspapers, too. In other words, if you developed a corner, you were protected by the circulation departments
and that corner was yours unless you wanted to sell it to another
kid. Later corners became so valuable that groups of adults would
buy them and put kids on them as sellers or sell on them themselves.

I sold papers down in the restricted areas where kids were not
supposed to go. The Skid Road and the Slot. My mother would
have killed me if she had known I was down there. That was the
habitat of all the gamblers and madams and everything else illicit
that you can think of. Oh, I saw many madams but at that time I
didn't even know what they were. It was a damn good place to sell
newspapers because people were likely to give you twenty-five
cents more for a newspaper than you could get north of there.
That was the free-spending life they were living.

Then around 1912 or 1913, when the prostitutes were driven
out of the Slot, they located all over the damned area where I drove
laundry wagons. I can remember delivering to them down on Lake
Union when they lived in houseboats.

When I got a newspaper route of my own, I walked at least seven
miles per trip, traversing back and forth throughout the neighbor-
hoods. Then I'd walk back down to Lake Union where we lived at
1207 Aloha and eat breakfast. We lived only about a block and a
half from the lake. After breakfast I'd go down to the lakeshore and
collect bark which had washed up from the log booms and mills.
Lots of times the lake would be covered with floating bark. We'd
store it for winter stove wood because it would burn as well as coal.
Then I'd go to school, walking from the south end of Lake Union
to Broadway High School.

I don't want to make it sound like my boyhood was all drudgery

There was time for some play. I was a pretty good ballplayer. When I was seventeen, I played some semi-pro baseball around Seattle. I was never good enough to qualify for organized ball but I was a fair player.

They talked me into playing golf one weekend. But I decided right away I was getting interested in the labor movement, and I found out very quickly I had to choose between golf and attending to business.

Both myself and my sister had to quit school and go to work to help support the family. After two years of Seattle High School I had to leave in 1911 during my sophomore year. I got a job delivering typewriters for the L.C. Smith Typewriter Agency at Third and Marion for five dollars a week, six days a week. [This typewriter company was then building the Smith Tower, for years the tallest building west of Chicago.]

We had a friend, Mr. Ragsdale, who was manager of a laundry. I was looking for a job, after I had been working as a deliveryman for the L.C. Smith Typewriter Agency, and that's where I landed.

The laundry owner had had a small brewery. In 1910 when the state of Washington went Prohibition before the United States did, he then gravitated toward the laundry business. He bought the Central Wet Wash Laundry here in Seattle, right over between Westlake and Ninth on Valley Street.

I started out as an assistant to the ringer man in the laundry for about sixty or ninety days. Mr. Ragsdale was the manager. Then I went on as a driver. I had no experience as a driver but I took to it fast. The laundry wagon was a Model-T Ford. I liked the Model-T. You only had a pedal for reverse. You had bands for brakes. When you needed brakes real bad, you'd ease in the reverse a bit. It was dangerous, because you could ruin the whole transmission and then you were on your own.

I first joined the Teamsters Union when I was working as a driver. I had been in the laundryworkers union before that when I had been working inside as a wringer man squeezing the wash dry. Part of my route as a driver was among eighteen, twenty, thirty Chinese laundries down in Chinatown and all through the business areas of Seattle, from First Avenue clear out north to Denny Way. I would go there and pick up the laundry that the

Chinese laundries had and bring it into the Central Wet Wash, where it would be washed. I would deliver it back within two or three or four hours to the Chinese laundries where I had picked it up. We did the washing, put it through the ringers, and sent it out damp to the Chinese laundries, which then finished it. Or housewives. Sometimes I had a large route on Queen Anne Hill and other places.

Never was there any strength to Communism in the Northwest. The lumber industry imposed atrocious conditions upon labor. The employers were united to destroy labor. So Communism got a foothold in the lumber industry. The old Wobblies. I opposed them, speaking on soap boxes when I was a kid down on Second and Washington, south of the Slot. I climbed up on the goddamn soap boxes and argued my head off at them. "You are too far on the left," I said. "You are trying to go too fast, too soon."

Nobody ever fought Communism in this country more than I fought it. From Labor I fought it. I was fourteen, fifteen, sixteen when I was on the soap boxes before I was ever in a union. I inherited whatever speaking ability I had from my father, who had been an auctioneer for many years. Soap box speakers weren't common downtown, but the Wobblies were primarily all south of Yesler Way, down in the old Skid Road district where the unskilled loggers were. The police wouldn't let soapbox speakers uptown. The Mayor and the council booted you off up there. But you were wide open south of Yesler.

I was engaged to be married just before World War I was declared. But when war broke out in 1917, I decided to hell with getting married. I enlisted the day after war was declared and I was afraid for Dorothy that I might never come back. So it was better not to be married.

I met my first wife through one of my friends, Paul Farrow, who was a fellow laundry truck driver. Dorothy Leschander was of French extraction. She was working as a salesgirl at Rhodes Department Store in Seattle.

I was training at North Island in San Diego in Balboa Park and I got five days furlough to come home to Seattle. When I got back, Dorothy still wanted to get married. She was living with my folks at 1302 Valley Street. She said, "We should get married." I said,

"No, wait till the war is over." Finally I relented because she was so disturbed about it. But I still didn't want to.

We were married in June 1918 at a Presbyterian minister's house over in the Wallingford District. I didn't know him from a bale of hay, but we didn't have time to look around long for a minister. Dorothy was Presbyterian and my family was Catholic. The minister's wife was the only one there. I left for San Diego right afterwards. I didn't even have any time at all with my new bride. I was off to war for fourteen months before seeing her again!

I remember a hell of a fight with her when I went back to my Navy base after we were married. I didn't want her to go back to work but she insisted!

I was only in San Diego forty-eight hours and I was on my way to the East Coast. I was shipped over to Killinghome, England, as a machinist's mate, second class. I served on station on the North Sea opposite the Kiel Canal. Our mission was to stop German submarines, destroyers, and Zeppelins from attacking our commerce and ships.

The Zeppelins often tried to bomb our station. When the lights went out because of a warning, we would take a blanket and go sleep in the fields. After the all clear signal, there would still be a lot of people sleeping in the fields.

The armistice was November 11, 1918. We were directly across from Helgoland, because we were the closest spot to Germany. They used the station we were on as a prison exchange camp. That released us to go back to the U.S. I was in London on Armistice night, the first night that the lights had been turned on in London for several years. Oh, Jesus, it was a wild night in London, I'll tell ya! Just raising particular hell. London will never see another night like that one.

I left England very soon on a troopship, the Leviathan, the largest ship in the world. We had twenty-nine thousand other servicemen bound for New York, including two or three decks of shell-shocked men. When the ship hit a goddamned thunderstorm at sea, the minute we hit thunder and lightning, they were back in the war in their minds.

Our ship tied up in New York just before Christmas. Immediately, all the guys in uniform started angling for early discharges. I was still under a four-year enlistment with the Navy, but I filed an application for release in the form of a letter. I explained that I was married and I emphasized that my young bride of fourteen months was very sick. I just made that story up but the letter went right out to Seattle where it was turned over to the Red Cross for investigation. Within three days a letter came back recommending immediate discharge.

I was amazed!

I got my discharge and caught a train out of New York that evening. My entire bankroll totaled about twenty-five dollars. All I had for three thousand miles to Seattle.

There was a brief stopover in Cleveland and I got out to buy donuts and coffee up the stairs from the train tracks. This guy came up to me, stuck a gun in my ribs, and took the money. Now I was down to one dollar and forty cents in change.

That's the God's honest truth. When I got back on the train and told everybody about my bad luck, they passed a hat around the parlor car and took up a collection. The result was that I landed in Seattle with *more* than when I left New York. Because of that collection and because somebody was always inviting us men in uniform to dinner on the train.

Now for the clincher. My father and sister met me at the train depot and drove me home. Where was Dorothy? Well, she had been staying with my parents and, by God, was sick in bed. For four months, she hadn't been able to hear a thing. She was stone deaf, a victim of the great Seattle influenza epidemic of 1918.

Thank heaven, she pulled through and her hearing returned. But just consider the coincidence: dreaming up a phony story to get out of the Navy, thinking I was lying like hell, and she really was ill!

As soon as I got back to Seattle, Jack Connors came to see me. He was an old friend of the family and a good union man. I was still in uniform and hadn't even unpacked yet but Connors said, "Dave, the newspapers are talking about a general strike here. Shipyard workers are walking off the job. Everybody is calling for a general strike in sympathy with them. It's the truth. The labor situation is very dim. Dave, you must do something."

The war had ended and there were hundreds of thousands of men returning to civilian life. During the war there had been a fantastic growth in industrial expansion. Now, because of the shutdowns of war plants everywhere, unemployment was rampant. Right here in Seattle the shipyards closed down practically overnight. That's what caused the city's general strike. The first and only such strike in the history of the U.S.A. It was a mess, I'll tell you.

"Me?" I said. "I'm just home from the war. Why me?"

"Because the fellows respect you," Jack said. "They'll listen to you. We're holding an emergency meeting of our laundry union this very night. Come on down to the hall and speak to them."

Before the war I had had a brief experience with a strike and hated it. I still hate strikes. Sure, the Teamsters had plenty of them under Dan Tobin and later when I was on the way to the presidency, but I have always regarded a strike as a last resort. I believe I was the first union leader to take that position, though I always demanded the *right* to strike. Any crackpot can work up a strike vote but it takes sensible effort on both sides to avoid one.

So the idea of a general strike in Seattle curdled my blood. I knew that Connors was no alarmist. Some of the Teamster unions already had voted to hit the bricks, and that concerned me more. The idea of a general strike was only a theory in America. It was something that happened in Europe occasionally and always raised the roof in the process.

Connors explained that the shipyard workers were demanding eight dollars a day for skilled labor and five and a half for unskilled. They wanted a forty-four hour work week. I told him that they must have gone crazy.

I wore my Navy uniform to the laundry union meeting because I had put on so much weight that I had no suit which still fit. I don't remember what I said that night. The meeting was not covered by the press so there is no record of it. But whatever I told them must have convinced the membership that a general strike was a revolution. Actually anarchy. I really stood them on their feet! And how good that felt to a fuzz-chinned kid in a sailor suit!

When we went into the meeting, one hundred ten unions had already voted for anarchy. When we came out, the Laundry and Dye Works Drivers Local 566 had said, "No." We were the only Teamster union to vote that way.

The general strike made a deep impression on me. I was a union member and always will be. Unions are part of the national economy, although even now there are still a few diehards trying to break them up. I believed in World War I and in the second World War, too. And I figured we had fought for democracy. But in 1919 before I could get back into a laundry truck, I ran into something that was the direct opposite of democracy. *Right in my own country* and *my hometown.*

That Anna Louise Strong they made such a fuss about was a fuzzy in the head. She was an old-time suffragette in the wrong pew when it came to labor. It was then and there during the general strike that I had it proved to me that Communism had nothing for labor. If ever they got the chance, they would crucify labor right off the bat. Look what happened in Russia.

My opposition to the general strike was not entirely due to my hatred of the Reds. Our local had a contract and so did the other Teamster unions. I was preaching the sanctity of contracts when a whole hell of a lot of union leaders were still preaching what amounted to class warfare.

When I came back from the war, I went to take back my old position at the Central Wet Wash Laundry. Under the war regulations, those who had enlisted for the war were entitled to their jobs when they returned. But I found out that the laundry had been sold by the brewery owner when Prohibition began and that my old boss Mr. Ragsdale had been demoted from manager to driver on the route that I was to have back. So I refused to take the job, because I could get another one easier than he could.

So I went to work as a driver for Mutual Laundry, owned and operated by the union. I was assigned a route out in the University District.

It was hard work but I made good money. More than one hundred dollars a week. I was on that job for about two years before I was made route manager. Then I had an argument with the supervisor driver over working conditions. He refused to change his order and I walked off the job. Back at Central Laundry Mr. Ragsdale was retiring and I got my old route back. I stayed there until 1924.

I took quite an active part in the union while I was a driver at the Mutual Laundry and after I came back to the Central Laundry when Mr. Ragsdale died. That activity led me to want to become a part of the Labor official family.

Later I ran for secretary of the local union, a position held by Fred Wyatt from the day of its inception. In my campaign against him I pointed out in my speeches that the drivers were not making progress, because wages, hours, and conditions were below par. I won the election rather easily and started as secretary-treasurer of Local 566 on December 1, 1924.

The following year the national convention of the International Brotherhood of Teamsters was scheduled to meet in Seattle. As secretary-treasurer of the Laundry Drivers Union, I became a member of Joint Council 28 and was elected secretary of that. Subsequently I was named chairman of the Arrangements Committee for the Teamster convention.

The first time in my life I ever met Dan Tobin was when he walked off the boat coming down from Vancouver, British Columbia. He had traveled west via Canada on the Canadian Pacific Railroad, then took a Princess boat to Seattle. I and Mike Casey of San Francisco, who was my superior officer on the coast, met him at the dock.

When the Railroad Brotherhood came into Seattle and invested large sums of money merging fifteen laundries into six, I was still secretary-treasurer of the Laundry Drivers Union. Those behind the merger offered me two hundred dollars a week if I'd quit the labor movement and go with them. I telephoned Mike Casey, who had been something of a mentor to me, and told him I was seriously considering the offer.

Mike said Dan Tobin wouldn't want me to leave. I wasn't yet on the Teamster payroll and I told Casey that my son had reached school age and that I had to make a living.

Casey asked that I hold off for a few days before giving them my answer. "I'll talk to Tobin," he said. He telephoned Tobin, who proposed that I accept an appointment as a part-time general organizer for the International. It paid five hundred dollars a month and five dollars a day for miscellaneous expenses. Tobin said I could keep my job with the laundry drivers as secretary.

I accepted. Later, because I had made such good progress organizing, I became a full-time organizer in charge of the whole Pacific Northwest and British Columbia.

That's how I got involved with the Teamsters. I don't know what I would have done with my life if I hadn't accepted Tobin's offer. I probably would have wound up in the laundry business in a managerial capacity.

In high school I had considered becoming a lawyer but I couldn't stay in school. That's the one regret I still have. But there was no way I could have afforded law school. Later, my father-in-law, superintendent of the Dexter-Horton Building, talked about me to an attorney who had an office there. The lawyer invited me to come down and read law with him. I did that in my spare time for three or four years and he urged me to go on to law school. However, I couldn't spare any more time because I was becoming successful in Labor. And because I *loved* Labor organizing. To me it was the same as if I was a priest or a minister of the gospel. The inspiration was the same. I felt that I was helping ordinary people by putting millions of dollars into their pocketbooks.

My whole goddamn life has been wrapped up in some aspect of Labor. But even when I was president of the Teamsters in Washington, D.C., my residence was always Seattle. And my wife continued to live in Seattle. And I would come back every weekend unless I was traveling in Europe or elsewhere on Labor business.

I wanted to live here all my life because of my associations from the time that I was a boy. Seattle is my hometown.

HU "SCOOP" BLONK:
"I HAVE SEEN MORE
CONCRETE POURED THAN
ANY OTHER NEWSMAN
IN THE HISTORY
OF THE WORLD."
Wenatchee, WA
Born: 1909

The project was so grand that in 1918 readers of *The Wenatchee Daily World* could be excused for thinking that it was a pipe dream. That was the year that publisher Rufus Woods ran the first story about a colossal public power dam proposed to harness the Columbia River for electricity and irrigation. Former *Wenatchee Daily World* managing editor Hu Blonk says, "The paper ran endless amounts of publicity and nearly everybody was against it. But Rufus loved big ideas."

Big ideas indeed! Grand Coulee Dam was finally begun as a make-work project by F.D.R. in 1933, using public relief funds from the Public Works Administration and the Works Progress Administration. The Grand Coulee project set many construction records; the first power was generated in 1941 and the first irrigation water applied to semiarid wastelands in 1952.

Big ideas. Big dam. Big fight. Grand Coulee Dam was not only the triumph of American engineering, but the triumph of public power advocates over their private power rivals. What is usually forgotten in this story, however, is the daily reality of the perhaps twenty thousand men who at one time or another labored to construct the West's largest public works project. Hu Blonk is the ideal chronicler of that story, since he wrote about almost every aspect of the dam from the beginning of construction to initial operation about eight years later.

The dam's plentiful electrical power contributed greatly to the success of the Northwest's aircraft and aluminum industries during and after World War II. Grand Coulee's irrigation waters transformed a sizeable part of central Washington from desert to cropland.

Hu Blonk was there and can tell of F.D.R.'s impulsive 1937 dinner at a burger joint, subsequently renamed "President's Choice." Hu remembers the colorful figures and the ordinary working stiffs who created the giant dam. He recalls the joints on B Street in Grand Coulee where rooms were used on average only about twenty minutes at a time. He remembers the dam's innovations and his own struggle to get by on little money while wearing oversized, hand-me-down boots.

Hu was a Dutch immigrant (1920) whose father was a dairyman. English-weak Hu had happened into journalism by accident and had graduated from the University of Washington in the Great Depression year of 1933. Eventually he became managing editor of *The Wenatchee Daily World.* As a noted champion of freedom of the press he served as chairman of the Associated Press Managing Editors Association's "Freedom of Information Committee." Not bad for someone who had had to delay beginning first grade until age eleven because he didn't know English.

Hu Blonk still writes for *The Wenatchee Daily World,* especially if he hears of a new Methow Valley subject which has human interest potential. But it was the Grand Coulee Dam which he shared for so many years with his readers.

I am the guy that really tabulated the number of deaths that occurred at the dam, although the company never did anything to hide the deaths. Seventy-seven men were killed on the job. The fatalities were due to men's falling off concrete blocks and other high places, and to things falling on the men. But the boys claimed, "You didn't report all the guys killed, Blonk." I don't have any virtues, but I am honest. It made me so damned mad. I finally said, "Alright you bastards. For every guy that was killed that I did not report, I will pay you twenty-five bucks."

Hu Blonk (no hat) eavesdropping on F.D.R. (Credit: The Wenatchee World)

That was a lot of money in those days. I never had to pay off.

Incidentally, before you ask me, *no one* is buried in the concrete at Grand Coulee Dam. That's a question that I have been asked every few months since 1933. It was impossible, because the concrete was poured in fifty-foot forms, five feet deep, by four-yard buckets opening within a foot of the surface. Men were in there with vibrators waiting to go to work. So how in the dickens could a guy be buried under there with all of these people standing around?

I was known as "Scoop" by some of my close friends at Grand Coulee Dam. I can always tell what phase of my life someone is from when they say hello. If they say, "Hello Dutch," that means high school days. At the University of Washington I was "Butch Blonk." There, we guys on the U. W. *Daily* each made up names like Bulldog Drummond and Killer Stevens.

I worked my way through the U. W. and about starved to death. I got a job on the *P-I* as a college graduate, for ten dollars a week for a summer. When the job ran out I became a newspaper carrier. I covered the paper route along First Avenue for a couple of months and always wound up on the waterfront at the Booth Fish Company plant. Then the school called me up and said they had two jobs: one, putting out a magazine in Seattle and the other, working for a guy who was promoting the Grand Coulee Dam with a weekly. So I said, "Where is Grand Coulee Dam?"

I got there in December 1933. They were just digging the first yard of dirt toward exposing the bedrock. I stayed until the dam was about completed in 1941.

In December 1933 I was working for that weekly and living in Almira. Later I covered the job for the *Wenatchee World* and *Spokane Chronicle,* being paid space rates, so much a column inch. I lived in the cheapest room that I could get in the Almira Hotel. I had a beautiful view of a window well.

At first people lived at the dam in shacks. There weren't many tents. Of course, when the dam really started, the contractor built barracks. Most of these construction stiffs were single men because they couldn't afford to bring their wives. They were mostly good people, but there were also shysters and pimps. Laborers were not getting paid very much. I think it was fifty cents an hour at first but it was work during the Depression. Total employment rose to eight thousand eight hundred men. All those men were away from home and I don't think that Ma got all their money back home.

Some of the workers eventually bought a lot in the sagebrush, drove up and unloaded their chairs and what not, and started building a house. Gradually more and more men lived in houses.

While the Bureau of Reclamation was located at Almira, I hitch-hiked to the job site at Coulee Dam. But when they moved the Bureau's offices down there, I moved too. I lived there in an eight-by-ten shack with a toilet outside.

Grand Coulee had wooden sidewalks at first. Everyone called the mud in the streets "gumbo." I remember a little kid standing in the mud of Main Street crying because he couldn't move back or forth. His boots were stuck in the gumbo.

Everybody remembered me because for a lot of years I wore huge boots. The truth was that I was so poor when I got out of the University of Washington that I didn't have any gear to wear in that cold climate. So this weekly's editor gave me a pair of boots that were way too big. I swallowed my pride and wore them. There wasn't any use to gripe about it. That's all I had.

But I didn't have any warm clothing. It was always cold in winter and I would wake up in the morning and find my water supply frozen in an ordinary galvanized pail. Most of the time I just prepared something to eat on a little stove in there. I don't think I ever ate a well-balanced meal until I got married two years after I arrived.

I was never a lady's man. I never dated in college. I was shy about women. But what happened was that when I was staying in the hotel in Almira, I would sit in the lobby and see this pretty gal coming across the street with this red polka dot dress on. I thought she was about the prettiest thing I had ever seen.

Martha Haskin was a daughter of Carl Haskin, an insurance man who sometimes gave me rides from Almira to Coulee Dam and who later was postmaster at Almira. Martha was a very reserved person, not outgoing like I am. She was a very kind person and everybody loved her.

She thought I was a very modest guy. I can remember her saying that.

She was a beauty operator and that was embarrassing to me because in those days I had a beautiful natural marcel. If you laid a pencil in there, it would stay in place. I was afraid that the guys would think that she was fixing up my hair.

I had been going with her for about a year when she said she was going to move to Wenatchee to take a new job. Later I was at some friends' house, where I said, "I'm not going to go down and compete with a whole bunch of guys in Wenatchee." I talked like that and these friends, who liked my wife-to-be, said, "Damn it, you dumb cluck. She's in love with *you!*" That's how stupid I was. She wasn't going to go with anybody but me.

In those days getting around was tough. Finally in 1935 I bought a ten-year-old Buick for seventy-five dollars. It was my first car and I would start up this steep hill at Coulee Dam to go see my girl in Almira. I always knew where the car would stop on that incline. I would have to get out behind it, take off the gas cap, and blow into the gas tank to make enough pressure to get the gas flowing. Then I would make it to Almira to visit Martha.

That was love, wasn't it?

In 1935 we were married in the parson's front room in Davenport, Washington. Then we moved into the Cozy Apartments in Grand Coulee Center. Workers were digging house foundations all over the place, causing a tremendous amount of dust when the wind was blowing. My wife was always very tidy and I remember how upset she got when the sand would come in under the door.

As Grand Coulee Dam progressed, we finally moved out of that little dust-gathering apartment in 1937 and bought a house for seven hundred dollars. Which doesn't sound like much of a house, but it was an attractive one, in a place called Electric City. It was so nice that it won the dam site's Home and Garden contest.

Not everyone was happy with the way things turned out. Sam Seaton, the ferryman, had owned part of the dam site. He was a little fella who loved horses and who liked to dance. He danced to about the day he died in his eighties. He and some others who had had property there felt badly treated because they never got paid for the value of the property as a site for a dam. They got paid only for scabland and sagebrush.

The Indians felt the same way, that they never got compensated. Now they are making quite a lot of noise, hoping that they will get paid at this late date for the flooding of part of the Colville Indian Reservation.

I have written more about the dam, of course, than anybody else ever has. I have seen more concrete poured than any other newsman in the history of the world. I particularly remember that great day when they poured twenty-six thousand, eight hundred and some cubic yards of concrete in twenty-four hours. That set a record that has never been approached.

One thing I learned as a news reporter was that you don't pour cement, you pour concrete. Cement is the powder. Engineers gave me the devil about that.

The concrete in the dam would circle the earth one and a half times as a sidewalk. We always used stuff like that. I wrote stories about changes such as when the first bathtub came to Coulee Dam in the Columbia Hotel. I wrote about anything, because I reported on a space-rate basis instead of a salary. In other words, I got paid by how much copy that they ran. So much for a column inch.

Sometimes the bus driver would forget to deliver the envelope with my copy. I would just roar at that because I would lose a day's pay.

One story has followed me all my life. It concerns the contractor testing different kinds of tractors. Caterpillars and other brands. He wanted to see which tractor would do the best job in the mud. I got there late, saw a group of fellas standing around, and I said, "What tractor won this?"

A man said, "Earthworm. The Earthworm Tractor."

I had never heard of the Earthworm Tractor so I double checked, as a good reporter should do. I went up to another group and said, "Fellas, what tractor won that?"

Someone said, "Earthworm."

What I didn't know was that the same guy who had first said "Earthworm" was answering me again. So it came out in the *Spokane Chronicle* how the Earthworm Tractor had won this test. Well, the Earthworm Tractor was a tractor sold by the fictitious Alexander Botts in a serialized story in *The Saturday Evening Post!*

I had been starving to death and I had never had any money to buy *The Saturday Evening Post.*

Subsequently somebody would say, "I was on a plane going to Boston and some fella told me a story about you." I always replied that I knew what the story was.

They *never* let me forget that.

I also wrote about the frequent raids on the madams and gamblers on B Street in Coulee City. In those days the Washington State Patrol was the police agency because the dam site was where four counties came together. Lincoln, Douglas, Okanogan, and Grant.

But I didn't write about some subjects. For instance, about Harvey Slocum, who was the head of the dam project for the contractor. He had never got out of the eighth grade but he had submitted the low bid for the job. Harvey was a heavy drinker and he would disappear to spend three days in the whorehouses up on B Street. I didn't write about that.

The whorehouses were always second-story places up above the beer parlors. One summer the girls were complaining about how hot their second-story place was, so Harvey sent up a plumbing crew and put a sprinkling system on the whorehouse's roof!

Sometimes when the city of Grand Coulee ran out of money, two councilmen took a pillowslip to the whorehouses and collected enough money to keep the city going. Some streets were graveled with the whores' money, if my memory serves me correctly. There was never anything criminal about it. Those fifty-five women just paid their taxes, I guess.

The reason that I know that there were fifty-five was that later I interviewed a doctor who retired in Wenatchee and he reminded me that he had been health officer at the dam site. When I asked him how many prostitutes there had been, he said, "Fifty-five." Then he added proudly, "And not one of them got infected."

Dancing was a popular form of entertainment in Grand Coulee. But it was so muddy in the winter that someone would have to get a shovel now and then and shovel the mud off the dance floor that the guys coming off the street would bring in on their boots. The summers were so dusty that they would sweep the dust out of dance halls at intermission.

I wrote about everything. About the mud. About the deaths on the dam. The new methods of doing something. People in the town, the city council. I even became a sandhog and went under the river under pressure. I did everything there was to do.

Being a sandhog was probably the most exciting story I did at the dam site. What was involved was a crew of jackhammermen drilling a foundation for a bridge pier on bedrock. A caisson had been built around the work area, but water kept seeping in so a pneumatic caisson had to be resorted to. That involved building up pressure in an airtight container.

In order for me to get to the bedrock I had to enter a can-like container about six feet in diameter and about eight feet high. Me and about a half dozen other guys entered it through an opening in the top. Then pressure was applied. When that pressure equalized the pressure of the work area, a hatch in the bottom of the container could be opened and I had to climb about fifty feet down a slippery ladder to the rock.

It was a scary experience because the jackhammers chattering away on the rock in that confined area made a noise that sounded as though they were drilling a tomb. After a half hour there I was glad to make my way back into the can by way of the bottom opening. Once inside, the pressure was lowered until the top lid could be opened. I've never forgotten how great it was to see the stars above again.

One of the most sensational stories I wrote involved the slide of a million yards of earth. I was in a shoe repair shop in Grand Coulee getting a heel put on my huge boots when someone came running into the place to say, "Blonk, get down there. They've had a helluva slide."

I yelled to the shoemaker, "Put that heel back on. Hurry!" Then I ran a quarter mile or more to the area he mentioned and got the facts.

A million cubic yards of earth had slid down the hillside where the highway makes a semicircle directly below where the dam now sits. The mass of earth had forced a steamshovel up onto a thirty-five foot high ridge it created, and had sent ninety or so men scurrying every which way to avoid the cracks which were opening and closing as the material moved down.

The slide had been caused by the men and equipment excavating for the dam having taken out the toe of the mass. Soap seams prevalent in the material had caused the earth to move.

Once I had the facts I dashed to the only public phone in the area. I had to hitch a ride on somebody's running board. I was also with the Associated Press and I wanted to beat the UPI guy. I got there in time and phoned it in for the morning editions. That was one of the last extras that the *Spokane Chronicle* ever put out in those days. Soon after that extras disappeared from newspapers.

The other big story that I enjoyed writing very much was when a cofferdam broke. Cofferdams consisted of cells made of steel piling filled with earth. One of them broke and the water from the Columbia started to flood the work area. Harvey Slocum, the construction boss, was down there in his red pajamas. His crews threw

Christmas trees, mattresses, everything in there without success to try to stop the flood. Finally they brought in some bentonite, which is a clay silt that, when water hits it, expands seven times its normal size. So it swelled up and, along with some steel piling driven into the ground, ultimately saved the day. Otherwise, that broken cofferdam would have tied up the job for a long time.

There was one memorable time for me when Franklin Delano Roosevelt came and went across the river on the power ferry. He wasn't supposed to, but he did. The next morning the fella who ran the cable ferry (which was there before the dam started), Sam Seaton, told me that it was lucky the president hadn't been there the day after, because he would have gotten a wild ride, the motor having stopped. Without checking it out I put it in the paper. It was lousy reporting because you always check *two* sources.

The next morning I happened to meet the fella that ran the power ferry. The angry Cap Tuttle asked, "You write that story?"

I said, "Yeah." Clunk, he hit me right in the side of the head and down I went.

He hit me because he said I had libeled him and made his ferry operator look terrible, by saying that the president of the United States had been endangered. I said, "Cap, if I am wrong, I will correct it. But otherwise you can hit me eight more times and I won't change it."

Cap Tuttle and I later became good friends.

Of all the characters at the dam, my favorite was Harvey Slocum, who ran the job for the contractor. He was a typical construction stiff. He drank, cussed. Just a rugged individualist.

Harvey finally got drunk up there one time too many and was fired by George Atkinson, who was associated with one of the companies in the combine that was building the first half of the dam. So I said to George, "What will I give as a reason, George?"

He said, "Oh, ill health."

Later when I came into the Continental Hotel up in Grand Coulee, I saw Harvey sitting across the room and noted that he had been drinking. When he saw me, he hollered out, "goddamn you, Blonk."

I walked up and I said, "What's the matter, Harvey?"

He said, "You put in that goddamned paper of yours that I was canned because of ill health. You know goddamned well that I was drunk.''

He was a lovable guy. Acted tough. Was tough. Later on, when he built the Bhakra Dam in India after having quit drinking, Khrushchev came to visit. Harvey was quoted in *True* magazine as saying, "I could probably do your job, but you would play hell doing mine."

That is typical of Harvey.

When he left Grand Coulee Dam the fellas bought him a car and he had tears in his eyes. He was just a great guy, an early day American construction stiff.

My friends called me "Scoop" but once *I* got badly scooped. The builders were having trouble filling a deep crevice in the bedrock with concrete. Gooey mud and dirt from above kept sliding into the hole. It kept sliding, so they built a little bulkhead, but the mud slid over the top of that. So they still couldn't pour concrete.

I was in the concrete lab when someone reported that Grant Gordon, who was a young Bureau engineer, had said, "Why don't we freeze it?" The boys laughed at the idea and I laughed with them.

But by golly, a couple of mornings later I read on the front page of my rival paper, *The Spokesman-Review,* that that was exactly what they were going to do, build an ice dam by feeding refrigerating brine through pipes sunk into the mud. When the concrete was high enough, normal concrete pouring could take place.

I had had that story but I got scooped anyway. I just hated to be beat on anything. To this day I don't want to be beat on even a PTA item.

After leaving the reporting scene at the dam site in 1941 when the dam was virtually finished, I became assistant project information officer there for the Bureau of Reclamation, and later was Pacific Northwest regional information officer with offices in Boise.

In the latter job we helped to get the potential water users to sign construction repayment contracts, agreeing to pay the share of the construction cost that was within their ability to repay, the rest to come out of power revenues. We had public meetings all over the basin and in distant parts of the state where the landowners lived.

So I got to know a lot of farmers. Jake Weber was one of them. I don't know how many agencies he belonged to, but he was on the Quincy-Columbia Basin Irrigation District board. The project was run by three irrigation districts and Jake was always in there pitching. They wanted water. It was the most precious thing there was. Land was worthless without water.

Dick Penhalluric of Moses Lake was a good promoter for the project too. I remember him particularly because during the 1950s, when I was Northwest information officer, I wanted to do something to draw national attention to the project by publicizing the initial delivery of water from Lake Roosevelt. So with the aid of Penhallurick and others we turned a sixty-acre piece of land into a completed farm overnight. In twenty-four hours the sagebrush was removed, the land leveled, the irrigation run in, and a cow, barn, and a completely furnished house set up. It was a sensational event we'd dreamed up!

It drew tremendous publicity. I'm still proud of what we did.

FRANK "BOW HILL" BOB:
CHIEF OF THE TARHEELS
Alger, WA
Born: 1902

Highrigger Hod Wood had encouraged me to search for his former mentor at the Alger Tavern. And sure enough I found the old logger at the bar nursing a beer[1] and killing time. Quite a change of pace, I thought, from the early years of this century when Bow Hill had participated with thousands of other men in one of the greatest, decades-long logging shows in history. Timber! How many trees had this man heard fall? How many board feet had he helped send to the mills?

Frank Bob is a Skagit Indian who got his nickname from the place where he was born. Bow Hill is one of my favorite environs because for many years I have been helping the Pacific Northwest Trail Association locate and construct new trail nearby. Over the years I have met a lot of Tarheels there. Of course, they are John-nie-come-latelies compared to Bow Hill.

When Bow Hill was born, the virgin forests of the Northwest had scarcely been touched except along the coasts and rivers. They still looked much the same as they had in his grandfather's time before the period of white settlement.

He worked in the woods all his life. I was most interested to hear about his river log drives, when he and the other shingle bolt drivers guided the big chunks of cedar down the Baker River from the original pre-dam Baker Lake to Concrete. And down the Sauk River above Darrington.

---

[1] A year after our first interview, Bow Hill suffered a stroke and gave up drinking.

That was quite a life. There were no cabins along the river to stay in at night. In good weather you slept out at night. In bad weather we set up a little tent.

We carried only two sets of clothes. We were always wet because we waded up to our waists every day and sometimes fell in over our heads. So we'd always arrive in camp totally wet. If it was raining, we couldn't dry our wet clothes out with a bonfire so we'd ring em out and put on our dry set. Then in the morning, if it was still raining, we'd put the wet ones back on again because we didn't dare let both pairs of clothes get wet.

Bow Hill was active in other aspects of logging, too. He horse-logged his own place and he worked with steam and diesel machinery and with spar trees. When he was no longer agile enough after age forty to climb and rig the two-hundred-foot tall firs, he became the assistant of a young highrigger named Hod Wood. "I'd send the rigging up to him," says Bow Hill, "and if he needed help, I always gave him a few pointers."

Bow Hill showed me souvenirs from his early days in the woods. Things such as a leather punch he had used on his horses' harnesses. But, like artifacts in museums, these suggested more questions than they answered.

How to sum up a life?

As Hod Wood had told me, "He was one of the nicest guys you ever could log with. He could get more work out of a crew. He did it the easiest way. He was just an artist at communicating with people of all different lives. Buy him one beer and charge it to me."

I was born April 6, 1902, right here about four hundred feet across Friday Creek from where my home is now. When I was a boy Alger was called Lookout and where my home is was called Desmond, Washington.

I was raised by Tarheel people. There had been a shingle mill, the American Shingle Company of Burlington, at Desmond for many years. It burned down in 1908 just before some logging families such as the Daveses and the Garlands moved into its cabins. In 1909 those loggers moved here from Camp Two at Cain

Lake because Bloedel Donovan was moving its operation south. Quite a few of those loggers were from Carolina.

My father, Johnnie Bob, had homesteaded at Desmond in 1892. (Four other Skagit Indians were homesteading then on Bow Hill.) And he died about 1910.

My mother died when I was a baby and I don't remember her. She was also a Skagit Indian.

I grew up more or less with the Daves's family. They didn't adopt me but Mrs. Daves always said, "One more don't make no difference." They had a large family of maybe ten kids.

Tom Daves[2] and I were nearly the same age and he and I went to Alger school together. Then I went to the Indian Training School in Tulalip which was mostly for orphans like I was or for kids whose parents followed the hops and potato or other harvests, and so they couldn't go to a regular school.

When Tom Daves and I were fifteen or sixteen years old, we went to work for Bloedel Donovan. In later years I worked for Scott Paper at Hamilton where there were many Tarheels.

When I first went to work in the woods, some boys had just come from Carolina. They used different words in their language. One day a boy came to ask me, "Bow, where can I find a branch?"

I didn't say nothing. I just walked off.

---

[2]Belle Garland was Tom Daves's aunt.

I came back to him in an hour or so, after I had figured out what he was looking for. By "branch" he meant a little stream where he could get a drink of water.

So I grew up with Tarheels and later worked with them. They're nice, friendly people. I felt we were all equal. I was Indian and they were Tarheel and it didn't make any difference. We were all working in the woods for the same purpose—to make a living.

Mrs. Daves's friendship made a big impression on me. She had a lot of children but she made room for me. [Tears and crying.]

She was very tall but not overweight, because she was always busy working so hard to take care of that big family. For instance, packing water from Friday Creek in a bucket. None of us had water or lights in our houses. The only lights we saw where when we went to town.

She had a Carolina accent but she and her family had been here quite awhile and did not have such a strong Carolina way of speaking and neither did I. I spoke only Indian language till I went to school, but then I lost it after my father died and I grew up with non-Indians.

Mrs. Daves was kind to everybody. If some of the women were having a baby, they called on her to help.

Her son Tom was my best friend. He was about my size. He took after his mother and I did, too. His old man was friendly but very quiet.

Mrs. Daves's husband, Cope Daves, was a good logger and I learned it from him. He never had too much to say but if you made a mistake, he'd show you how to do it right. Like setting chokers and being sure that I was out of the way when logs were moved. I looked up to him like a father.

Carolinians are the friendliest people in the world. The nicest. They'd help you any way in the world if you needed help. You bet! That's Carolina people.

They live from where Hod Wood is [Hamilton, WA], clear up to Marblemount and up to Darrington. No matter how many of them there are, they are all one family. No matter what, they help each other.

I am way older than Hod Wood. Gosh, I don't know what year I met him. It was at Scott Paper at Hamilton. He was the second rigger, them days. See, the big operations, they have a head rigger and then they have a couple of seconds.

We worked together a few years at Hamilton and Baker Lake and Phinney Creek. When he got this job at Baker Lake, I went up with him. He was a rigger and he was the foreman of the operation. Hod was alright. He was good to work for.

I'd been through what he was doing but I was working for him. I don't know how old he was when I first met him. But he was always a good, friendly guy. We got along fine. If he needed help, I always gave him a few pointers. The same things happened to him that had happened to me when I was in charge of an operation. Like you break a cable half as big as your wrist and it has to go back together. After a couple of days, you couldn't even find the splice.

And then a lot of times something would go wrong up in the trees. A cable would break and run out through the block and have to be rethreaded and hoisted up again. A lot of things can go wrong up in a tree.

I wouldn't say that I was more responsible than Hod Wood. I liked Hod's hunting but I never went hunting like he did.

Tom Daves, whom I grew up with, liked work and had dogs. He'd work for a period of time and then take the dogs out hunting. Deer hunting. Bear hunting. Fox hunting. His wife, Blanche Daves, taught school in Alger for many years.

My wife never drank, smoked, or used foul language. If it hadn't been for my wife I wouldn't have had a nickel. I wanted to buy what I wanted. There is a difference between what you want and what you need. She'd buy what we needed. I'd see something that looked good and I'd think, "God, I want that. I'd like to have that. I want it." She'd say, "Think it over for a few days." She wouldn't tell me not to buy it but to think it over a few days. By the time I thought it over, I'd woke up. There's a difference between what you want and what you need, especially with a large family like I had. Eight kids.

Phyllis Kimball was from the Arlington-Oso area. Her sister Beatrice had married Ben Cline in Everson and Phyllis would come over to pick strawberries and raspberries. I was a good friend of Ben and Beatrice. I met Phyllis at their place when she was picking berries. She was very religious and I liked that. I was religious in my own way. The church is one way, but my way was in helping people, like Mrs. Daves had.

We married in Bellingham soon after we met.

I got married young and immediately had children. On the weekends I couldn't go hunting. There was always something to do here. The older ones in the family would help me work in the garden, and with the cows and the pigs and the chickens. I'd stay home with my wife and our eight children.

A lot of my Indian friends didn't drink. One nondrinking friend would just visit. He'd go into the tavern and order pop or a cup of coffee.

When I was young, all of them drank. Indians. Non-Indians. In the early days it was homebrew and moonshine. But I never started. I never thought about it. As soon as I saw the first bottle I'd say, "Good-bye boys" and I'd leave the party.

I didn't drink until my sons Herb and Tony came home from World War II. Raising a family, I never thought about drinking. But when the boys came home from the Army, I was so happy that they had come home in one piece, I went to Bellingham with them and drank some beer with them at a tavern. From then on I drank more, until I drank too much.

When Hod and I were working together, we'd stop at the tavern up at Hamilton. Hod never drank. He'd have a bottle of pop with us. One day I told him that I was the chief of the Tarheels.

Now when I drive up there, the old loggers will still say, "Shape up, you guys. The chief is here." We laugh. We always had a good time about that.

LAURA BORDERS:

4-H HORSE LOVER

Curlew, WA

Born: 1971

A century after statehood the horse is alive and well in Washington state. In fact, horses have never been more numerous since their great decline in the 1920s and 1930s. Of course, today's horses are not engaged in logging, freighting, and farming. True, some are used for working cattle, but the typical horse today is probably a quarter horse owned by a member of the Washington Backcountry Horsemen, the American Quarter Horse Association, and dozens of other horse groups. If there is such a thing as a typical Washington horse, it probably belongs to someone like Laura Borders.

When I met fourteen-year-old Laura at the Ferry County Fair, she and her quarter horse "Rocket" were on a winning streak. Laura had had Rocket for two years and had been training him for at least an hour a day. Her work was paying off in blue ribbons and, according to her instructor Debra Powell, in increased poise and leadership. "Laura is real devoted," said Debra. "She has real style and carries herself well. She has a certain amount of natural ability but she works at it, too. That's why she is a particularly good rider."

Debra Powell thought that Laura might go on to become a trainer, as she herself had done after many years as a 4-H girl. I had a vision of the generations of kids maturing under the banner of "Head, Heart, Hands, & Health." Of course, unlike the old days when horses were an *essential* part of rural life, boys are no longer likely to be a part of the horse world. "Ninety-five percent of my riding students have been girls," said Debra. "It's some type of maternal thing. The guys are into engines and motors. There aren't a whole lot of cowboys now and the few cowboys that are left are riding helicopters and motorcycles. But I don't care. There will always be enough girls out there wanting to ride horses and compete."

When we got Rocket two years ago, he had quite a bucking problem. So my mom took him to a trainer, Debra Powell, who retrained him. Then I started riding him. He still bucks occasionally and every once in awhile he bucks me off. Yesterday in the bareback class I had trouble with him bucking, but I still won.

Winning ribbons is fun but I do lots of things before the fair which are fun, too, like trail rides. And we have an arena on our land that I ride in. I take riding lessons all the time from my trainer, Debbie. She's better than most trainers. She handles horses real well. She usually comes down to our house and some of the other 4-H kids come over and she gives everybody lessons.

Rocket is hotblooded. He's bred to race. It's in his blood. I like him because he is exciting. Other horses are kind of boring.

I like racing and he wanted to race back there in that last event. But I don't race him, because it would ruin him. He'd be ruined in one race. [Sigh.] It's hard. He wanted to race back there but I held him in as tight as I could. He was crow-hopping. He wanted to take off.

It takes a good horse to ride well. It's hard to look nice riding a bad horse. If I show Rocket a lot, he probably won't have many more years left, because he'll get sour. I'm fourteen and Rocket is eight.

I have another horse in the barn but he's just a young horse so he doesn't work too well yet.

My events are Western riding, English riding (I like riding that way better), halter classes, pleasure, trail, and show. About a third of our school is doing 4-H. Most of them are in horses. There's not many boys. A lot of boys don't like horses. They are in beef and hogs.

It's fun. It's a lot of work, but it's fun. You've got to ride your horse every day, but if you ride them too much, doing the same thing all the time, they go sour.

Mom became a 4-H leader after I got into 4-H. We have other projects besides horses. I have to do some housework and help take care of all the animals: horses, calves, cows, dogs, chickens, ducks, kittens, cats. I have hamsters and guinea pigs and gerbils. Probably about one hundred animals all together.

I buy my own stuff for Rocket. With all the feed and stuff Rocket costs me five hundred dollars a year. I get an allowance and sometimes I work for Debbie Powell.

Debbie has inspired me because she is so dedicated to horses and because she is so skillful. Her specialty is show jumping and I would someday like to be as good a rider as she is.

EARL BRYANT: CAPTAIN, "LADY OF THE LAKE"
Chelan, WA
Born: 1908

Earl Bryant came by his career as a freighter captain via Omak orchards and sawmills where he was "big and husky and could get out a day's work." In 1931 he gravitated to Manson on Lake Chelan to another ten-hour-a-day, six-day-a-week sawmill job. By 1947 he had moved up the lake to operate a tugboat for Holden, Washington's Howe Sound Mine. When a job as a pilot opened up on the lake's freight, postal, and passenger boat, Earl jumped at the chance. Soon he was running the show, every day of the week for much of the year. The former apple picker was now "Captain Bryant."

It took Earl about three and a half hours to guide his seventy-five foot, wooden "Lady of the Lake" the fifty-five miles from Chelan to Stehekin. He carried passengers, mail, and freight to supply the isolated pioneer community at the head of the lake. Today's Lady of the Lake is a one-hundred-foot steel ship, but the work is essentially the same as when service began at the beginning of the century. In 1927 a dam raised the lake level and moderated its seasonal fluctuations. Creation of North Cascades National Park and Lake Chelan National Recreation Area in 1968 accelerated the Lady's transformation from backwoods freighter to tourist excursion vessel.

In a short period of time Lake Chelan has gone from trappers, homesteaders, and miners to condos, congestion, and regulation.

It is as if we had awakened one morning and the lake's old-timers had slipped around the bend taking their history with them.

Earl Bryant retired in 1968. I asked him how he had originally qualified as captain.

The Lady of the Lake (Credit: Puget Sound Maritime Historical Society, Inc.)

On my first run in 1957 I asked the boss and owner, "Who's in charge?"

He said, "You are, because you are the captain. You make a decision and I'll decide whether it was right or wrong when you get back. I will give you hell or praise you for it."

I never got any hell.

But lots of these guys are either pilots or engineers or navigators. When I took out a boat, I was the pilot, engineer, navigator, *and* everything else.

You had to be smart enough to figure out what to do to save your life, the boat, and other people's lives. I worked fourteen, sixteen, twenty hours, sometimes in emergencies. If someone had an emergency up the lake and there was a storm so that the plane couldn't go, I would get in a passenger boat and bring them out to a hospital. I was always available for that.

I have seen waves. . . . They never did get over five feet high but when you take a seventy-five mile an hour wind, it's not the waves so much as the hard blowin' wind. You can lose control of your boat fast if you do not know what to do, whether to keep the stern to the wind or the bow to the wind.

Twice the lake froze from Twenty-five Mile Creek on down. The lake was down low and extremely cold. After the propeller had stirred up the water you could see it glaze over. We had a steel landing barge that we used to break a trail through. It would chop through the ice and we would follow along close behind.

It was always interesting. Different storms, winds, snow and ice. You always had to be on your toes.

From April 15 to the middle of December the Lady of the Lake used to go up to Stehekin every day. In the wintertime we ran three days a week because the mail needed to go three days a week. I've made lots of trips up there with no passengers at all, just to deliver the mail to places along the shore.

Our boat held a hundred and fifty passengers. Lots of times in summer we would have that loaded down. Then we would hit a storm and have to run it by ear and be damned careful. As pilot and captain I had to see that the boat landed safely. Driftwood was the worst danger. In the spring, washouts up in the hills would wash timber down into the lake. We had to be careful that we didn't run over a log and wreck the prop or knock a hole in the boat.

Only one time was there so much ice that we couldn't go. Except for that one time in, I think, '49 we always went, because we had a mail contract and the mail *must* go through. If a storm came up, it might be blowing across the lake, down the lake, up the lake, a head wind or a tail wind, and I had to run her according to what the situation was.

I can remember during that big Entiat fire in 1970, the wind kept adrivin' and drivin' for two weeks. I put in fourteen hours a day making a good many trips with firefighters. We had two boats and we loaded them down to take people up the lake to get to the fires. There were no roads. The only other way to get in there was to bail out of an airplane and parachute down to a fire.

One time we got a message that a fire had some firefighters surrounded at the edge of the lake. The wind had changed, had brought the fire down through the timber, and had trapped them at the water. They got all excited about that, but there was no need for it because the men could have gotten out in the water. Hell, they didn't need to be rescued at all because they could have swum out into the water. But we sent up both boats, and a big wind came up and damned near swamped both of them. Rocked them over far enough that they flooded. Inexperienced pilots! Lucky it didn't sink them.

A lot of the packers like Ray Courtney were working that fire bust. I sure liked some of those old-timers. Guy Imus was a packer that hired his horses out to take people into the hills for pack trips. A friendly and all-around good guy. Oscar Getty was another one. He had a string of horses. When the mine was running at Holden he packed all their supplies and building materials into the mine to get it started.

Harry Buckner ran the post office up at Stehekin in his little store. Raised a family up there. He was pretty quiet, just an ordinary guy who was friendly and liked people. He would set down and talk to people in his store and tell them the history of Stehekin. He could remember all the old-timers.

Gordon Stuart lived at Domke Lake at Lucerne. He had come in there as a young man in 1925. He trapped cougars, coyotes, beavers, mink, or whatever. He was quite a character. Gordon had traplines in the area up from Domke and across the Chelan Mountains to the Entiat side. He lived by trapping minks, martens, and stuff like that.

And huntin' cougars for bounties. He had one dog named Rupert and he would go out and get on a cougar track. He would go out without any supplies except a tarp and some food for Rupert. That dog would track and tree the cougar and Gordon would shoot it. Until then Gordon would just build a fire in a rock shelter someplace and live in that.

There are lots more people going up the lake now. It has gotten commercialized. The National Park took it over and started pullin' people around. They had their businesses set up and the National Park come in and upset the whole deal. Bought out property that they weren't supposed to. It has been an upset, dissatisfied community ever since.

People up there had their own way of doing things. That's the way they lived it. The National Park came in and started telling them what they could do and what they couldn't do. People used to hunt, trap, fish, whatever they wanted to do. Now they've got to where they can't even keep a dog around.

Of course, the people on the lake have changed, too. It used to be more like one big village all up and down the lake. Everybody knew everyone and everybody was doing something for someone else. Helping other people out. If anybody got burned out or got robbed or something, everybody moved in and helped them out. Now when you are burned out or get robbed, you are just on your own.

I used to be able to name everybody up and down the lake. Knew when they came in and when they left and why. But it's gettin' so built up so that nobody knows who's who and who's where and why.

SOUTH BURN:

BUILDING WITH LOGS

Waldron Island, WA

Born: 1924

Nothing symbolizes more the vast changes that have overtaken Washington during its first century of statehood than the status accorded the home-built cabin in our laws and folkways. In my early interviews across the Northwest I encountered homesteaders whose accounts of log construction rang with pride and nostalgia. And I have listened to urban back-to-the-landers tell the same tales of cutting logs, peeling bark, raising courses of walls, cutting windows and doorways, and roofing and enclosing the new wonder. That this thread continues throughout our short period of American settlement is one of the many charms of Washington.

Today's cabin builders are a quirky, competitive bunch—much like their predecessors were. Standardization is not their forte and the results are often amazing and sometimes beautiful.

What has become increasingly clear, though is that today's burgeoning, highly mobile population is not the old homesteading society on which many of our mores have been based. For example, if everyone in Seattle were permitted to heat with wood, the city's air quality would often be extremely hazardous instead of merely dangerous. And if everyone in newly populous areas were permitted to build noncode houses, property transactions and liability claims might be in chaos.

Yet the old "put 'er up, by God, and hope she don't fall down" approach has undeniable appeal.

South Burn knows all about it. He grew up with his brother, North Burn, in a literary (and log cabin-building) family in about the farthest point of the San Juan Islands. Waldron Island to this day still does nicely without either electricity or telephones. (I remember that when I visited there in the 1970s, little children spoke of electricity with the same awe which mainland children reserved for Santa Claus or the Tooth Fairy.) South Burn has lived a lifetime in log cabins and he believes that his experience is valuable to preserve for the next generations of by-the-seat-of-the-pants builders.

South Burn outside his Chuckanut Mountain cabin.

What is different now? Why must the county become inserted into this essentially personal equation in which one's personal concept of habitability, regardless of how eccentric or ignorant it may be, should be the only consideration? Something is irretrievably lost by each of us when some one of us is prevented by bureaucratic, irrelevant rules from living in a home we have built on our own place for our own use.

I asked South Burn to tell me about the ties he remembered between family and home.

The first house I knew was the "Carter Cabin" on Johns Island. We spent summers on Johns. My folks, Farrar and June Burn, were rich and successful. (They were always successful, but only this once, rich.) I was young and my images are randomly focused and blurred at the edges. I remember dark logs, the back door (leading to the privy), head-high room partitions, and a green-painted platform swing in the yard. I remember rock outcroppings, beach logs, and the brown beach. I also remember that my brother North could pull the starter rope out of the giant ten-horsepower Johnson but I could not.

The "Carter Cabin" was still usable a few years back but the porch was rotting and the platform swing only decayed remnants.

The next house, of which I have more vivid memories, Dad had built on a 1922 Dodge chassis. It was painted yellow, with black trim and with red brick fenders (fake), running boards, flower pots (on the fenders), and a fold-down chimney atop a real shingle roof and attic. On the back was hung the "grub box" containing all our food and cooking supplies. On each side, in huge black letters was printed *BURN'S BALLAD BUNGALOW,* and in smaller letters, "Sings and Sells His Own Songs."

The running boards were cases full of Dad's songs, which he sang while dressed in troubadour costume, standing atop a fold-up stage over the engine.

Our year-long, U. S. song-selling tour ended in 1929 in South Bellingham, Washington. There, on two acres gotten in exchange for Mother's boat, Dad built the first of two log cabins while we camped in the Dodge.

The first one-room cabin later became the "kitchen" cabin and North's and my bedroom, after Dad built another cabin which had a graceful bird-wing, curved roof and an arched door and window. This second cabin became the main living cabin and was called the "study cabin" because in it Mother wrote her daily column, "Puget Soundings," for the *Bellingham Herald.* Into this cabin, also, came an organ and running water.

These cabins were the base office of Dad's and Mother's monthly magazine, the *Puget Sounder,* which faded away early in the Depression. The two acres and cabins (now part of Fairhaven College campus) were deeded to the printer in exchange for the printing bill, and we moved to our place on Waldron Island, bought with Dad's WWI veteran's bonus.

Dad liked tools. He kept them clean and sharp. He built, first, a nine-by-fourteen-foot tool shed. It became our Waldron home for the next twenty years.

It was built of logs set right on the ground with a floor of beach planks and sandstone slabs. One corner was made into a fireplace by cutting a hole in the roof for a cedar shake, quarter-funnel smoke catcher, and by haphazardly lining the corner with smeared clay and stone slabs. In the other front corner were North's and my bunks and the organ.

That house had magic. With friends in, lamps lit, fire crackling, shadows flickering on the log walls, Mother playing "Heart Songs" on the organ—or singing duets of Dad's songs, accompanied by him on his guitar—that cabin was a never-before and never-again experience. No silver-spooned child could have had a richer childhood.

Dad built Mother a nine-by-nine log study cabin on a rock point over the beach. One wall was built entirely of filing cabinets with a small bunk tucked in. It had another of Dad's instant fireplaces. This cabin violated every known rule of good construction: too-small-for-*any*-use, unpeeled logs set right on the ground; a fireplace certain to catch fire; and a shake roof too flat to shed rain.

It was perfect!

That cabin is still there and still usable over half a century later.

Not so the "Boys' Cabin," a five-corner log cabin so precisely divided (fireplace in the fifth corner) as to be virtually argument-proof. In 1934, as a complete surprise, the Folks gave it to North and me for Christmas.

A few years later two visiting girls accidentally burned it down. Years later, I married one of them, Doe.

Not wishing to go to high school in New York (where Dad and Mother then lived), I returned to Bellingham to live with friends. They owned a lot of the forested west slope of Chuckanut Mountain, south of town. They let me build my first real cabin there. I lived in it for most of my last two years of high school.

My childhood heroes had been cowboys because they were stoic and nonverbal. But in high school my hero was Thoreau of *Walden*.

I built my cabin eleven by seventeen feet, one room set on cedar sill logs on stone piers. It had pole floor joists, plank floors and ceiling, and moss-chinked log walls with traditional and not very skillful corner notches. The roof shakes were hand split from logs found nearby and the building logs were cut and dragged to the site by a borrowed workhorse.

A freshly-peeled, spring-cut building log is very slippery. When dragged downhill, it will shoot ahead between the legs of the horse, upsetting its tranquility.

The cabin had a corner fireplace, shipmate stove, closet, double bunk below for guests (rare) and a single above for me. It had a bench and log ends for sitting and a tree-round fixed to a dugout stump for a table. And there was a row of windows looking out over virtually the entire upper Puget Sound.

There were only two other houses on the mountain, both miles away, and deer, perhaps intrigued by my rhythmic chopping, frequently stopped while I was building.

Each weekday I ran down the mountain trail from my cabin to catch the school bus to high school. Each evening I studied by Aladdin light at a log-round table in front of the crackling fireplace. That cabin was the cocoon, essential to me, in which the chrysalis which was to become me was formed. I grew up in Seattle, Bellingham, San Francisco, and New York, but my inner self was formed in those cabins.

In later years, North's house was something special. When he found he had terminal cancer in the mid-70s, I suggested that he come back to Waldron where he had childhood memories and loving friends. He camped in a beach shack while we planned his cabin.

After looking at all the available sites on his property, we decided on a site on my property, facing west. Actually it wasn't on my property either, but straddled the property line between my place and that of my best friend and ex-wife, Doe, who had been a friend to both of us since childhood.

With North's cabin as with all the cabins mentioned before, there were but two groups of considerations—where to build it and who was to use it. The *where* considered the site, its size, character, outlook. The *who* considered its purpose, money available, and the imagination and capability of the owner and builder.

North's house was personal. He was an immaculate housekeeper, a gourmet cook, and personally fastidious. He loved fine music, was a prodigious letter writer and a gracious host. He needed a cabin designed, but not obtrusively designed, to accommodate his near-total leg paralysis from polio. The point of North's house was that it be beautiful, comfortable, easy to live in, and that we get him into it fast.

To build it I simply planted three rows of cedar logs solidly into the ground and built a roof over them. I dragged other cedar logs alongside each row of uprights and built a floor over them, and walls supported by the floor between the uprights. The spaces between uprights was filled with cedar chunks, rough-sawn cedar boards, and pleasing patterns of windows (using secondhand sashes). With completion of the bay window, desk, and cabinets, North moved in.

North's cabin glowed with love, and soft lamplight reflected off satin brown, red, and yellow woods of several textures—planed, sanded, or rough-sawed.

North loved his cabin with the intensity of one who knows his loving-time is nearing an end.

I am still living in the log cabin Doe and I built in 1951 on the site of the torn-down "Tool Shed." On the right the fire jumps and crackles. I've just finished a bowl of chili which simmered over the fireplace all afternoon.

This house, loaded with hazards and code violations, is my home. It was the home of my family for several years. Three of my children were born in this house and several grew up in it. This house has seen lots of loving, lots of happiness, and a share of sadness.

In that Waldron "Tool Shed" cabin of my childhood, built by my father during the Great Depression for less than two dollars and fifty cents, I learned how to be wealthy, to have a bountiful surplus of everything money could buy—without money.

I learned, too, that a cabin should not jerk and jut and try to assert power over its piece of earth. It should rather express gratitude.

Each separate piece of a house must be treated with respect and assembled into a harmonious whole. Even showpieces of exceptional beauty or artistry should blush shyly when admired and not jump out saying, "Look at me, aren't I cute?"

SAM CASSEL:

SALOONKEEPER

Republic, WA

Born: 1910

Ferry County's county seat began its existence as a prospectors' tent city at the end of the nineteenth century. Then as now, Republic's primary underpinning was gold.

Sam Cassel operated a combination hotel and tavern in Republic for three decades. Although his stories centered on the town's rough and ready characters, Sam himself was colorful enough when he served his barroom customers from atop his pony, Pistol.

I'm tougher than a boot! I came to Republic in 1948 and ran a hotel bar and grill till I sold out in 1976. Most people would have quit long before that!

I had been in the entertaining business with my own band at State Line Gardens on the Idaho-Washington line. One day a tire salesman said, "Sam, there's a fantastic cardroom and tavern for sale up at Republic made of varnished tamarack slabs."

So I became the owner of the Bailey Hotel, changed to Cassel's Tavern. The tavern was built in 1934 when the liquor laws changed. A sign on the side of the hotel said, "Meals 35 (cents)." Bea Van Meekeren took care of the hotel and was the cook. I had a nice dining room in the back with white table cloths. It was real home style cooking.

They called that part of town Buttercup Hill. I tore down twenty-five old log cabins where there had been many saloons and a cathouse.

The hotel often had unusual guests. Like Stanley Dempski. Stanley was a New York gangster who bootlegged here and stayed in the hotel. He'd come downstairs and steal everyone's money off the bar. He was a kleptomaniac. Honest!

But he was awfully clean. If anyone sat in his chair, he'd wipe it off afterwards. He kept a car in the back and every once in awhile my tools would disappear into it. I had a special key and once a month I'd go out and get my own tools back from Stanley's car.

Morrie and Dick Slagle at the drugstore used to say when they saw him coming, "Leave everything else and watch that man."

I borrowed money from him, and when he died he left me twenty-five hundred dollars. Isn't that strange?

Another hotel guest would shoot his rifle into the hill from inside the hotel. And when he was mad, he'd jump into his car and drive all over town with one hand on the horn!

Prospector Days were pretty wild, too. They combined a rodeo and a prospectors' celebration. In the beginning it was mostly genuine prospectors. But those guys are down the drain now.

Any town you go to there are always a few people that when they get a few drinks in them they get wild. And when brothers get together, watch out! Brothers will gang up on anybody who gets out of line. It used to happen quite a little bit here in the 1950s. We had a big gang of brothers, local guys, come into town one night and start fighting. The sheriff, Fred Murray, was locked in the ladies' room while the brothers went on with their big to-do.

Every night somebody passed out at my tavern. We had one cop here, and every night he took 'em home.

And there were fights. We had a gang fight in there one night during the rodeo. There was a group from Curlew and a group of rodeo guys, cowboys up from Deer Park and all over. A group of Canadians walked in and began playing pool for money. The rodeo guys said, "Your goddamn Canadian money isn't worth a crap."

They started arguing and here they come. They started battling. They hit each other and they kicked each other when they were down. The bartenders hollered at my wife in the back in our apartment to come out and help get everyone out. We got them out into the street and we closed up.

Next, the Canadians and rodeo guys went down the street to

Henry's and Jim Hall challenged 'em. They fought with beer glasses and hit each other over the head with pool sticks. The city cop looked in the window and didn't even attempt to go in there. They broke all the beer pitchers. It was a real free-for-all. Oh, that was a bad one! Then the Canadians went up to Curlew and cleaned that tavern out.

In the 1960s when we first had the Job Corps up at the old military base near Curlew, there were a bunch of coloreds there and the local yokels didn't like that. One night the Job Corps foreman called me up and said, "We want to take our group up to Grand Forks. Could you cash their checks?"

I cashed all the checks for the San Poil lumber mill and the Knob Hill Mine—ten thousand dollars worth each week—because the banks were always closed after three P.M. The banker would give me the money and I would keep a little percentage for cashing the men's checks.

Them colored boys that come in from the air base, I cashed their checks. They were real nice. Real quiet. But some local yokels started shouting, "Jesus Christ Almighty, get them niggers out of here."

It got so bad that I told the guys that were yelling that nigger stuff to cut it out. But when those colored boys took their belts off with the square buckles, right on Main Street, they laid those locals out like cordwood. After that the sheriff wouldn't let the Job Corps come to town for several months. But it wasn't their fault. They were nice kids who hadn't said a word. It was your local guys that done it.

We had such spoiled locals here! Any other place, they would have been in jail. One night a black man drove an Allied Van Lines truck into town and stopped for hamburgers at my place. Some local yokels took off after him. He ran across the street and jumped into his rig. I ran across and gave him his hamburger. I didn't charge him anything.

One year I bought a pretty good-sized Shetland pony as a pet for one of my daughters. I paid seventy-five dollars for Pistol.

Everyone had attempted to ride their horses into my tavern. The Burbanks had great big horses and they wanted to ride them straight into the bar. I didn't want that because the linoleum floor was slippery and I didn't have that kind of insurance.

But I put my little girl's rubber overshoes on Pistol's front feet so he couldn't slip and finally some on his back feet, too. I'd buckle those overshoes on up and Pistol would just walk on in there. God almighty, it was fabulous!

I began riding him in the tavern because I had gout in my feet and I couldn't get around. It was a huge bar with plenty of room in the back. I used to come in riding Pistol bareback and go right up to the cash register.

Women would get on his back and have their pictures taken. He'd yawn. He just loved girls. He'd nibble on 'em and they'd give him a little piece of candy.

Once when I was going around to customers on Pistol with a full tray of beer glasses, some local yokel poked Pistol in the flank. Pistol was startled. He got going one way. And the beer glasses got going the other way.

It was a horrible thing for a guy to do. He did it to cause some excitement. I was so mad! If I could have got off, I would have hit that guy!

I kept Pistol out back in a little barn. If he wanted a drink of water, he'd jump up into the back end of my hotel and go to the sink. At night I'd play them spoons to the jukebox and he'd nod. He had a mind just like a human being.

He was a lot nicer than some of our customers.

OME DAIBER:

LEGENDARY BOY SCOUTS

LEADER

Bothell, WA

Born: 1907

"I think it's a real pleasure for a leader to develop kids." Yes, that's Ome Daiber talking. The legendary Boy Scouts of America leader. One of the founders of Mountain Rescue. Inventor of all-season outdoor gear, both military and civilian. Alaskan wilderness surveyor. Ome was the climber who with Jim Borrow and Arnie Campbell made the first ascent of Mount Rainier's Liberty Ridge, one of the nation's most classic climbs. Ome was a beloved, cussed, respected figure, as ornery as a mountain storm and as concerned about kids as a mother hen.

Most of all, Ome was leadership. His old friend Max Eckenburg thought of Ome's concern for everyone on his team as being similar to that of Shackleton in the Antarctic. Ome's approach to mountaineering leadership was to choose his crew carefully, see that they were well prepared, and never demand something of them that he was not willing to do himself. What interests me about him is that although Ome Daiber looked like a changeless chunk of the mountains, his leadership had evolved with the seasons.

Ome joined a Scout troop in 1921 and quickly became the only kid in the unit who had a patrol leader rating. It happened that the Scoutmaster, George B. Dunn, was a clothing salesman who was often away selling suits. So at the age of sixteen Ome Daiber fell into the role of trying to play Scoutmaster to boys his own age or older. "I made a lot of mistakes," says Ome, "because I expected my peers to respond to me like they did to the Scoutmaster. Which they didn't. And being of the nature that I am, we had many a slugfest because they wouldn't follow my directions." Eventually he found that persuasion and discussion worked better than bullying, and his troop became such a success that fifty years later more than half of its members attended its reunion in Seattle.

In the years since 1921 when Ome joined that Scout troop, the Seattle area has become a national center. I have wanted to choose a person for this book who represents the best of what we have to offer. That's a heavy load to put on one person's shoulders, because the Seattle area boasts leaders in aerospace, medicine, education, business, the arts, and other fields. But I have chosen Ome Daiber because the essence of his work with kids, Mountain Rescue, and Scouting, is that "Leadership starts with knowing how to get along with people and to inspire their actions."

Here's a good example of Ome in action. In the '60s he took a group of black VISTA workers up Mount Adams as part of an outdoor leadership course and one of the "mass climbs of Mount Adams," about four hundred people, sponsored by the city of Yakima. Ome said that it was not what color they were that mattered but what he could make out of them. After a classic Daiber pep talk, one unlikely mountaineer said that he would climb that mountain if it was the last thing he ever did. The man succeeded and Ome says, "My point is that I sold the idea and then they were more than willing to do it."

I was surprised when Ome told me that it is not enough to be qualified for leadership with skills such as first aid. You also have to be humble, he said. Ome, humble? That was a new idea! "Are you always humble?" I asked politely.

Basically, yes. If I don't appear to be, I can guarantee you I am. And I can back-water like nothing. If I'm wrong, you're gonna hear about it in a hurry. No one is so good that he can't be wrong.

Well, humble maybe. Outspoken definitely. Ome did not mince words in his mountaineering narrations. There have been many famous climbers who have died tragically in our mountains, he said, because they were "as ignorant as dirt when it comes to snow and avalanches." And, "Doctors get strange ideas," meaning that they may have the temerity to refute part of Ome's decades of first aid know-how. But he was quick to heap blame on those whose errors led to death and disaster. And as he put it, "I've told people more than once. They don't like me."

Ome was usually so frugal that if he had to spend a nickel, you could hear that buffalo bellow all the way back to Nebraska. But fortunately he was not stingy with praise. If you planned your expedition as thoroughly as possible (meaning down to the last minute detail of equipment) and if you prepared yourself for every possibility, Ome could be downright effusive in his endorsement. For instance, he said of expedition leader Lou Whittaker, "He's good. He doesn't let personalities stick out. On Mount Everest in 1982 and 1984 he had men with him who had been on any number of climbs and who would stick with Lou regardless. Now that tells you something."

An Ome Daiber story is an experience. I've heard many of them. If you can wade through the blood and guts, you come to the heart of the matter.

Leadership comes down to little details. The leader has to know the answers. I led a hike once where one of the kids had new shoes and within less than a mile he was limping. His problem was that he had not cut his toenails. And if the leader doesn't know these damn things, he's stuck. The leader doesn't have to cut the guy's toenails but I've cut ingrown toenails off of people in the Tetons.

I mean, you can't let a guy cripple up on a mountain. You take care of it!

Ome told the following story about Delmar Fadden to a meeting of the Pacific Northwest Trail Association.

In May 1960 we had a rescue on Mount Rainier. One Delmar Fadden. A tremendous guy. He was only nineteen. He was the most wonderful combination you can imagine. He was an artist; he was a poet; he was a sculptor, a good student, and a powerhouse.

Delmar loved the out-of-doors. His life ambition in those years was to climb Mount Everest. The year before he had made the climb up Mount Baker in the wintertime.

He and his twin brother Don Fadden thought that Mount Rainier was about the best training Delmar could undertake to get ready for Everest. Don took Delmar up to White River, near the entrance, probably on skis. And Delmar circumvented the ranger station so he would not be seen starting up the mountain [without a permit].

Don came back to pick him up around New Year's and no Delmar. He then apprised the Park Service of what had taken place, which was, of course, against the rules. But when things become that urgent then you drop your guard and tell the authorities. Anyway, then he came downtown and told me. I got together some guys—Jack Hossack, Joe Halwax, Bob Buschmann (who was a friend of Delmar's), and Paul Gilbreath to do something about Delmar. Paul apprised the Park Service, of course.

We went up the White River. We had a toboggan, Joe and I did. Bob and Jack did, too.

We split at the White River/Frying Pan Creek junction. Joe and I continued up White River towards Starbo, an old mining camp, and on up to Interglacier. Jack and Bob went up Frying Pan Creek. We would rendezvous at Steamboat Prow, which is ninety-seven hundred feet at its very topmost point. The Prow where people can stay is one hundred feet less than that. An immense volcanic formation at ninety-six hundred feet. We were planning to make a snow cave for our sleeping bags and to have a tarp over the entrance.

I'll never forget that night. The snow was deep, clear up to your ears. One guy in front of the heavy toboggan and the other guy underneath holding it up. We got into Starbo after dark, using lights, and went on up Interglacier to the Prow, dug our snow cave, and got into our Penguin sleeping bags that had arms and legs. We covered the entrance with a tarpaulin and got ready for dinner.

How many of you like raw meat? My mother liked it totally dead. Cooked and cooked and cooked. Anyway, after leaving town, we stopped at Bob Buschmann's home. His dad was Eigel Buschmann, who was the head of Nacket Packing, which was a subsidiary of A&P stores. They served filet mignon an inch thick. Eigel told of a time up north when he and a companion were marooned on an island for a week or two and they had no means for producing fire. He told of eating the meat raw.

Of course, you don't eat bear or other carnivores for the reason that they carry trichinosis. But, anyway, Joe and I unpacked our packs after we dug our cave and covered it with a tarp over the entrance. Eigel had given us each a steak. The temperature was well below zero. So Joe said, "Well, let's try it". We were remembering what Eigel had told us and our knives were good and sharp and we shaved off a little bit. It was not hard to chew or swallow.

It was good! I've eaten my steaks rare ever since. Mother would be shocked!

Poor Delmar planned his expedition beautifully.

Except that he chose Eskimo mukluks for foot gear. They, if you don't know, are a soft moccasin boot.

There is no better footgear for keeping your feet warm than mukluks because they flex. Like a glove but soft and roomy, and thereby you stimulate circulation. You don't constrict circulation like you would in a rigid shoe.

He failed, however, to reckon with the fact that a crampon stays on your shoe where it belongs as a result of a rigid sole. Now, these words that I'm giving you at the moment were conclusions from what we found when we got to him, his body. The crampon on his left foot had come up around on the inside so that the prong was sticking out on the inside of the right leg, toward the pants, and the coroner later told us it lacerated the leg.

So he must have been making a right traverse. But the load of man and pack were such as to cause the crampon to slide around from the bottom of the foot up to the inside.

It's like the time that we had a rescue mission on Mount Stewart in July, 1952. The men we went to rescue had been struck by lightning.

I think to a large degree most people are not too capable in their analytical abilities to approach something that's new to them. You may remember some years back, the late '40s or early '50s, maybe, when a group of climbers, Sierra Club, were climbing in the Canadian Rockies and a storm came in on them. They got back in a cave, high on the mountain, and were electrocuted. From that, of course, a lot has been learned.

You don't get back into a cave that's wet as the conductivity is enhanced tremendously by the water. Now pure water is not as good a conductor as is salt water, but there are a lot of salts on the mountain.

And, as you may remember, Mt. Stewart is a very steep mountain. It is just under ninety-five hundred feet. And even if you think you're in good shape, that would take the starch out of you.

Paul Brickoff and Bob Grant were alone on Stewart. A third man who had intended to climb with them didn't feel good and he waited in camp. After the others didn't return, he came out and reported to the parents. He said there had been a severe storm and he was worried.

They climbed the West Ridge in ever-worsening weather. They continued to climb even though they observed lightning kickin' around on peaks nearby. And Paul stood on top of that mountain near the summit register. Bob waited just below the summit but he was roped to Paul.

Bob, not taking time to sign the register, had gotten down off the top to the south. And poor Paul stood on top and wrote in the register. I read it and I can't remember all of what he said, but the last part ended something like, "Lightning, thunder, what hell!"

And they were struck three times. Bob was struck because the static charge hit Paul and traveled down their very wet climbing rope. When it hit Bob it paralyzed one of his legs and scorched his back and buttocks with third degree burns.

Paul died when his diaphragm was paralyzed and, unable to control himself, he fell down headfirst and ended up near to where Bob was squatting in a shallow overhang for protection from a direct exposure hit. (He forgot that he was still roped to Paul.)

Bob sat beside him the rest of the night. Paul died of a paralyzed diaphragm and multiple fractures of the skull from his headfirst fall.

Bob dumped all of his provisions out of his pack and took all of Paul's to take home to Paul's parents. Anyway, Bob got down off of that mountain the next day. He just did. He was a tough young man and as he descended, his leg improved. What a nightmare that kid must have lived!

He came down off of that mountain—I'm sure he came down the Ulrich route. We didn't know it had a name then. Any of you know Herman Ulrich? He's a native-born Swiss, lives in Yakima.

Anyway, that guy came down there sitting down, one foot, two hands, and came clear down to Ingels Creek, where we found him the next morning. He had third-degree burns, but he had what it took.

So a lot of people who climb don't really come to grips with what can happen under certain circumstances.

Getting back to Delmar Fadden. After a few days of searching, we got chased off Mount Rainier by a storm. Later I flew over the mountain with a professional pilot named Elliot Merrill. We discovered something unusual at thirteen thousand feet which we at first thought was a tent. So we circled around to the east for a better look and approached the spot on a south wind updraft. We cleared the top of Mount Rainier by eight hundred or a thousand feet as we tested the winds and currents. Then we came in much closer, to maybe one hundred feet, and we realized that what we had thought was a tent was really Delmar Fadden's body.

On January 31, 1936 nine of us set out on skis up the mountain to bring Delmar home. Our summit team consisted of Chief Ranger John Davis, Ranger Bill Butler, Paul Gilbreath, Bob Buschmann, and myself. We pushed up in evening darkness to Starbo, where there was an old hut, and we climbed the Interglacier to the Prow. When we finally reached the body on the upper slopes of the Emmons Glacier, Delmar was sprawled in the position to which he had come after skidding. His mittens were gone and the flesh of his fingers was ground down to the bones from trying to stop his slide. The crampon on his left foot had slipped up to the inside of the foot and had lacerated the lower part of his right leg during the fall.

Delmar had come to rest in a bank of soft snow, most of which had blown away in the meantime. There he had died of hypothermia.

I cut the pack from Delmar's back so that we could wrap him in a tarpaulin. We rolled up the tarp and tied the two ends with separate ropes.

Then while we were descending, we had come down quite a distance, taking turns letting Delmar down, when I heard a scrambling noise from above. Down came the body *and* the two men from that end. They skidded by like an express train and went out of sight.

I went down to find them. Seeing them fall, we couldn't imagine that they would still be alive.

You pray at times like that.

My only reaction was, "How could I tell their wives?"

John Davis, the Chief Park Ranger, was not a climber. He must have edged his crampons, which can be fatal. It was the first time he had ever climbed on crampons.

Fortunately, the body and the two men stopped in soft snow and were OK.

We continued on down the mountain in the same fashion as we had before. Two at the top, to let the body down and two below, to take up the slack and to keep the body from sliding out of control. At Steamboat Prow we met our support party and all of us retreated to Starbo and down to White River Campground.

Delmar was only nineteen. He was an artist, poet, and sculptor. He was a great athlete. The world lost a lot when he died.

Of course, in instances like this, you meet his family. His parents.

We Mountain Rescue men have been welcomed into many a home through the years.

[The next summer Ome recovered Delmar Fadden's pack and camera, which proved that Delmar had successfully made the first solo winter ascent of Mount Rainier. The first *unauthorized* winter climb.

But during that trip to recover the camera, a boulder rolled over one of Ome's feet, causing an injury which would bother him for the rest of his climbing career.]

ETTA LEIGHTHEART EGELAND:
"WE LIVED BY THE TIDES"
Friday Harbor, WA
Born: 1896

When she was a girl growing up on San Juan Island, Etta Elizabeth Leightheart could look across Haro Strait from her grandfather Aaron Jackson Leightheart's homestead at Vancouver Island. Victoria was the nearest capital and little Etta once saw that city's namesake, Queen Victoria (1819–1901), riding there in a royal coach.

Grandfather Leightheart had homesteaded at the southwest moorage at Smuggler's Cove in approximately 1892 after coming West from Michigan.

Etta's other grandfather, Peter Lawson, had come around the Horn from Denmark to the California gold rush and had drifted north to the Fraser River gold rush. "He went up the Fraser River in a canoe with an Indian guide" in about 1852. Eventually he acquired a sloop, and in 1856 he claimed squatter's rights to land at Eagle Point on San Juan Island, an island still in contention between Britain and the United States.

After Emperor Wilhelm I awarded San Juan Island to the United States in 1872, my grandfather Lawson took up the patent on his one hundred seventy-three acre farm. He married an English girl, Fanny Dearden, from Manchester, England. She had come here to Vancouver Island on a bride ship to find a husband because so many Englishmen had been lost in war. Peter and Fanny Lawson raised eight children. Their daughter, my mother Anna Lawson, was born in 1874. She married Alex Leightheart in Victoria in July 1893 after they had traveled there in Ed Scribner's boat. It was customary in those days to go back and forth to Victoria because it was the largest settlement near San Juan Island. In 1896 I was born at my grandfather Lawson's squatter's rights house at Eagle Point.

The Lawson/Leightheart mix was very fruitful, and Etta Leightheart grew up in an extended family with many cousins. In her mother's family were four boys and four girls. In her father's were ten children. In her father's sister's family were ten also.

Though all the families were very close, Etta's favorite sibling was her half-sister Winifred Leightheart, with whom she used to ride the great drifting logs where the tides, currents, and winds made for "very rough water."

The San Juan Islands were a rowing, paddling, sailing country. The water was a way of life. For instance, Etta's uncle's lighthouse keeper parents once moved with all their belongings and animals from Port Townsend to Smith Island on a sail-equipped raft. Another time, when a cow broke Etta's mother's leg, an Indian paddled her to the Jubilee Hospital on Vancouver Island. Water transportation was so crucial, says Etta, that "you had to know your weather, your tides. You knew when to go and how long it would take by rowboats and canoes. We rowed to go someplace, but paddling logs on the North End [southwest side] at my grandfather Leightheart's farm, that was for fun!"

Out by Smuggler's cove on the southwest end of San Juan Island was where my grandfather Leightheart had homesteaded. He had a daughter named Winifred by his second marriage that was the same age as I. Her birthday was May 5 and mine was November 10. We were rocked in the same cradle in her home and as we grew up we were together a lot. She was alone so much at that end of the island that they would let me stay with her. She had the most wonderful mother, a former Michigan schoolteacher. I just loved her mother. Some women are born mothers. Everything about them makes you feel warm inside.

When Winifred Leightheart and I were about nine, ten, or eleven years old, we used to ride on big logs that would come rolling in, out in front of my grandfather Leightheart's log cabin a mile west of Sunset Point. Winifred and I would get on them and paddle around. We were hardy little rascals. If I saw *my* children doing that. . . . I had two, a girl and a boy. I wouldn't let them get out there in those tides in the Strait of Juan de Fuca!

Etta Egeland (left) and
Elizabeth Leightheart, circa 1912.

Not in my day, you didn't wear jeans! Little boys when they were very small, they wore dresses. Then they had short pants first before they were allowed to wear long pants. Girls always wore dresses.

I was wearing a dress while riding on a log. We didn't fall in the water. I don't know what we'd have done. We straddled the logs but getting our dresses wet never bothered us. I imagine we were just like ice when we got out of that water.

Winifred Leightheart and I knew the tides. We knew when the tide was going out and when it was coming in. And we didn't go out on an outgoing tide or we would be in some other country by now.

But a few years later, Winifred and a boy that my grandfather got from the orphan's home in Seattle, Frank Miller, he and Winifred made a raft and started out, going south, and a purse seiner saw them and took them aboard, much against their will, and set the raft adrift into the tide rips. Winifred had a great desire to be adventuresome. We were very close but we were very different personalities. I was much less venturesome. Those fishermen really gave them a talking to!

She always laughed about it later.

When you are growing up on an island, you very quickly learn. You see the stormy weather and hear those logs pounding on the beach. They're thrown up into the air. That wind and water have a terrible, terrible force. I've never gotten over the logs pounding onto the beach during a storm. I still shudder when I remember hearing them at night.

I can say this for our families, they took good care of us. Smuggler's cove was not far from Grandfather's log house. There was a certain area that we were never to go north of. Because that's where the smugglers came in. I was a grown person before I ever went down there. But the boys went down there. Tell them not to do something and they are apt to do it right away.

Oh, they smuggled Chinese and dope. Smuggler Kelly was well-known on the island. He went in the bay to get out of sight of the Coast Guard. Well, I don't know if he was any more of a pirate than some of the fish trap men. Smuggler Kelly used to go up to see my Aunt Nellie Leightheart Flinn for farm produce. He was always nervous when he was there in case someone came along. If he saw anyone coming up the road, he was out of sight immediately.

My father often went fishing. He'd take a rowboat and go out in the fall of the year, catch silvers and salt them for winter. In the early spring he'd have the spring salmon. And then the sockeyes and the humpbacks and the coho. Humpback bellies were the best salted fish there was.

My mother loved to fish. She loved to go out and spend a day fishing just to get away. She was an efficient manager of her home and was always cooking, washing, crocheting, gardening, and drying apples and fruit. Once I rowed the boat for her when she went fishing. Fishing never appealed to me after that. I am not a boat person!

But I have done a lot of rowing. We'd go to the beach and go places. Sometimes it was in dories, those big boats that they had on the fish traps. That's what they liked to give us when we were young because we couldn't fall out. They were so high up from the water and the weather couldn't affect you.

When I was fourteen or fifteen, Winifred and I used to row out to the fish trap at Mitchell Bay where our cousins and uncles worked. We used to walk the planks from piling to piling and we could identify the types of fish coming into the trap on the tide.

My parents were farmers. My father wasn't really a true farmer (he had a livery stable down in the ravine behind Whitey's grocery store), but my mother was. When she was growing up, my grandfather Lawson just took land from the wilderness and built a farm out of it. And that wasn't easy, but I never heard any of them say they were overworked. They all took up homesteading claims up there on Mount Dallas on San Juan Island.

Instead of marrying a farmer, I married a shingleweaver. He came from Stavanger, Norway out to Cedar Rapids, Iowa. When the hotel that he worked for there burned down, he came out to Washington in 1909 during the Alaska-Yukon-Pacific Exposition. His sister and a friend came out, too, to visit their relatives in Bellingham. Harry went into the shingleweaving business on the mainland.

Do you know what a shingleweaver is? It was a very common job years ago when there were so many cedar trees on the mainland. A shingleweaver works in a shingle mill where shingle bolts go down a conveyor and are sliced into shingles. The shingles come out in a bin and the shingleweaver picks them up and binds them into a bundle.

Shingleweavers have to be very fast. Their eye tells them at a glance what size to pick out and where to set it in this bundle. So that when they get through, the bundle is the proper shape, width, length, and flatness.

My mother was running the Friday Harbor tourist hotel and its dining room, and I was waiting tables. Harry Egeland generally came in for a meal every day. He had come here to Friday Harbor in approximately 1910 to work in the Templins Shingle Mill.

After the shingle mill burned, Harry became quite well acquainted with the business people around town because he and George Frank bought a cardroom where they had card tables and pool tables.

Harry came in as a dining room customer when I was a waitress and going to high school. He was older than I was. As far as I was concerned, he was very eligible.

He had a good personality. He met people easily and was friendly and well-liked. Of course, he had been around a lot, which was very interesting to a young country girl. At that time even the town of Friday Harbor was country-like. Harry Egeland, he danced well and he wore his clothes very well. He could put on a pair of overalls and he would look fine.

Yes, he danced well. That was worth a lot to me!

Now, dances are so different. There used to be a community feeling at them. They were always held on special occasions like St. Patrick's Day, New Year's, and the Fourth of July. Christmas was a different type of a holiday. It was spent with family and friends, not dancing.

There were other dances in between holidays, though. If there wasn't a big dance at the fraternal halls, then we'd dance on Saturday nights in the homes. We'd dance all night through. Someone'd play the piano. Someone'd play the fiddle, not the violin. It was just lots of fun.

I went to a lot of dances with Harry Egeland, mostly in town. By the time I met Harry in approximately 1911, my parents and I were living in Friday Harbor and there were now a lot of public dances, because the Woodmen of the World Hall, Masonic Hall, Mitchell Bay Dance Hall, and Odd Fellows Hall had been built. We all crowded upstairs into those lodge rooms to the supper dances. The stairways must have been well-braced, because *everyone* went!

Those dances cost a couple two dollars to attend. (The man always paid.)

Generally dances were held to raise funds; for example, for a degree of honor lodge. The organizers provided good-sized sandwiches since the people were hungry because they had come a long ways. Plus, they were dancing and building up an appetite. In summer we danced from nine o'clock till four or five in the morning.

In 1913 I was the first girl on the island to have my hair cut off and bobbed. Irene Castle was a famous ballroom dancer and I had seen pictures of her in the paper with her hair bobbed. I was in disgrace, but I didn't mind.

I was dancing right up to the time I was married and after I was married. If I had someone to go dancing with now, I'd still be dancing! It's good fun. But I wouldn't want to be dancing with the same person all the time. That's what they do today, but not what we did during the Teens and Twenties.

I always went to dances years ago by myself, or some young man would take me, or I went with girlfriends and cousins. Many men would dance with me, not just the man that had brought me. We women would be sitting on the benches and men would ask us to dance. Men were standing back by the door of the ladies' and men's wrap rooms and would come and ask us to dance. We'd have a waltz, a two-step, a three-step, and maybe some square dances if they had someone there to call them.

In 1906 when I was staying down there on my Grandfather Lawson's squatter's rights farm, my Aunt Lizzie Lawson was running the farm because her father was elderly and had given up farming. At the Woodmen of the World Hall near the Corner Store, Aunt Lizzie's boyfriends—she had plenty of them, she dressed beautifully and was good-looking—taught me how to dance. They would dance with her and then ask me to dance. I was surely delighted.

I still love dancing. I can look at T.V. and if they are dancing, I can be entertained all evening. It's just movement. I like action. And there's a friendliness about dancing. Years ago some men were shy but if you looked at 'em and gave 'em kind of a come-along look, then they'd ask you to dance. I'm sure you know about that! You made them feel more comfortable about asking you to dance.

Harry Egeland knew his way around and did not need any enticement.

Harry and I were going to elope, but my parents knew and Father tried to talk me out of it. My parents were not particularly fond of Harry. But we were married June 5, 1915 in a chapel across from the courthouse. For our honeymoon we went to the Panama-Pacific Exposition in San Francisco. That was exciting and a lot of fun.

Harry Egeland and I raised our daughter, Juanita, who still lives near me here in Friday Harbor. I have three grandchildren, four great-grandchildren, one great-great-grandchild. They are always curious about what San Juan Island was like when I and my parents were young.

I like people, but I think that the recent crowds of latecomers since 1973 have been changing the island. Until 1936, when ferry service commenced, the island used to be much more of a community and much more separate from the mainland. Our canoes, rowboats, and sloops were a big part of what it meant to be an islander.

Like I said, I am not a boat person, but I spent a lot of time on the water as a girl. We lived on an island cut off by water, but neither one of my parents believed in staying in one spot all the time. Many of the farmers couldn't spare time or cash to leave because they were building their farms up from scratch. But my parents believed in getting off-island and seeing something. A trip off-island to the city was a very big occasion for us because we had little contact with the outside world. No radio or TV. Electricity arrived in the early '20s, but we only had lights from six A.M. to midnight.

I must have been five years old when I went to see Queen Victoria. The twenty-fourth of May was always a big celebration in Victoria. My parents never missed it.

The whole city of Victoria was out for the parade. We Leight-hearts were all dressed up and there were lots of people around. I remember Queen Victoria greeting everybody from her low carriage with beautifully harnessed horses and with footmen sitting up high.

She was very old.

Quite a few people from San Juan Island went over to Victoria in rowboats, canoes, and sloops. After Queen Victoria's death in 1901, we still went over every May 24 in Mr. Bailer's launch with only our own group or family. I remember going into Cadboro Bay on an incoming tide. From shore we'd walk a puncheon trail through a large alder swamp to the end of the streetcar line that took us into Victoria.

Living on San Juan Island was an adventure. Any time you went anywhere in a boat, you went by tides.

We lived by the tides.

JIM ELLIS:
CIVIC LEADER
Seattle, WA
Born: 1921

Seattle is often lauded by national surveys as America's most livable city. The 1962 World's Fair first put the city in the limelight, but the almost simultaneous cleanup of Lake Washington and the subsequent preservation of huge acreages of parks and open space lent the city and King County a glitter which still shines.

The amazing thing is that the World's Fair (1962), the Lake Washington cleanup (1958–1969), Forward Thrust (1965–1972), the campaigns for farmland preservation (1974–1979), and even the new Washington State Convention and Trade Center (1982–1988) were projects created primarily by citizen activists and not by politicians. In fact, during the last three decades, Washington state has offered America two distinctly different models of large-scale, tax-exempt bond projects. The first, METRO, became a widely emulated success. The second, WPPSS, was an egregious failure. The former was the result of widely debated grassroots elections. The latter was a creature of the state legislature and never subjected to voter approval.

Jim Ellis and his wife, Mary Lou Earling Ellis, were young optimists in the early '50s who had survived the war, started a family, begun a career, and who needed a cause. In the 1950s that cause was the creation of METRO, the unification of greater Seattle's pollution and transportation efforts. "I had learned the hard way," says Jim Ellis, "that we couldn't rely on changeable government zoning to protect open land. Zoning protection simply doesn't last when confronted by persistent development pressure." Instead, public acquisition through the sale of publicly-voted municipal bonds was to become his answer.

However, bond lawyer Ellis had not counted on the enormity of the political tasks ahead, an effort which would consume his whole life and that of his wife (who died in 1983). What was it about the Ellises, I wondered, which had led them into a series of quality-of-life, conservation campaigns, each one more difficult than the last?

Jim and Mary Lou came from pioneer families which had ended up in Seattle. One of Jim's paternal great-grandmothers was born on a wagon train in 1846, and a great-grandfather settled in Dayton, Washington in 1862. Mary Lou Earling's maternal grandmother was the first white child born in Spokane. Her maternal grandfather came to Seattle just before the great fire, after working at the Indian Agency in San Carlos, New Mexico. Mary Lou's paternal grandfather had come to Seattle as the engineer in charge of building the Milwaukee, St. Paul and Pacific Railroad from Minneapolis to the West coast.

In 1925 Mary Lou's father moved his family to Nome, Alaska, when that territory was as frontier-minded as anywhere in North America.

In both Mary Lou Earling and Jim Ellis there was an old-fashioned brand of Western public-spiritedness.

Of course, a century after Washington statehood many people are just as civic-minded as any barn-raising, let's-pitch-in-together person ever was. But the scale of what the Ellises helped to do made me wonder how anyone could actually go about beginning something like the Forward Thrust three hundred thirty million dollar program of park, sewer, and highway bond levies. Jim explained it to me this way:

After the cleanup of Lake Washington by METRO in the late '50s and the success of the business community in staging the World's Fair at a profit in 1962, Paul Seibert, the Seattle Downtown Association's young executive director and a good friend of mine, encouraged me to spell out some of my ideas for transportation, recreation, and open spaces. I began putting them together and took them to Mary Lou. I had this feeling that we ought to go for broke. We ought to try to assemble all of these things in a single big crusade and see if we couldn't unite the community behind it.

She said, "That's a fantastic idea and it will capture people's imaginations. But you need some kind of a slogan or something that people can relate to easily. You have explained it to me for a half an hour. If it takes that long to explain, nobody is going to be able to follow it."

So she came up with the name of Forward Thrust. Paul and I decided to test the idea in a speech to Seattle Rotary in the fall of 1965. But first we went to the business community for help. We met with Bill Allen of the Boeing Company, Eddie Carlson of Western International Hotels, Walter Straley of the telephone company, and Bill Jenkins, of Seattle First National Bank. I said, "I am not going to do this work unless you guys will back us up with fifty thousand dollars so we can organize a major community effort. A speech without any follow-up will just be wasted words." We agreed that Eddie would chair a finance committee and he sent me a letter before I made that speech. "This is your authority to commit fifty thousand dollars," he said. "We will take the responsibility for getting other businesses to help."

So we had something tangible to start with.

We prepared for that Forward Thrust speech the way that only Paul could do.

The press and media were much more community development-oriented then. They gave a tremendous boost to Forward Thrust. A few politicians were initially jealous of the fact that this was enunciated by a lay person. . . . Paul had refused to let me talk to anybody about these ideas. He said, "If you do that, it will be dead. As soon as you tell an elected official and he likes the idea, then his opponents have to be opposed to it because they have to run against him. So let's do it as a business and civic effort. If the idea is good enough, the elected officials sooner or later will come on board.

Dorm Braman, the mayor of Seattle, sat next to me when I made the speech. He was very annoyed with me. He said, "Why didn't you tell me what you were going to do?"

But I knew he loved his city. I knew that in a week or so he would get over it, because Forward Thrust would do all the things that he had wanted to do. He came around within a week and said, "Alright, what do we do now?"

For awhile after the speech the county tried to run its own show. It took three months before they backed away from a separate effort.

Then we all got together at the old Olympic Grill for breakfast—County Commissioner Scott Wallace, Mayor Dorm Braman, and I. We organized a committee of twenty-two people who were charged with the responsibility of creating an organization that would move these ideas forward. Two hundred people were selected by those twenty-two to form the Forward Thrust Committee. Each committee member agreed to commit to four hours of time a week. It was a tremendous group of private citizens and public officials. Ultimately of course, it grew to include thousands of people during the campaigns.

That breakfast kicked off by far the biggest effort we ever undertook. We hoped to obtain voter approval for rapid transit, major highways, a domed stadium, and a magnificent parks program with miles of new public waterfront. These projects would be put together under a single umbrella.

The timing couldn't have been better. There was a Boeing boom in full progress. After the World's Fair and the successful lake cleanup the people believed that their business leaders, their civic leaders, and their public officials (who in a short time were very closely working together) could do damned near anything. At first the program sounded like a wild and far out idea (it was more money than anybody had previously thought of spending for the city), still, the public became convinced that these weren't crazy people and that this proposal would work.

I am offering Jim Ellis's story in the hope that it will inspire *you* in Washington's second century to "go for broke."

John Muir and others have written about the importance of people committing themselves to the environment and to its transmission from generation to generation. Commitment to do something beyond self.

Today I remain optimistic but not quite as optimistic as I was in 1953 when we started METRO. Civic work is now much harder to accomplish, because there are so many forces in the media and in local constituencies which can be arrayed against large-scale pro-

jects. And the processes of approval are more complicated and offer more opportunities for attack. Building the State Convention Center was bitterly fought by many people, including some who should have been helpers.

Jim Ellis, Mary Lou and two of their children.

Mary Lou was a very optimistic person, with great common sense and a smile in her voice all the time. Every civic activist should be as lucky as I was to fall in love with a woman like her.

In the last few years before she died, she and I were growing more and more concerned that society was becoming loose at the seams. Some fundamental values which we had taken for granted when we were growing up seemed almost to have fallen into disuse, creating huge problems for the next generation.

If Mary Lou and I were starting over today, we would be most concerned about strengthening families and encouraging the pub-lic spirit which produces community.

It is, of course, more important that we care about people *than about land or buildings. We saw conservation and urban improve-ments as meeting the needs of people. I have been working this week on practical ways to assure the long-term availability of hous-ing for low-income people. That doesn't mean that the people I am working with pretend to have a solution for such a big problem, but the fact that we are working on it is an encouraging thing.*

There are very impressive satisfactions inherent in civic work, but unless you have experienced them, they are quite difficult to communicate. I could say to someone, "It is a great thrill to stand in Freeway Park and watch people enjoy that park." But that sounds a little corny. If, on the other hand, newspapers say "Forward Thrust is a concrete bust" or "Bond lawyer cashed in on Freeway Park," even though such stories are false, readers will wonder if they are true. A public perception that civic workers are bad guys would discourage most people from becoming civic workers. We have to find psychic rewards which will motivate people to get into public activity.

The struggles for Farmland Preservation, for METRO, for Forward Thrust, were very demanding. You can't say to a potential volunteer, "Look, take on this new job, it will be easy and you'll be a hero." It just doesn't happen that way. It will take a lot of time, a lot of hard work. To be an effective civic worker you have to be a catalyst—somewhat sponge-like—cushioning the sharp edges of advocacy in order to achieve acceptable compromises.

Being a sponge between sharp edges of advocacy isn't exactly fun. In fact, it is exhausting to try to pull people together that are pushing and pulling in every direction.

It is tiring if you have to be this catalytic leader to pull all these people together that are pushing and pulling in each direction. The task itself is demanding, but today's climate also sets you up for both fair and unfair criticism. This is what I call "the day of the critic" or the "free shot." If you are running for elected office, you must say, "That's the way of life. I'd better be able to handle it or I'd better not go into it."

However, the civic person isn't like that. He or she is not going to make civic work a career. Most volunteers are not likely to move from a successful park campaign to a regular political job. Rather, such a person is more likely to take time out from his or her career and family life to do a one-time community good deed. And if the effort is controversial, he or she may end up being portrayed as some kind of a crook or person with some evil conflict of interest.

Who wants to be portrayed in the community as a bad guy? For a volunteer in today's world there is a high risk of such portrayal. And it is a risk that some good people may not be willing to take. If they think about it, they would probably say, "Well, I don't want to see a lot of personal attacks in the newspapers. I just want to do something good. People can disagree with my ideas as long as they understand that I am trying to do good. If, on the other hand, people will think that I am evil, I didn't bargain for that."

Today there is a greater tendency towards negative personal reporting. Reporters feel a duty to find out what is in it for each person who is playing a leading role.

I have been through it up to the horn. I can't tell a newcomer that unfair personal criticism isn't going to happen. I have to say that it is likely to happen.

Under these circumstances it is not hard to see why people might be reluctant to become activists. Also, civic work takes away heavily from the time that a person can devote to his or her job, profession, and family. Such sacrifices are very difficult to make.

As we look for people to be sparkplugs for major improvement programs, many will say, "I don't want to give up that much of my family life. I don't want to take that much away from my business or professional duties. I have a heavy enough burden with those."

In looking back on our own experiences over forty years, I guess that Mary Lou and I have lost two elections for every one that passed. We had to vote three times to pass Farmland Preservation. There were four elections before metropolitan public transportation passed. It took two elections just to get the lake cleanup started.

In other words, you don't win all the time. You have to hang in there because it may take a long time to make something happen.

There have always been people in the West who cared about the land and there have always been those who just wanted to rip it off. Whether you have lived here all your life or have just arrived is pure coincidence. But whether you have a high degree of concern for the land and the community of people is a matter of personal choice.

My great-grandfather who settled in Dayton was noted for the fact that he organized the school district there. His community lacked doctors so he took care of the sick and the dying. He had a concern for other people. My father and mother transmitted some of that concern to their children.

My grandfather, Dr. James Reed, and my father, Floyd Ellis, had great influence on me. I didn't join the Scouts as a youngster because my grandfather and father often took me camping in the woods. I learned a lot from them. When I was fifteen years old, my father decided that my thirteen-year-old young brother Bob and I should have some experience in independence. So in 1937 he bought a piece of undeveloped property in the foothills of the Cascades, dropped us off at the end of the road with our dogs and plenty of food to spend the summer by ourselves.

The first week it rained pitchforks. We slept in a little tent with two soaking wet English sheepdogs. I thought, "This is supposed to be fun, but it isn't any fun at all."

But when the sun came out, we learned to find dry wood in a wet forest and we learned a lot of other things. It was a marvelous, marvelous experience and my brother Bob and I became inseparable.

In the late '20s and early '30s I went to school at John Muir Grade School in Seattle. The school was run by a principal, Jesse Lockwood, who had tremendous charisma with her youngsters, and who was totally dedicated to the conservation principles of the school's namesake, John Muir. I can recall Nature pageants in which everyone in the school was involved. I played the part of youth and this was a big deal. My brother Bob was a bear and the little children in the first and second grade were part of a "glacier" under a sheet.

That school background had a big influence on me.

Both my wife, Mary Lou, and I were taught to be optimistic. We believed that if we worked hard, that something good would come of it. We believed that the world was more good than evil.

We had a hopeful view of society. We respected the natural heritage and we loved the natural wonders of the West as a God-given gift. We believed that most people shared our feelings of stewardship.

Mary Lou was a remarkable person. She grew up in Alaska and had been sent down to Bush School in Seattle by her folks who then lived in the mining community of Fairbanks. We met at age sixteen at a party that my mother had organized to get my brother and me to become a little more sociable. We were sort of tied up in the woods and we weren't. . . . My father said, "They are eating like animals."

At first we only dated occasionally and didn't really start going together until World War II, when I joined the Air Force as a weather forecaster and Mary Lou entered a pilot training program designed for women to ferry airplanes so that more men could fly combat. She was quite willing to take on challenging things like that.

In November 1944 we were married and stationed at an air base in Mountain Home, Idaho.

In February, 1945 my brother Bob was killed in action.

I wasn't prepared! I had never experienced death in my family. I became disoriented, even self-destructive. I wouldn't talk to people.

Mary Lou and I had been married for three months and were living in a housing project. One night she grabbed me and said, "You have got to get hold of yourself. It won't do any good to throw your life after Bob's. Why don't you make your life count for his?"

I said, "Do you mean give part of our time to public service in memory of Bob?"

When the war was over, we lived for six years in the log house on Raging River which my brother and I had built when we were fifteen and thirteen. Mary Lou and I lived there while I went to law school and started my practice. We didn't have a dime.

But we began to perform our commitment to Bob. Her Alaskan upbringing and my summers in the mountains were a natural fit. We both shared many of the same values. Her parents had instilled the same kind of personal and family values in her that my parents had instilled in me.

Mary Lou taught me a lot about what is important (experiences), and what is not important (things). How far to let your dreams run, and when they need to be reined in and put in balance with family needs.

She was courageous. She was persistent and extraordinarily innovative. Without her commitment to our public service goals we never would have done the things we did. The public service work was like having an extra full-time job in addition to earning a living. Working twelve- to fourteen-hour days, means you need a lot of support.

Mary Lou had inspired me in the first place and as time went on she was able to keep me rolling. I would come back a beat-up carcass in the evening and leave in the morning charged up and ready to go! She accomplished that. She kept the family together. She gave a great deal of common sense advice during difficult, controversial public situations.

I learned to listen to her advice very carefully.

Most people would say she was an extraordinarily unselfish person, whether it was in the family, the neighborhood, or in the larger community that we were working for. But she wouldn't describe it that way. She once said to me, "I'm not unselfish. It pleasures me to do these things. Love is where I am coming from and where I am going."

DIANE ELLISON:

LOG ROLLER

Aberdeen, WA

Born: 1941

Log rolling is one of those sports like rodeoing or rock drilling which grew out of men's work on the land. But that is not how Diane Ellison, independent lumber company owner, became a champion log roller.

The original log rollers were burly, big-shouldered men able to move heavy logs around ponds and sloughs with merely a pike pole and a sense of balance. Despite the grip of their caulked (studded or nailed) boots, the old river pigs and log boom men had to be "catty," agile as cats.

The new breed of log rollers was different, after logging railroads and then trucks replaced much of the need for this skill. The new competitors tended to be slender athletes, less attuned to mill pond or boom work than to showmanship.

The new breed included women. Diane Ellison had been trained since early childhood for life on the logs. She absorbed her father Russ Ellison's skills and competitiveness and, as she mentions below, his land ethic.

Diane raises timber on property her father acquired in trades for Toyotas. She has tried marriage several times. She has successfully grown European truffles. She is president of the Washington State Folklife Council and has helped the Grays Harbor Historical Seaport's efforts to build two tall ships. However, none of this compares to the show business thrills of life on the logs with her father. "My father was a unique person," she says. "I have performed our trick and fancy act with other people, but when I did it with them it was only an act. When I did it with my father, it was magic."

Diane Ellison, World Champion Log Roller, at the opening of Log Ride, Knotts Berry Farm, 1969.

Two loggers challenging each other on a log is the way logrolling started back before the turn of the century. I picked it up as a girl because I was a good athlete, very competitive, and because there weren't any sports for girls in a small town grade school in the '40s and '50s. So I took what was available and I ran with it.

But I was embarrassed when they called me a tomboy. The first time they whistled at me when I was thirteen years old and I came out in a bathing suit, I quit for five years. I thought I'd never logroll again because I was so embarrassed at doing something that was so unfeminine.

And yet I loved it! But I let what people thought drive me out of my sport. I lost some good years trying to find my own identity as a woman. Finally I was able to say, "——— on you, World. I don't care if it is a man's sport or not. I do it. And I do it well, and I love it and I'm going to do it, no matter what you think."

That was hard. I had to be nineteen years old before I got the courage to do that.

Then one day when I was a sophomore at the U. W., I saw two big forestry majors trying to roll a log on Frosh Pond. Obviously they knew nothing about it, so I said, "Excuse me, but if you'd turn your feet parallel to the end of the log, don't turn them sideways, and do look at the other guy's feet instead of your own, then you'd do better."

Oh yeah," one of them said. "If you know so much about it, come show us."

I knew they didn't mean it but I asked them to push the log over to the edge of Frosh Pond. I put my books down and jumped on the log with the guy from the Forestry fraternity. He fell in.

I continued rolling and giving instructions to the guy in the water and to the guys around the pond. I pivoted in the middle of the pond, rolled to the edge, got off the log, picked up my books, and went up 17th Avenue to the Alpha Chi Omega house, my sorority, for dinner. The phone was ringing when I got there. The president of the Forestry fraternity wanted to know if I would log roll in Frosh Pond for Forestry Day. The Channel 7 evening news covered it and we had a ball!

My log rolling actually started with my grandfather, Robert Ellison, who was a log boom man on the Wishkaw River, where there was a log boom five miles long where logs were sorted into log boom rafts to be towed by tugboats downstream to lumber mills. He was the boom gap swinger, which was the man who kept the loose logs from getting in the way of the tugboats. We don't know to this day what happened, except that he went out on an extremely stormy day and was lost in the river.

The boom men were not married. They lived in the Wishkah Boom logging camp. My grandfather was one of the few married men. He lived near the camp. He and his wife had originally come from Kamilchee near Shelton, Washington. The family had come from Canada in 1884 to settle in Mason County in order to log.

The boom men banded together and helped save my grandmother from losing her farm. They lent her money and became father substitutes to her three boys, including my dad who was then an infant. Eventually my grandmother married one of those men.

When the three boys got older and their stepfather was in ailing health, they all did boom work for extra money. The two older boys did it to help put themselves through college.

My dad left school at fifteen when his stepfather died. There was no money to keep the farm going, so he went to work as a full-time boom man for three years. Many of the river men were originally from Nova Scotia and had made log drives back there. A lot of them had come across as the logging moved westward. Dad got so intrigued by the river men that he rode the rails back to Nova Scotia for a winter to participate in one of those log drives. Once was enough, because apparently it was extremely cold and at nineteen he got very homesick.

Impoverished is probably the right word to describe what it was like when a woman was widowed in those days, because there was no compensation, no life insurance, nothing like that. Grandmother hung on tight to the forty acres that my grandfather had originally bought. She paid off the notes and that became one of the deepest things she instilled in my father, which was to own your own land and to get it paid free and clear.

After my father did some years as a log roller, it became more of a hobby than a profession. There was obviously not a great deal of money to be made in traveling with shows. Enough to eat, but not enough to really get to the point he wanted in life.

Dad went to school and became a journeyman mechanic, and learned more and more until eventually he owned his own garage, working from the bottom up. He became a Pontiac dealer. Then later, on a log rolling trip he saw the first Toyota that was ever shown in this country and he fell in love with it. Then he sold a lot of Land Cruisers. People who enjoyed the woods like he did really enjoyed the four-wheel drive. He helped design the first winch. So he really fell in love with the Toyota. What he did on a lot of car deals was that when someone had a piece of land that they really didn't want anymore and they needed a car, they worked out an arrangement. After a number of years, he had over four hundred acres of land.

He had a great deal of reverence for his land and he found it very hard to harvest it even though the particular land near the homestead at that point in the early '80s was mature and ready to be cut. Every tree that fell pained him even though it was a crop and he knew that it was time to cut it. That is why he was so anxiously replanting it.

My father died in 1984. He was seventy-four years old at the time, and in excellent health as far as anyone knew, so it was a shock. He simply went to sleep and didn't wake up, which is the way that he would have chosen to go. The day of his death he planted over seventy trees on a hill which had just been logged because he was quite anxious to get it replanted.

When I was cleaning out his closets, I found his suitcases. They were packed with his log rolling gear, his jump rope and his caulked boots. He had never quit log rolling.

Shortly after that, the International Log Rolling Association decided to give the only perpetual trophy they have ever given in their one hundred years. I think they were formed in 1898. And it was the Russ Ellison trophy for perseverance, which has been given each year since.

They asked me to go back to Hayward, Wisconsin, present the trophy, and give a speech for "ABC Wild World of Sports." So I just took his suitcase and moved his things over. I took his shoes and lucky shirt, and I put my stuff in and went back to present it at one of the original Weyerhaeuser mill ponds.

His trophy celebrates persistence, because Dad was still log rolling in the men's division at fifty and fifty-five, and winning the trick and fancy in his early fifties. He never quit and was still at it at age seventy-four when he died.

He had begun at age fifteen and he had never quit log rolling. He taught me that when I started to fall, not to just fall but to reach my hands up as high as I could and pretend like I was literally grabbing the sky to hold me up. It gave the illusion that I was higher on the log and it won the championship for me in a close call in 1961. Because a fall is not a fall until you are wet above the waist.

The year that I won the championship, when I started to fall first, I kept that fight going that he drilled in my head for so long. When the fall actually came, although it was very close, I was reaching for the sky and I was just a little higher than my opponent.

My dad did something that I have not seen very often. In fact, I have never seen anyone do it with quite the dexterity that he did. And that was making a pivot turn on a log. A lot of your log rollers now have a shoulder that they feel most comfortable looking over. If they get into a position where the other person turns, then they will have to run backwards because they can't turn. Dad's feeling was that you were to practice over both shoulders so you never had a "good" shoulder, one which was easier to look over than the other. He would be up on his toes and into a quick pivot, and he used to do that back and forth maybe three or four times. Sometimes for show and sometimes for confusion of the opponent. He pivoted fast enough that he didn't get in trouble with it. I see it done very seldom nowadays.

My character was very much influenced by him. I was an only child. He was planning on a boy and he definitely wanted another world champion log roller in the family. I was raised probably for the first thirteen years of my life as if I was the boy in the family.

I found that the things that my dad did were more interesting to me than the prescribed stereotypes of what a woman should do. And I am talking about the '40s when sex role stereotypes were pretty well solidified. Taking care of the house. Cooking. Clothes and all the things that my mother did were fine, but what Dad did I found a lot more exciting.

I could never hunt. He tried to take me bird hunting once and although he had taught me to be a very good shot, I cried when I hit a bird and it died. So he gave up on that.

And so, from then on, I enjoyed the woods with a great many walks with him. We both very much liked to photograph the woods. We particularly liked the Olympic Mountains. Mount Colonel Bob was our favorite climb together.

We fished a great deal together.

But I liked his business. I liked his garage. I liked the excitement of the car business. I liked the car auctions. He kept a nursery in the back and experimented a great deal. So I started planting trees with him when I was just old enough to barely walk. And we log rolled at the same time.

He had a great deal of nostalgia for the way logging had been.

I feel that way, too, but I also like what's going on today. I just went to the Pacific Logging Conference because I like to keep up with what's going on. I like what's happening in the new logging, such as trade with Pacific Rim countries in a global economy.

Yet I am somewhere in the middle because I very much see what the ecologist is saying. I see a need to coexist with Nature and to preserve the spirit of our logging heritage while promoting sound forestry practices that will ensure the perpetuity of this great timber resource.

I hear a lot of opinions and I frequently find myself in the middle. To me there is nothing in the world more beautiful or pristine than virgin timber. And I hate to see it cut. But at the same time I make my living by forest management.

In later life, in the late '60s, I was still log rolling professionally at loggers' and sports shows. I'd gone through the little girl phase with father-daughter, which the public liked a great deal. Then I had come into a phase where we did a lot of trick and fancy log rolling where I wore a very fancy, sequined bathing suit. I had done several sport shows for Werner Buck in Hollywood, which is certainly a different area to be log rolling than the sloughs and bays of Duncan, B.C. and Grays Harbor, Washington. So in 1968 Werner Buck was doing a new show for the first time in Anaheim and he called to ask me to perform.

It was the first time in my life that I had ever performed when one of my children was in the audience. I was doing the show with my husband, whose family owned Lumbermen's Mercantile, which originated as Simpson's Company in Shelton, Washington and which was the company store offshoot of Simpson Timber Company. They had taken that over in the Shelton-McCleary area and then expanded all the way to Southern California. Thomas Rowe and I had met and eloped at the University of Washington and then had gone south with the expansion of the store. I had taught him to log roll and he got very good.

So we were doing the trick and fancy and I was going down on the back bend and in the silence of that dark arena with a spotlight on me, this clear voice goes, "Be careful, Mommy." That was my daughter, which sent me into peals of laughter, enough almost to send me off the log.

We finished that, and then we asked if anyone in the audience could stay on the log with me for two minutes. Obviously no one in the audience could stay on a log two minutes even if they had had a little experience. But we had set it up so that during the Saturday night show, the last and the biggest show, my dad would be in the audience.

Dad came down out of the audience as a volunteer. We didn't tell anyone who he was. He was wearing a street suit and no one looked close enough to realize that he had caulked shoes on. He got on the log and did what a clown does. He did a thousand times of almost falling off, but didn't fall off. And then, of course, in the very end, I fell off and the crowd was completely befuddled.

You couldn't befuddle a crowd like at Albany, Oregon or at any other timber show because they would know that no novice could log roll like that. But in Los Angeles you could get away with it.

And then I grabbed the mike. And I can't even talk now without my voice breaking. [Pause.]

I said, "This really isn't a stranger out of the crowd. This is my teacher and my father."

BELLE GARLAND:

TARHEEL

Alger, WA

Born: 1879

Belle Garland, like so many of us, came to Washington of her own free will from a home place far away. She immigrated here at the age of thirty, a married woman following her husband out.

We always speak of America in general as a nation of immigrants, as a great "melting pot," and as a last frontier. These bromides long ago lost their piquancy. Unless, that is, *you* happen to be an immigrant, too.

In my first summer in Washington, 1968, it seemed like everyone I met was a native. In succeeding years, though, a greater and greater percentage of the people I met in urban areas had come from California, back East (wherever that is), or points south of Walla Walla and east of Spokane. By the time I began to live full-time in Washington in 1977, I had traveled the state so extensively that people began to mistake me for a native.

I thought of my birth region, New England, where, as I wrote in *Vermonters,* you are not accepted as really belonging until you have been in one place for at least three generations. Until very recently the only Washingtonians with that type of longevity have been folks like Frank "Bow Hill" Bob's father, Johnnie Bob, a Skagit Indian.

And few have ever minded if you talked and looked as if you just got off the boat. Oh, there have been subtle differences. My Eastern friends and I sometimes detect a subtle resentment against newcomers among longer-settled Puget Sounders. But that hint of chauvinism is often coupled with a perverse feeling that the Eastern person or the Eastern degree are part of a wider, more knowing world.

I have known people who work in Seattle, but whose universe is so national and international that they never begin to come to grips with their new home. They neither vote there nor read the local papers. Their work in computers, aerospace, banking, and other professions is generic and nonevergreen. And then there are people like Belle Garland, who sink into our forests and valleys and take on the local coloration.

Washington's regions have been culturally influenced by their northern European ethnicities and natural resources occupations. After the period (still within living memory) when Chinook was the major *lingua franca,* the Washington newcomer has had few more difficult hurdles to overcome than the pronunciation of odd place names, such as Puyallup and Sequim and Inchelium.

Yet it *is* different here. Not as different as it was, but still different. Belle Garland remembers a stump between Alger and Arlington which was so big that a car could drive through it. I remember hearing old-timers greet each other in Chinook just for fun. Just to identify themselves to each other as people who remembered when this country teemed with game. When there were so many fish that you could hardly find a buyer at any price. When homestead land was free for the taking. And when opportunity beckoned to those who had only to come and seize it.

Belle Garland did not talk about it in these terms. At first, she had not even understood what the attraction of this new state was. Belle was old when I spoke with her. So old that she would not smile for my camera. "Honey," she said, "I ain't got no teeth." Communication was difficult through her deafness and blindness. Anyway, it wasn't actual history which I sought but a feeling for the country when it was new to her.

Because I remember my own excitement in 1968 when the Cascades Mountains shimmered with mystery and wonderment.

I came out on the train in 1909. Not nice, it made us late. We started out late and it made us late the whole way. We came to the Sound, honey. My husband was out here already. We came to his house. I had a sister and my husband had a brother. They came the year before.

My sister and I married a pair of brothers. I married the oldest and she married the youngest. Barney was the name of Bess's man

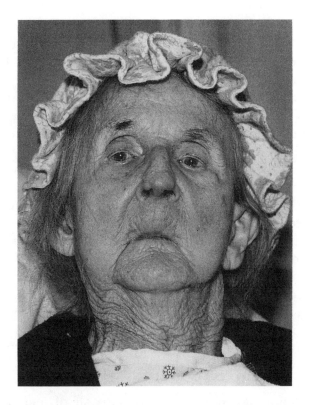

and Bob was mine. It was kinda funny being married to two brothers. I was the oldest. She married later. We married a good family.

My father had one hundred and six acres. He tended it by himself. My mother never did move. She came out here visiting. I
wanted to have her more, but her home was in North Carolina.

I didn't think much of Skagit County when I first moved here.
I thought, "How do people live here?" All these stumps!

We were used to farming. I didn't see how they lived here. We
saw the shacks. They didn't have no cars. They didn't have no
paved roads or streets.

When the checks started coming in, I understood. North Carolina was farming country and this was logging country. That's the
difference. This was timber money. We didn't have much to bring
in money back in North Carolina. Wasn't any industry there,
honey, to bring in money. And the timber here was bringing in big
money.

Donovan was the head man for the Bloedel camps. He gave the

church an organ. He built a cookhouse pretty close to me. Alger had a cookhouse and a bunkhouse that Donovan built. It was a logging camp. That's it. There was nothing in Alger then.

My husband had a brother there who helped him to get straightened out. When you move somewhere, you do things. My husband didn't work in the woods much. He worked for the county and state as a road man. He kept the road open clear to Bellingham. When the Depression was on, he worked for two days and then was off for two days. My husband worked the people on relief two days and then laid them off for two days.

In 1909 there were many Tarheels in Hamilton but not so many around here. Do you know how they got that name? The Yankees didn't like to fight North Carolinians because they were so fierce. They would stick. General Lee called them Tarheels. During the Civil War my husband's father worked under Lee in the cookhouse where he could get something to eat.

Grandpa was rich. He owned one hundred and sixty acres of land. He willed Mother sixty-five acres.

My great-grandfather raised 'em because their mother and father died young. He worked eight slaves. Yeah, I knew former slaves.

We had churches at home. I went to all of 'em. Baptistism. Methodistism. Presbyterianism. Went to one in the morning and another in the afternoon. We went to church and Sunday school. I always wanted to go to church.

When I came here I didn't go to church much. I wasn't very well. I couldn't walk it. Then Donovan and Bloedel, the head men of the logging, gave us the land and some timber to make us a hall and a church. I could see it from my house.

I had a pretty good farm. It was down the country road a ways. I had chickens and pigs and cows. We shipped milk. The milkman came every day. Later we had an association. Truck picked it up every morning. I had a good fifty-five-foot artesian well. I hated to leave that.

There was much land, them days. My husband kept buying and buying land. There was just one store when I came. We had cattle. We bought our feed from Knudsen in Burlington. Knudsen's boy delivered everything two or three times a week.

I had three children. At first I had a doctor at home. We lived down the country road a ways from Alger. The doctor rode horseback to get there. He didn't have a car.

I didn't have my children in Alger. I had them at Saint Luke's Hospital in Bellingham. The first child died. She was a girl.

At first Bellingham was paved with bricks and the roads were dragged with a horse scraper. Later we had the Interurban and a bus. Later Alger had a big school with three teachers. They were good teachers, too. My kids were like all school kids.

Frankie Bob went with them too, and then he went to the government school. Frank had a pretty good education. Frankie Bob and his father were the only two Indians that I knew. Frank's father was a regular Indian, Johnnie was. In the summertime, he had horses, Johnnie did, and he went up there in the woods to get bolts and float them down to the railroad. He was a full Indian. Frank is half Indian.

I was married at twenty-four in Carolina.

I was thirty when I came to Alger.

My sister had come to Alger before me.

I wasn't disappointed.

ERNIE GIBSON:
BUSH PILOT
Chelan, WA
Born: 1917

Ernie Gibson says that flying Lake Chelan in all kinds of weather is "just a job," but if he really felt that way, he would not be so attached to the good old days of one of America's most out-of-the-way places.

Although he sold Chelan Airways in 1977, Ernie Gibson still arrives at its lakeside office at six A.M. and leaves at eight P.M. He says that he thrives on work.

Certainly, flying used to be much harder work when he began his career in the biplane era. He has seen aviation go from flimsy craft to sophisticated moonlanders, but what this bush pilot still likes best is flying into the backcountry.

Though Ernie laments the U. S. Park Service's effect on Lake Chelan's old pioneer ways, he says that the change has been good for business. "But it isn't near as nice as it was before," he says. "The local people don't like to be regimented like that."

The North Cascades National Park was lobbied into existence by a small group from distant Seattle. One can argue that the distress they brought to the Stehekin community helped to prevent later environmental problems by transferring scenic U. S. Forest Service lands to the U. S. Park Service. And that the old trapping/packing/prospecting/homesteading lifestyle was doomed anyway. The truth is probably somewhere in between the versions of the urban backpackers and the Stehekin country folk.

What remains is a legacy of stories. "Sometimes," says Ernie, "the miners would get what they called 'stake happy.' They would *have* to get out to the outside world. So they would pay me a hundred dollars to fly them out to get a haircut!''

Throughout Washington, old-timers have told me of this century's material progress arriving at the expense of familial and community cohesiveness. Each of us, however long or short our claim on Washington, knows the relative value he or she places on progress or tradition. For me one sad symbol of all these changes has been the disappearance of Ernie Gibson's "flag stops."

We would take a few prospectors who wanted to be dropped off at some little crick along the lake and then they would hike back up into the hills. We would make arrangements that when they got back they would signal us from the shoreline. The first time we went by, they would wave to us. The second time, they would put up a flag if they wanted to be picked up. We'd rock the wings to let them know that we would pick them up the first chance we got. If we had a load, we would catch them on the next trip back.

No, we don't have any more flag stops. Chelan, Lucerne, Stehekin, and Domke Lake are the only places we will stop now.

It was a bush operation. We did everything they did in Alaska, except we have better weather to do it in. For instance, years ago when they were mining up in the Horseshoe Basin, we would drop supplies to them from the air. The plane was a lifeline. Even the Lady of the Lake, in the wintertime ran only three days a week. *We* flew every day.

We had no radar, no nothing in those days. No radios of any kind. We wouldn't fly at night, except for emergencies, because of the risk. You would never know when you were going to hit a deadhead on the lake. Or boats without lights. So night flying was not too safe. I just did it in an emergency.

One night a miner decided that he wanted to get out to town from the mine because he got stake happy. So he called down and left a message that he wanted to fly out. It was too late; so we said, "No, it's too dark to fly."

The Howe Sound Mine had a primitive telephone system that went down to Lucerne to a Forest Service station where the ranger had a line goin' down here to Chelan to another Forest Service station. That way, the miners got word out that there was a man there with a compound fracture of his leg and the doctor said he had to get out right away. So I flew up to Lucerne in the dark to pick him up. It was the same guy that had wanted to come out earlier!

He and two other friends flew out with me and the two friends put him in a car down here at Chelan to take him to the hospital. Later on that night I had some reason to go downtown. Lo and behold, I saw him walkin' down the street, well as can be! He had faked the broken leg just so he could get out. It's characters like that that always keep you wondering what will happen next. We got to be pretty good friends later on. After the mine closed in 1957, he would bring his wife in and go fishin' at Gordon Stuart's Domke Lake resort. He always felt that that broken leg had been a pretty good joke.

We had a lot of real emergencies, though. We still have three or four emergencies a year. Accidents. Climbers fallin' down and breakin' bones. Heart attacks and stuff. We have the airplanes now so that we can put stretchers in them and bring the victims out.

Since the Park Service took over in the late '60s, the upper lake has all been changed over. Seattle people tried for years before they got that through. The park increased business by a lot, but it took away the old family feeling that they used to have up there. Stehekin was a little rural town of fifty or sixty people. They would all come to meet the boat and stand around and talk.

Harry Buckner ran the little general store and post office. He had lived there all his life. I really admired his philosophy and the way he treated people. He was like Will Rogers. Everybody was his friend. He never had an enemy in his life. I got to know him at the post office/store. We would get to talking and once in a while I would fly him out or bring in supplies for him.

There is still some of that old community spirit at Stehekin. There are still a few of the residents that were there forty years ago. It's still a pretty friendly place, though there is still a lot of friction between the Park Service and the community. They don't like to be told what they can do and how they can do it.

Ray Courtney, he was one of a kind, too. For years and years he packed people back into the hills until he and his horse fell off a cliff in 1977. I think he had more friends than anybody in the valley. Dudes were coming back year after year because of the way he treated them and because of his philosophy of life. He was just like an old-time farmer. Very likable and very capable.

Then there was an old-time trapper named Gordon Stuart. He gave up trapping to run the Emerald Park resort. At the end of fishing season, he would close up the camp and go out on his trap run. He had a trap line that was about forty miles long. He had a dog that went along with him when he would be out for a week at a time on snowshoes. He could get ten to fifteen miles per day on snowshoes.

He was really a super man. For example, one winter up there, around Thanksgiving, he got real sick. He went to bed and finally got over it. He came out the next spring for an examination to find out what had been wrong with him. He found out his appendix had burst on him. He had just laid there and lived through it!

Yeah, he was very independent! He just let people into the resort that he liked. If someone came in that irked him, rubbed him the wrong way, didn't clean up the cabin when they left, he would say, "Goodbye. But don't bother coming back again." He had a lot of friends. Right now I am flying the third generation of people that started going in there.

I began flying in 1945 and was a flying instructor in World War II, first for the Army and then the Navy. The last hitch I had was a contract for Navy cadets. They flew the old N3N two-wing jobs with open cockpits, goggles, and all the rest of it, right there at Fancher Field in Wenatchee. It sounds romantic but it was just another job. Nice and cool in the summer and you like to froze to death in the wintertime. No heat in those biplanes. No canopies or anything. You were right out in the open. No matter what you put on, you just about froze to death.

I think about that every once in a while, especially when I see another biplane. When I see one, it takes me back to when I was instructing in them.

In 1945 right after the war I began training people under the GI bill in Piper Cub seaplanes. We started in the fall, October. We built a bonfire on the beach to keep the students warm when they weren't flying. Eventually we built a little office and a ramp to get the aircraft in and out of the water.

We had three very light, two-place airplanes with sixty-five-horsepower engines in them. All they could do was get two people off the water and that was about it. They were so underpowered that they wouldn't take any kind of a load at all.

Today we have powerful planes and modern electronics but the weather can be as bad as it ever was. In the wintertime we have periods of fogs, especially in the morning. We have to fly anywhere from fifteen to fifty feet off the water and stay close to the shoreline. The minute you lose the shoreline, you land and taxi so that you can see it again. It isn't really dangerous because you have a landing strip under you all the time. All you have to do when you can't see, is just land. Cut the throttle and put it down.

It took you a long time to make a trip sometimes. It generally takes thirty minutes to go up to Stehekin. I have been as high as four hours trying to get up there.

We have had lots of heavy wind storms. If you get caught in one, you just try to find a sheltered spot and get down and ride it out on the water. Of course, occasionally the waves can get pretty big on this lake, especially in the middle. With the airplanes now, you can handle a lot heavier water than you could then.

Ice can still be a problem though. When it gets super cold, every time you make a landing or a takeoff, the water splashes up over the floats and onto the tail and forms a sheet of ice. When it is below twenty degrees, everything freezes instantly. It blocks up the little rudders on the back of the floats that we steer with. If they freeze solid, we have to get out, crawl back on the floats on our hands and knees, and knock the ice off to free them up so we can steer over to a dock. You can get very wet doing that while the waves are washing over you and bucking you up and down.

One time in 1950 I had a big fog bank from Manson to here, and I had to land and taxi on the water. I had a little bit of wave action and it splashed freezing water all over the airplane. We were getting so much ice that the airplane was starting to sink. By the time I got to the beach, the airplane was almost ready to sink!

I had to run it up on the beach. Another pilot had to get rubber hammers to beat the ice off the doors so that we could get out of there. Yeah, I came pretty close to sinking that time. I was getting a little nervous because I knew I couldn't open the doors. They were frozen shut!

Did I ever get scared? Well, there was one time when we were dropping supplies to the Horseshoe Basin copper mine, twenty-three miles past the head of the lake near Cascade Pass. We had to drop a bottle of oxygen and we had it on a parachute. I was flyin' and I had a man in the back seat. He threw it out and the parachute opened partially and hooked onto the rear of the float on the water rudder. It put the airplane in a stall where I couldn't fly. The nose was up and we were starting to slide back. Even with all the power I couldn't control it.

The guy in the back seat crawled out on the float, took a knife and cut the shroud, and got back into the airplane.

I tell ya, that's as close as I have ever really come to getting worried.

FRED HARRIS:

PUTTING DOWN ROOTS

Pasco, WA

Born: 1887

The best source for Northwest history, said historian Robert Cantwell in *The Hidden Northwest,* are the personal narratives of the pioneers who created the region only a few generations ago. My favorite Northwest reminiscences are stories of making-do, homely recitals of ordinary people progressing toward personal dreams.

Like so many other Northwesterners of his generation, Fred Harris quit school at an early age to become a farmer. He started from nothing and built up to owning a "showplace" spread on the Columbia River at Big Pasco. His laconic account of how he did this is short on details and suspense, but long on sincerity. Fred Harris today still lives beside the Columbia River (though about ten miles away from his original farm). His large garden flourishes in the Columbia Basin sun.

Nowadays the vegetables which Fred grows do provide him and his descendants with valuable food. But more than that, they bring the continuity of a long life, quietly spent on the land. As his daughter Lucille Olsen says, "Pop likes to see things grow."

I went to school till I was in the eighth grade. Because I was working more than I was in school, in the spring of the year, why I quit. I never went back again. I worked from then on.

There was a woman named Mrs. Crotty who was running a little dairy. They peddled milk from house to house with a horse. One of her boys went to Seattle. Seattle was not much bigger than Pasco but it was on a boom. This boy, why he persuaded his mother to sell the dairy.

She had forty-nine acres of land out where Big Pasco is. Where the Port of Pasco is, down there where all those big buildings are towards the Snake river. I wrote and asked her if she was interested in selling. She wrote back from Seattle that she would sell it for twelve hundred dollars.

At that time you went to the post office to get your mail because there was no rural free delivery yet. My stepdad opened her letter at the post office and when he come home, he wanted to buy her dairy. I had saved two or three hundred dollars and he had enough to make the first payment of six hundred dollars. We bought that land and, well, I quit school.

My stepdad worked for another year for the Northern Pacific and then we moved out to the place from Tenth and Sylvester in Pasco. The second year we was down there we dug a well and put in a gas engine and started growing garden stuff and sold it. Tomatoes and beans and radishes. Onions. Anything that we could sell. We had a few cows and sold milk.

I worked on the farm there till I was twenty-two years old and then I went in town and worked for one and a half years for another party on a dairy. That was the only time I worked for wages. I married my wife during that time. She had been born in Pasco, but her father was a doctor and he lived in Rosalia in Oaksdale. They lived out there until she was eighteen years old and then they moved back to Pasco and they farmed for two or three years. That's where I met her. And then they moved to Whidbey Island. My stepfather drove her by horse-drawn vehicle to Whidbey Island, hoping to alleviate her brother's asthma.

When I married her she lived on Whidbey Island. When I got married, I took fifteen acres of the ranch we had bought from Mrs. Crotty. I quit working at the dairy when I got married and built a little cabin on there and started for myself. I put in a well and pumped water to grow garden stuff. Just a little of everything.

In two or three years I started a dairy myself and I run a milk wagon with horses in town. I grew garden stuff and I sold my produce to the local stores and to my milk customers. It was all local customers. There was nothing shipped out. At that time there were just a few little five-acre farms. They raised strawberries and melons and stuff like that and very little stuff was shipped out.

By the time my kids were growing up, why we formed an association in 1928 and shipped stuff out by railroad. I was one of the directors of the association. We raised lettuce and onions and melons and all kinds of garden stuff. We packed that stuff up and shipped it mostly to Seattle.

Our producers' association gave people about all the income they had. Lettuce is what started it. There was a company in Walla Walla that run greenhouses and they furnished lettuce plants. We planted the seed in August and then had head lettuce in September and October. Then we planted plants in the spring and had the spring lettuce.

It was about the only income they had. There was no industry around.

I built up and accumulated forty to fifty acres of land. I got up to where I was milking forty-five head of cows and had all the buildings and everything. And I built a pretty fair house. It took me several years before I finished it. It was a two-story house with an open porch three-quarters of the way around it. It had two bedrooms, a kitchen, dining, living room, bath, and sewing room downstairs. Upstairs was later finished into three bedrooms and an open room. It had a full basement, thirty-six by forty feet.

The place was pretty nice and the Northern Pacific Railroad company would bring tourists down there off the immigrant trains to show them my place. The railroad company had gotten every other section of land along the railroad when they had built the railroad and now they were trying to get settlers out here to sell their land to. My daughter, Lucille, was about twelve to fourteen years old at that time, so it was about 1919.

Well, anyhow, we had a pretty nice place!

This story of gradual progress and hard work came to an abrupt end in 1942 when the Harrises lost their hard-won farm to the U. S. Army for a reconsignment depot. Fred Harris had to start all over from scratch. He bought another farm, the Wexler place, and moved his dairy there.

After World War II the Army's Big Pasco Reconsignment Depot became the Port of Pasco.

The following letter from the Harrises to their customers gives an idea of their sense of loss. *All* of the farm improvements were leveled, except for some outbuildings and the farm house which were sold. (The latter still stands today on Sylvester Street in Pasco.)

It is with a feeling of genuine sadness that we present you this view [a photo was enclosed with this letter] of the farm house that we built with our own hands and we loved so dearly. It is hard to give up something that has become a part of yourself through the long years of loving labor. But we are doing it without complaining since it is our government that demands it, and the most important job for all of us is to win the war. Our sacrifice, great and painful as it may seem to us, is gladly made since the cause is so important and vital to our country.

Thank you and may you keep some small part of our beloved home in your memory for the future.

Mr. and Mrs. Fred Harris
June 1942

KONRAD HARTBAUER:

BAGGING BUCKS

AND BUCKING CORDS

Northport, WA

Born: 1896

Konrad Hartbauer grew up on a homestead at Leadpoint in the lead and silver mining country east of Northport, Washington. At the end of the nineteenth century when he was born, that area was aswarm with prospectors hoping to strike it rich. The Hartbauers never struck pay dirt but they cashed in on the folksy rewards and hard work of the homesteading lifestyle. "When I was a kid out at the ranch, if we went to town every three months we were getting extravagant. We raised our own food, threshed our own grain, made our own flour."

It was a different time in all respects. Take the matter of wild game, for instance. Konrad, who is deaf from years of rifle practice, is still a lusty hunter (one buck in 1988) and cannot tolerate modern Game Department ways. Once he killed thirty-two bears who were enjoying his apples. "The game was in our way," he says. "You could take a dog and go down in the brush and shoot all the pheasants that you wanted. The deer came in and ate up the crops. You had to kill them to get rid of them. I really killed things. Fifteen bears and fifteen shots. Sixty-six coyotes and sixty-six shots. Twenty-nine deer and twenty-nine shots. My .257 Roberts kills everything it hits and I seldom miss. Big enough for anything in this country!"

Konrad's more pacifistic side is occupied with making knives from fine steel and with gardening. "I'm garden crazy," he says proudly. But bring up the subject of the Game Department and you will wish that you had kept to beets and beans.

These guys making the laws, they don't know beans. I don't think any of them know which end they are sittin' on. They read in a book about conservation and that's what they go by. All they care about is the dollar. Raise the license every year. They don't care if you get any game or not!

Thanks to Northport postmaster Ollie Mae Wilson, I met Konrad and his German-born second wife, Angie, in 1983 when I was hiking the Pacific Northwest Trail. Konrad had lived in Northport on the Columbia River since 1946 and had carried the rural mail from 1941 until 1953. In 1957 he switched to full-time firewood chopping. Angie is the ideal partner to locate, fall, buck, and cut tamarack cords. "Cutting logs is my fun," she says.

Konrad Hartbauer, old homesteader, says he doesn't dare tell how many deer he has killed during his lifetime. But he has plenty of hunting stories and a string of buck head photos dating back fifty years.

I went to a hunt on the other side of the river where I could see all around. I got up there and it was all fog. I couldn't see fifty feet.

But I kept lookin' toward the mountain. Pretty soon the fog parted a little and there comes a big buck. I shot it and the fog closed up just like that. Now if that ain't a fairy tale, I don't know what is.

Everybody has a notion that they like some certain thing in particular. Like me, I'm crazy about guns and ammunition, fishing tackle, and chain saws. Gettin' out in the woods and havin' a good time. I don't like to stay in town.

On my dad's homestead I never had time to grow up. I'm in my second childhood now. I feel just as good as I did fifty years ago. Maybe better. No aches, no pains, no nuthin'. But I get tired. I can't put in sixteen hours a day anymore like I used to.

During the hottest weather we had fifteen or twenty years ago when I cut lots of wood, I would leave town an hour before daylight. I would get up in the mountain in my woodyard just in time

Angie and Konrad
Hartbauer.

to turn my lights off. I would do my sawing before the sun got too
hot. After my saws once got hot, there was no coolin' them anymore. If the chain laid out on the bare ground, I would almost have
to have gloves on to pick it up. It was that hot. I would get home
at twelve o'clock with a load of wood and let it set till evening, then
I would unload it and start out again the next morning.

I've taken the trees out of this country, to where I don't know
where to look for another one. From Sheep Creek to Old Baldy,
Sherlock Peak, and Black Canyon. It is just about impossible to find
another dry tamarack. Of course, there are dead trees back in the
brush but there is no way to get to them. I cut trees as close to the
road as possible. I fall them toward my truck and then I drag them
out with block and tackle. Maybe spend three hours getting one
tree out.

Everybody cuts wood. We're running out of dead trees.

My father, Chris Hartbauer, was born in 1863 in Germany and
came to America in 1883 or 1884. Eventually he opened a bakery
in Mullen, Idaho, where he wrote his brother back in Germany to

send him a good woman for a wife and helper. When Mary Hubner came over, she was eighteen; they married and opened a bakery in Wardner, Idaho. It went broke after a few years when the miners went on strike.

So they moved to a new boomtown, Boundary, Washington on the Canadian border, where a railroad and a bridge across the Pend Oreille River were under construction. From 1892 to 1894 my dad had the store at Boundary when there were prospectors all over. They kept on bringing samples of ore in, showing the nice stuff they had found up in the hills. My daddy had lived over in the Coeur d'Alene country where the mineral is. Daddy thought maybe this would be another Coeur d'Alene some day. So when he had a chance in 1893 he bought the homestead rights on a hundred and sixty acres a mile north of Leadpoint, for two hundred dollars. It was all thick good cedar, tamarack, and pine. It took about a year for him to build a road to the ranch to get the family up there.

I was born there in 1896.

Oh, my goodness! We cleared a hundred and twenty-nine acres of swamp, timber, brush, boulders, and stumps and started a farm. Put up all those nice big buildings. Kept everything in shape. Every barn, every door, every gate, every bridge was always in first class order. Now the people that bought it can't even keep the roof on the buildings. They don't farm the land. They just turn the cattle in. No more hayin'. The place is goin' to the dogs. Makes me sick to look at it.

Every place was heavily farmed until about 1940 or 1945. Take old Purdy O'Hare. He had the homestead next to my dad's on the northwest side. He was a cowboy from Texas. He got tired of Texas, so he come up here to Boundary. He lived down there where it was pretty dry. When he left he said, "When I find a place where there is water, grass, and woods, that's where I'm goin' to settle."

He settled right against a hill where the water that came out of the spring back of his house always kept at about forty degrees in the summer time.

So he had ice water and good soil. You can see some of the old shack yet from the road. You come this way from Cedar Lake about three-quarters of a mile and you look right straight across and you will see some of O'Hare's buildings. Right against the hill, that's where the main house was. All the barns and stuff is torn down.

He first come into the country about 1895 and he had that ranch for over thirty years. I knew him pretty well. I used to go over and butcher pigs for him. Shoot squirrels for him. Took the threshing machine over and thrashed grain for him. I thrashed grain for all the people up and down the valley up there.

We were like one big family. Two or three times a year we would have a big picnic somewhere and everybody went. In winter they had dances. They usually danced in the schoolhouse there at Leadpoint. Then about 1912 or 1914 all the neighbors got together, put up a big community hall about forty by eighty or ninety. That's what they had their picnics and dances in. Waltzes, square dances, two-steps and whatever they could think of to dance. The schottische and I don't know what all else.

Everybody took something. Made a potluck out of it. My mother used to take a dishpan of raised donuts. She cut them diamond shape. They would puff up and get hollow inside. People would tease her about that. That dish pan was empty when it went home. They sure went for those big donuts!

It was just a community affair, year in and year out, for people spread out from Cedar Creek clear to South Fork. That's over fifteen miles.

There used to be a pavilion at this end of Deep Lake. They had lots of big doin's there. Especially the Fourth of July. Somebody usually set off two sticks of dynamite first thing in the morning to wake everybody up. No Fourth of July parades though. No, nothing like that. All they had in the country until 1912 was horses. O'Hare, he bought a Ford, 1912 or 1913. We got a 1914.

But they used horses for years and years after that. We had eight most the time to do the farm work. When I was a kid we didn't use any gasoline out on the farm. All horse power. We used the horses to pull the threshing machine. There were two units, the power and the thresher. We fastened the two together with a fifty-foot belt. The power was gasoline for threshing but not for any of the hayin'. We mowed with horses, raked with horses, used horses on the hayloader wagon.

There used to be three cream trucks runnin' in the valley, pickin' up the cream from farmers. Now you can take a cream truck up there and *sell* cream to all those people. That's the difference! You can sell vegetables up through the valley, eggs, meat, everything. Years ago they had it to sell.

It's so easy to go to the store and buy stuff. It is too much work to raise food. They can't be bothered. They would rather sit down with a glass of beer and a cigarette, and let the farm go to the dickens.

I wish I had let more grass grow under *my* feet. When I look at my hunting, fishing, and farm pictures I wonder how I ever had time to do all those things besides the work that I did. I farmed, trapped, ran the mail route, bought houses, looked after sixteen units, cut timbers. I averaged a hundred cords of wood a year for fifteen years, moving it in as many as five trips a day in my half-ton Chevy. My woodcutting territory was about five miles wide and forty-five miles long. I'm sure I've cut more sixteen-inch firewood than any other person in this area! When did I get time to do all that? I can't figure it out.

Even today I got energy to give away. We went out in the woods yesterday and got a load of wood. I'm weaker than I used to be. My wife did pert' near all the sawing. She is crazy about a chainsaw. She cut up a log up there in about ten minutes.

Yeah, she just loves that red chainsaw, it cuts so fast! She's gettin' good with it. Then she loaded the truck. When we come home she half unloads it. She can't find enough to do, she's worse than I am.

She'll be sixty-seven next month. I'll be ninety-three.

DOCTOR BILL HENRY:

COUNTRY DOCTOR

Twisp, WA

Born: 1929

As difficult as the lot of a country doctor may be today, conditions have improved greatly over those at the turn of the century. Phoebe Yeo of Stevenson, Washington remembers the following emergency.

It was in 1905. My dad at that time was superintendent of Wind River Lumber Company—of Camp No. 3, where Hemlock Ranger Station is today. A man who lived there and worked for Dad, by the name of Jim Taylor, said, "I want to stay all winter" as someone to look after the camp. Well, shoot, no one had ever bothered. There wasn't anyone that could get in there, 'cause the snow got so deep. But Mr. Taylor was a good friend of Dad's.

We had a phone where we lived that went into Stevenson, but Dad's phone at Camp 3 only went as far as our house. So to call Stevenson from camp he had to call the house and relay the call down to town. Our house telephone was hooked up to the Stevenson's telephone lines.

Oh, we had an awful lot of snow that winter!

Mr. Taylor, we always called him Uncle Jim, had a little girl, younger than me. We just loved that little girl and we played with her all the time.

This one morning, why, Uncle Jim called Dad and he said, "My little girl is terribly ill. If we can't get her to a doctor or get a doctor here, she's going to die."

Of course, when they told us kids about it, we were just sick. It was right before Christmas.

Dad said, "Well, Jim, I'll do what I can."

So Dad called Stevenson and asked Doctor Thomas Avary to go as quickly as he could up to Camp 3.

Doctor Avary said he'd try but he didn't know if he could make it or not, because Camp 3 was twelve miles north from Carson and seventeen miles from Stevenson, and the only way to get there was by horse and sleigh and the snow was probably too deep to get through.

Dad didn't know whether Doctor Avary could make it, either. So Dad said, "Well, you start out with your horse and sleigh in Stevenson from Bert Douglas's livery stable and when you get to Carson, I'll have a fresh team for you at Fred Estabrook's livery stable."

Beyond Carson the road was not where it is now. You had to go wa-a-ay down deep, clear to the bottom of the canyon of Wind River. And up the other side was a steep grade. Uncle Billy Anders lived where Ackers lives today, at the top of the steep grade, and the road went west of his house. Uncle Billy had his own team and so Dad said, "I'll have a fresh team for you at Carson, and then I'll have a fresh team for you at Billy Anders's place, and then I'll have a fresh team for you at the forest ranger's."

From there on, there wasn't anybody. Doctor Avary would just have to get there!

Camp 3 wasn't that much farther. It was where Hemlock is now. Before there was any town of Hemlock, Dad had built a dam and a logging camp there on Trout Creek.

I can remember those horses going by on that road, where there hadn't been a wagon or a horse or anything over that, and the snow was up to the horses' bellies. Trying to go through that and pull that sleigh, and Doctor Avary sitting in there, wrapped up in a big fur coat and a big lap robe, trying to keep warm.

All of us were just sick about poor little Lottie because we were sure she was going to die.

Doctor Avary got there and she had acute appendicitis. If they'd had any way of getting her there, they would have had her in the hospital and operated. But Doctor Avary stayed at the camp all day and, by golly, he saved that little girl's life.

He told her she had to take a teaspoon of castor oil for the rest of her life. I can remember her doing that with a little pickle that she'd eat afterwards to take away the taste of castor oil.

When Doctor Avary came back, he stopped at the ranger station to change horses. Elijah Weigle was the head ranger and the station was Weigle's own residence. Doctor Avary stopped again at Uncle Billy Anders's place, and he changed horses again at Carson, too.

When he finally got back to Stevenson and we kids heard that Lottie was all right and was going to live, that was the best Christmas![1]

Bill Henry of Twisp, Washington does not fit that low-tech stereotype of the country doctor. His modern clinic is equipped with defibrillators, I.V. pumps, X-ray, treadmill, and Macintosh computers.

But this workaholic is definitely a *family* doctor. "In the same family, I deliver the babies and take care of grandpa's stroke." That connectedness to the community appeals to this Pittsburgh-trained outdoorsman who has said, "I could never hear the silence around Pittsburgh. Not even when I visited my grandparents' grave."

Twisp, Washington is still genuinely rural, but in the 1980s an influx of urban refugees was attracted by the proposed Early Winters ski resort, the sunny climate, and the relatively low land prices. Several waves of back-to-the-landers have rippled across the back forty, leaving eccentrically-designed log cabins, new ideas, and even, since 1988, an *art gallery* on Main Street. Every once in a while some good old boy stumbles into the gallery from the Antlers Tavern next door and backs out again in bleary-eyed shock.

Well, that mix of second generation ranchers, urban professionals, back-to-the-landers, artists, and tourists is the milieu of Doctor Bill Henry. Mostly he thrives on it. He *is* the medical establishment

---

[1]Phoebe Yeo adds, "Dr. Avary was the best kind of family doctor. He would go anywhere he was called, day or night, in his horse and buggy. In 1914 he built a small hospital which still stands on Main Street in Stevenson and which is known as the Avary Building. Today we have a clinic with two, three doctors and nurses, two ambulances with paramedic drivers, and also a life flight helicopter to take patients into Portland!"

there and his influence can extend as far elsewhere into the community as he wishes. In the early 1970s he was a member of the school board, but resigned because the community was not willing to accept education reform. Bill sent his five children to finish high school in Bellevue and Wenatchee. Also, he had been active in Twisp's Methodist church but gradually drifted away in search of spiritual solitude.

Dr. Henry has taken time from his hectic schedule to serve on numerous Okanogan County and state medical boards. In 1967 he founded his own ambulance and rescue service. In the early '70s he was chairman of the governor's Advisory Committee for Emergency Services. There his eastern Washington needs came up against the reality of western Washington power.

It was our committee that defined the law that established the emergency system throughout the state for ambulances, emergency medical technicians, and paramedics. On that committee, east met west. Seattle's MEDIC I[2] ambulance standards could not be imposed on the east side ambulance services. Nor could our special requirements for power winches on the bumper, pulaskis, and peevees be imposed on the urban units. City ambulances did not even carry spare tires, because of the ready availability of back-up units. Their average rescue runs lasted between ten and fifteen minutes, but ours was over one hour. We therefore had a need for more "in vehicle" support than did MEDIC I. These committee meetings gave us a chance to ventilate our differences and to reach a compromise. I had to see to it that state law did not reflect just the King County perspective. Henry was the loudmouth who said, "Hey fellows, there is something east of Snoqualamie Pass and we have a different set of problems."

"I still get into arguments," says Dr. Henry. "They have learned to listen to me."

The dichotomy between the "have" Puget Sound and the "have not" rest of the state is part of the basic character of Washington.

---

[2]MEDIC I is Seattle's pioneering fast-response emergency medical service, founded in 1970, and widely copied nationally.

So, too, is the untamed nature of much of the countryside. Washington is such an outstanding showcase of untrammeled mountains, glaciers, coasts, forests, and lakes that it annually attracts legions of outdoorsmen.

Some stay. In 1960 that included Dr. Bill Henry, then a Navy search and rescue officer at Kodiak, Alaska.

In Alaska it was high-tech and complex rescue work. But this Twisp area needed a doctor and it was surrounded by the type of mountains that I liked. I thought I would spend a few years here and then become a big city specialist. But I would have had heart attacks and angina and everything else if I had had to fight that Seattle traffic going back and forth to Swedish Hospital every day. And, in fact, I am doing right now pretty much what I said I would do the first year I went to medical school.

I remember a young teenager in Denver, Colorado who told me that kids at his school had adopted the "Northwest look," meaning the practical duds sold by Seattle's many backpacking stores. Washington is a vast state where few men except downtown commuters wear neckties. Washington is so outdoors-oriented that climbing tragedies are always front page news. Washington has an unusual medical specialty, wilderness medicine.

The backcountry doctor must treat both normal problems such as broken bones and the special disasters of the wilderness such as frostbite, hypothermia, snakebite, avalanche injuries, and high altitude sickness. Often in very remote places, two or three days from the nearest trailhead.

Dr. Henry is constantly training his crew of ambulance people, volunteers, smokejumpers, EMT's, and paramedics. He goes to most accident scenes and participates in most of the backcountry tragedies. "Nobody is going to give their instructor any credence," he says, "unless he has been there. So I have been there! I know what it is like to see the bones lying in the dirt. Most doctors don't get out of their emergency rooms. They see them after we put them together and get them to the big city specialists that get out some nuts and bolts, and screw the legs back together."

"But someone has to get those people off the mountain."

Bill Henry beside his ambulance.

As a rural doctor I have to shoot from the hip, to work on the basis of intuition. I make an educated guess and sometimes I am right and sometimes I am wrong. We don't have access to all the electronic diagnostic gear. But in this fairly sophisticated medical center here in Twisp, I can do major procedures.

But those poor old doctors back before the big war, they didn't have a hospital or a clinic. They just worked out of their saddle-bags. The people could not come. The roads were not good enough, the cars were not good enough, so some poor doctor would spend half a day on horseback going up Beaver Creek to see somebody who had pneumonia. (Sometimes they gave them a dollar for that.)

Our rescue work involves a lot of uncertainties, too, but we minimize them with rigorous preparation and training. Let me tell you about the most difficult and dangerous rescue that Aero Methow Rescue has ever been involved in. On August 4, 1984 we were notified by a telephone call from a mountain climber in the Diablo area that there was an injured party on top of Liberty Bell. We learned that the accident victim had a two-bone open fracture of the leg with bone showing and that he was in highly-technical rock-climbing terrain about two hundred feet below the summit of Liberty Bell. At approximately 03:00 August 5 we left Twisp for the Blue Lake Trail servicing the backside of Liberty Bell. On board our ambulance were myself, Cynthia Button, paramedic, Charlie Chamberlain, E.M.T., and Darren Higbee.

We met the Liberty Bell Alpine units and the Chelan County units at the trailhead at approximately 04:30. The combined parties ascended to the notch between Liberty Bell and an adjacent mountain. A fixed rope was established to the summit and five of the Chelan County rescue personnel ascended to the summit. Mark Shipman, an emergency room doctor from Wenatchee who worked with me on this, discovered that the climber was hypothermic, and in shock and severe pain. But Mark was able to get those bones back in place, put a plaster of Paris cast on to mid-thigh, and set up an intravenous to take care of the man's shock.

We decided that the man had to be airlifted off Liberty Bell, but before the chopper could arrive from Boeing Field a thunderstorm hit. The helicopter had to put down between Washington Pass and Rainy Pass to wait out the severe rain and lightning.

Over the next fifty minutes the rescuers and the patient were each hit more than once by lightning. They were soaking wet. It was raining. Those guys said that never in their lives had they been in rain like that. They all remember the shocks.

One man was unconscious for about a minute and a half because he couldn't breathe. The muscles that controlled his respiration were just in chaotic fibrillation.

The victim recalled being hit twice but neither shock left any burns. He was dragged off the summit to decrease his susceptibility to the lightning. But while doing that, his rescuers took a few more strikes themselves.

At all other times all personnel were flat against the mountain, trying to hold as low a profile as possible in cracks and crevices.

When the helicopter finally arrived after the main storm had passed, the pilot, without putting his skid down, was able to hold a stable enough hover to receive the patient. The crew tried to jump in the helicopter, but the pilot wouldn't take them because of the severe winds.

But the rescue party was able to rappel off the exposed peak and to hike out approximately four miles cross-country to the road. I X-rayed the patient at our Twisp Medical Center and transferred him by helicopter to Virginia Mason Hospital in Seattle for further care.

The crew was convinced that the lightning had taken the way of least resistance, through their wet clothes. The lightning splashed onto them. One rescuer jumped about six feet because it stimulated the jump muscles in him. One boy was unconscious. Some of the men had numb spots on their legs that lasted for a couple of weeks.

But they all survived. That's the sort of thing that nobody hears anything about. We only hear about the tragedies. We had six people struck by lightning, each of them twice. Nobody died. Everybody survived.

Everybody has some residual of that trip in the form of maybe some inflamed nerves, holes in their memory, or just the memory that says, "I am not going back on that mountain again."

We got this man off and he has healed and is walking around. That's because we knew what to do and knew where to go. We knew the trails and we knew the mountain.

That's wilderness medicine. We didn't have to do this. We didn't get paid. We all left active jobs to participate in this rescue. The point is that we make our reputations and get our satisfaction out of doing what we don't *have* to do. And doing it well.

MONTE HOLM:
HOBO RAILROADER
Moses Lake, WA
Born: 1917

The Mon-Road Railroad of Moses Lake, Washington is not going to compete with Amtrak any time soon, but it does possess a formidable amount of rolling stock. I inspected an executive Pullman car (which had been used by presidents Wilson and Truman) and a giant steam locomotive (in the photo below). But it was the owner of this funky one-quarter-mile line whom I had come to see, not his cabooses and tenders.

In 1930 Monte Holm became a thirteen-year-old runaway from his stepmother and Lutheran minister father. He bummed around the country sheepherding, doing odd jobs, riding the rods, and wishing that he *owned* a railroad so that he could legally ride inside for a change. A chance beginning in Everett, Washington's junk business led to his acquiring many defunct logging railroads for scrap metal when trucks replaced trains in Northwest forests.

Nowadays Moses Lake Iron and Metal is a quarter-mile-long salvage yard where old this and that is piled up in a way described by one local wag as "from hell to breakfast." Monte Holm's museum is like that, too. Where else could you see cheek by jowl a foot-powered sewing machine "owned by a member of the Jessie James family" near a school bell, a butter churn, Monte's first car (a 1917 T-Model), and whistles from a Bellingham sawmill called Big Oly? Monte says, "Everything works in here but me."

Obviously, Monte Holm enjoys playing the role of local celebrity hobo for touring school kids and passersby like me. But I could not have spent much time in his cluttered office, as I did beside his vintage dog Buck, without realizing that Monte was a very savvy operator. Our conversation was frequently interrupted by buy and sell calls. The free scale outside his office door was constantly in use by farm produce truckers, each of whom left the old hobo a sack of carrots, cabbages, or Walla Walla sweets, many of which are likely to end up in the hobo stews which Monty still makes.

Judge John Langenbach[1] was never a hobo but he spoke with many railroad tramps during his daily two and a half mile walk to school along the tracks. So here in honor of every man or boy who ever rode the rods or the blinds is Judge Langenbach's "Hoboes' Convention."

> I'm just a tuckered out hobo—
>   I want to rest a while;
> I ain't done harm here on your farm.
>   It won't hurt none to smile.
>
> You've heard of great conventions—
>   There's some you can't forget;
> But get this straight there's none so great
>   As when the hoboes met.
>
> To Portland, Oregon, last year
>   They came from near and far,
> On top of blinds where cinders whined
>   They rode on every car.
>
> A dozen came from New York State;
>   Some came from Eagle Pass—
> That afternoon, the third of June,
>   They gathered round en masse.
>
> From Lone Star State came Texas Slim
>   And Jack the Katydid;
> With Lonesome Lou from Kalamazoo
>   And the San Diego Kid.
>
> Denver Don and Boston Red
>   Blew in with Hell-fire Jack

[1]See pages 171–180.

And Curly Lang with the Northshore gang,
  And Mac from Mackinac.

There was Phil the sleek from Cripple Creek,
  And the Philadelphia Sparrow,
And Lucky Sid, the New York Kid
  Came frozen from Point Barrow.

Chicago Bill was dressed to kill,
  Shook hands with Frisco Fred,
While half-breed Joe from Mexico
  Shot craps with Eastport Ed.

St. Louis Slim and Pittsburg Paul
  Whipped up a jungle stew,
While Slippery Bim and Bashful Tim
  Upset the whole menu.

The jockey kid spilled out a song
  Along with Desperate Sam,
And Jack the Shark from Terra Park
  Clog-danced with Alabam.

All night we flopped around the fire
  Until the morning sun;
Then from the town the bulls came down—
  We beat it on the run.

We scattered to the railroad yards;
  The bulls were left behind.
Some took fast freights for other states
  And some rode on the blinds.

I'm headed out to Denver now,
  A hungry, tired-out "Bo."
The flyer's due—when she comes thru
  I'll catch her and I'll blow.

I hear her whistling for the block,
  I'll make her on the fly;
It's number nine, Santa Fe line—
  I'm off again—Good-bye.

Monrad is my real name. I'm named after the king of Denmark.

I was raised in Montana. My mother died when I was six and I got a stepmother and we didn't agree too good. So at thirteen I left home. Three hours is all I've ever been home since.

I spent six years hoboing all over the United States on freight trains. In those days the work was very, very hard to come by and a kid didn't have much chance.

Underneath the railroad cars there were truss rods. Hobos would get underneath a boxcar with a grain door about eighteen inches across. They would stack these across there and lie on them. The cinders would come up and ashes. It was kinda miserable. They only fell off once.

I rode inside the boxcars more than I did underneath. Underneath and on top was miserable. But inside, you could lay there and sleep. Railroad bulls [train detectives] would kick you off. I was kicked off many trains out in the desert and all over. I used to tell them, "Some day I'm going to own my own train and you're not going to kick me off."

I was determined to buy a train afterwards to prove to them that I could get my own. That's what led to the House of Poverty Museum.

At the hobo jungles you could take something to eat but you always left the pans, such as they were, clean, so the next hobo that came along could use them. Every town had a hobo jungle. The first time that I was in one. . . .

I've got to tell you, I was brought up believing not to steal. And I didn't. But sometimes you get put in a situation where you get hungry. When I left home, I had two dollars. The first night in the boxcar, someone reached in my pocket and got it. They needed it, I guess, more than I did.

I didn't eat for maybe two days. It was dark and maybe there were twenty-five guys. And they used to use five-gallon cans to make stew in. They needed more meat in that night's stew. Twenty-five guys is a lot to feed.

Somebody knew where there was a chicken coop. And they wanted someone who could run and I was the only kid there. So I was picked, see, and the others went out to get vegetables out of gardens.

The chicken coop was dark and full of chickens. I grabbed two in each hand, see, and then they came to life. You know how chickens are. They made all kinds of racket. This farmer, he came out with a shotgun and started shooting at me. I ran out and I dropped two chickens, but I was proud that I got back with two chickens and had not been shot.

The fellows fixed the chickens up with the vegetables they had stolen. I kept smelling that stew cooking. I figured that, being as I got the chickens, I should be the first in the pot. They informed me that I was the youngest and that I would be the last in line. When I got to the pot there was a little broth left, is all.

But it taught me the best lesson I ever was taught, that I was going to have to take care of myself. Nobody else was going to. And it taught me not to steal any more chickens, which I never did do.

Speaking of chickens, they were shipped in a kind of cattle car which had a little opening. You'd reach in there and slice off a leg. When you're hungry you go to extremes.

The first time I begged, I asked for work. I would always work. The first time I begged a house. . . . I had a lot of pride but I was awfully hungry. I went up to the doorstep ten times before I ever knocked. They gave me a sandwich and I split wood for them.

I first came to Washington to pick fruit in Yakima. I didn't get a job doing nothing. I slept there on Front Street for a couple of weeks. I came to Tacoma and I stayed there about two weeks. The night agent let me sleep in the old railroad depot. I'd lay up there and look at that high dome.

Here about two years ago they had a promotion deal to recuperate that dome and they were looking for donations. So I sent them two hundred bucks and a letter telling them I was paying for my rent when I had slept there.

Another hobo that I knew said that there was some work going on in Everett. They needed section hands there on the logging railroads. So I said, "I sure could go for that."

We walked from Tacoma to Everett. It's quite a little hike the back way. I landed in Everett with a dime and not much schooling, and I never did get that section hand job.

Every town had a hobo jungle. It was usually down along a creek so you had water. In Everett it was down along the river. Them days, you could drink the water anywhere. You could drink out of every stream or lake, even in town. Now everything is poison. There weren't any pulp mills in Everett then and there weren't so many people. And the foliage has grown so at the old hobo jungle!

Sometimes people would build a little shack out of boards they found. In Seattle they had what they called Hooverville. It was a hobo town built out of discarded boxes. Just anything. There were thousands of people in there and most of them got along fine with each other.

When I got to Everett I figured that that was enough of my hobo years. I tried to settle down. But I had an awful hard time getting anything started. I finally got on my feet by going into the junk business, something that didn't require much education.

When I came to Everett in 1936, there was no work. I finally got enough money to rent a room on Norton, down on the waterfront. It was one twenty-five a week and I had a stove in there so that I could cook if I could find food.

Mostly hobos stayed there. There were three hobos taking junk out of a sawmill. And they wanted to know if I wanted to help because I was so ambitious and always wanted to work. We were getting a dollar a ton and could get out about one ton a day. It was mostly bolts, pulleys, and bearings. After a week, I asked the other hoboes, "Don't we ever get any money?" They said they didn't know.

We went down to the junkyard that was buying the stuff. There was a Jewish woman running it, a real nice lady. She said that the fellow who had been supplying her with our junk had got paid but that he had left the country. So we didn't get paid.

So we asked this Jewish woman if she would pay us if we kept bringing in the scrap metal. Sure. So then we got our money. That went on a couple of weeks and one hobo left and then another hobo left and that left me alone. So I hired hobos to salvage metal and I would make a dime a ton on them. And they would make ninety cents.

When I got through with that, they had a whole pile of brick there at the sawmill. So I asked this Jewish lady if I could clean those for her and we came to a price of a penny apiece.

We had to clean them and stack them on the truck. No forklifts in those days! It was all hand work.

So I hired hobos and paid them ninety cents a hundred. I'd make a dime on them. Hobos still come here. The old-timers are nice fellows.

When I was a kid I promised myself that when I could afford it I'd eat whatever I wanted. Now that I can afford to do that, the doctor tells me differently. It's awful.

Let me explain to you the conditions in the Depression. You have probably never really gone hungry. And you have probably always had a nice place to sleep normally every night. You've probably wanted things but didn't need them.

A few years ago my niece and daughter had never been to Chicago. So I said, "I'm going to hire the nicest chauffeured, stretched-out limo and we're going to go on skid row where I was when I was a kid. We did. But the driver wouldn't take us down on the roughest parts. We toured through the Loop at high noon. Unbelievable! We had fun.

I was on the bum mostly during the Depression, when there was just no work. In them days there was no Social Security or workman's compensation. They didn't know how many people were out of work.

I always go on trains because now I can ride inside, see. I take my grandsons around to these various skid roads where I used to live.

In Minneapolis I spent four months one winter living in lines for a bowl of soup. After I ate my soup I would go right back in line because I was hungry.

I was like sixteen years old that winter. I bedded down in a room with a thousand guys sleeping in it. Smells! Some of them hadn't had a bath since their mother gave them one.

At least I was warm.

I take the grandkids down to all these places. Took 'em down to Texas and places where I'd left a memory.

BILL HOTTELL:
THE EDUCATION
OF A FIGHTER
Spokane, WA
Born: 1916

Bill Hottell was a twelve-year-old kid in the rough and tumble world of loggers, miners, smugglers, teamsters, squawmen, cowboys, and sawmill hands which was 1928 Curlew, Washington. That Depression backwater, hard by the Canadian line, had "without a doubt more unusual characters than anywhere else in the world."

Even today Ferry County is so remote that it is difficult there to get a dial tone out, never mind a bus. Sixty years ago the forgotten mountains and valleys around Curlew were yet horse country. Many Indians, rumrunners, moonshiners, loggers, and hardscrabble farmers still worked horses. The Hottells, for instance, had a horse that bootlegger Mac McColough had sold after it had dumped a load of whiskey while crossing the Canadian line. "We owned that horse for a long time," says Bill. We called him Booze because he had bucked that pack of booze off."

In such a horse country a good blacksmith was an important man. And a source of inspiration to an impressionable boy. Another source of inspiration was Luther "Lute" Brown, a "rounder" and "fighting man" who had lost several fingers from sawmilling.

All four of us boys did some boxing. My oldest brother, Andy Hottell, was a successful professional boxer under the name of "Ace Conklin." Jack Dempsey refereed two of his fights and in

1932 Andy fought a draw with the second- or third-ranking welter-weight in the world.

Bill Hottell grew up working in the mines (for his brother-in-law Evan Brown), loading railroad cars with lumber, firefighting as a "plowshaker" on a fire line at the 1934 Aeneas Creek fire, helping out at the blacksmith shop, and ending up married and homesteading with only ten dollars to last him through a winter. He was a gregarious fellow who "liked everybody" and who "was not a very good speller" but could "sure work to beat hell."

A good Bill Hottell story always involves colorful friends and neighbors, involved in some violent escapade, preferably fist-fighting. For instance, Bill tells of rumrunner Ambrose Lamby who pulled off a Montgomery Ward holdup in Spokane. Or Bughouse Dick, an Indian who won the Keller Suicide Race with his feet tied underneath his horse. Or loggers fighting at Curlew dances. Or Dutch Tonasket (whose brother Two Jump Joe refused the Colville tribe's chieftainship because he was not fluent enough in that Indian dialect). Once, at a dance at the Curlew Community Hall Bill Hottell saw Dutch Tonasket come in looking for a fight.

Dutch was about my size and was always looking for a fight. It was just before the dance was starting and we had a big potbellied stove by the door. There was about a one-by-two-inch board for stirring the stove. Earl Brown, who was an ex-Marine, says, "Sure I'll fight you." He just grabbed up that stick that was about four feet long and broke it over Dutch Tonasket's head and threw him out. Somebody says, "Brown, that's no fair way to fight." He said, "Who the hell wants to break their hands up on an Indian?"

As we talked, Bill Hottell kept coming back to the story of Harry Lavin, Curlew's blacksmith. That story takes up most of this chapter. But before we get to that main event, pull up your chair next to the spittoon and imagine that we are at a Republic "smoker" (a fight between scholars from different schools).

I was the second for Evan Brown, my future brother-in-law, in a grudge fight against Oliver Davis. Oliver Davis, one hundred seventy-five pounds and Evan Brown one hundred sixty-five pounds. So I jumped in the ring and said, "Folks, there's been a mistake in the weights. I saw them weigh in just before the fight and Oliver Davis weighs one hundred eighty pounds and Evan Brown one hundred forty pounds.

But the weights didn't matter because this was just a plain grudge fight.

The first time Evan hit Davis it put a big welt over his eye and knocked him out of the ring. That punch ended the fight.

Evan was strong. He worked at the mill turning two-foot logs by hand. No cant hook. He just rolled them by hand.

Another time, at a smoker in Curlew my brother Jake was boxing with a sawmill kid from Republic. A husky kid. Jake and he were fighting and just going at it to beat hell. It was just a knock-down drag-out, and the referee didn't hear the bell. Slug Walker, the Republic boxing coach, just steps through the ropes and pulled Jake right flat on his back. I was second for Jake and I was about half looped anyway. Over the rope I come. I was dressed in white pants and I went over and started pouring it on old Slug. I was just beating the hell out of old Slug. I had him in the corner and. . . .

I was fascinated with anything to do with perfection or anything people did with their hands.

And Harry Lavin was without a doubt as good a blacksmith as anybody in the world. He was very, very capable. He could do all kinds of welding. He could do anything and everything. He was a real professional perfectionist.

We moved from the Greer Grade, Idaho to Curlew in 1928 and Harry was there then. I think he was still blacksmithing when we left in 1941 for Spokane.

I used to stop at the blacksmith shop to see what Harry was doing. I just worked with him. Sometimes he paid me. He said that I was probably the best worker in the country because I could do what he wanted.

Harry didn't let the work interfere too much with his drinking. If he needed money, he would work. For instance, he put new noses on plowshares. Just a low-bar plowshare that you would take

and drag around. The plowshares would wear out and they were expensive to buy so he would put a new nose on them. Hoof rasp is what he used a lot because it was a good, hard steel. A hoof rasp was a hand file, to grind down and shape the edge of a horse's hoof.

He sharpened steels for mine drilling. He was capable of doing any blacksmith work. He made horseshoes right from scratch. He could do anything. You showed him what you wanted and he could make it.

Once I helped Harry Lavin to put iron rims on wooden wagon wheels. Makin' them right out of a straight flat iron, putting the arc in them, and measuring them so that they fit absolutely perfectly. It was quite a simple operation if you knew how to do it, but it was exacting. Harry was a great blacksmith.

His shop was just at the edge of Curlew, not far from the school. I preferred fishing or going to the blacksmith shop to going to school. I remember a time when I was seventeen or eighteen years old (I had left school at the age of fifteen). Some Indians had a team of horses that weighed about a ton apiece and needed to be shod to go logging. Harry had been drunk for probably a month at least. He was too weak to shoe the horses himself and he asked me to help him, because I happened to be going past the shop on the railroad track into town. The Indians were scared to death of the horses and Harry was too weak to do anything with them. He offered to pay me two bits a shoe.

Anything was good money in those days because the average wage was only a dollar a day and board, or a dollar and a half if you boarded yourself. But I happened to be seventeen or eighteen and I was making between two-seventy and three-sixty a day, piling lumber for Fred Buddo. He bought lumber from all the sawmills and was more or less a lumber broker. He made a lot of money, especially in pine lumber. We would get it green from the mills and pile it, one stick at a time, lots of it, on the truck and haul it a half mile down to Bright, at the edge of Curlew right by the Ansorge Hotel, and load it into the box car. We handled that lumber twice and we would load a box car in six hours. That's what you call movin'. I could pile lumber faster than any two guys could ever push lumber into that baby. I was very efficient. I'm not a very good speller, but I can sure work to beat hell.

Anyway, Harry Lavin, one of the greatest blacksmiths in the world, lived only a quarter mile or less from me. But I didn't spend much time around the blacksmith shop because my dad kept me so busy working all the time. Even when I went to school, I would come home at noon to work during the noon hour. Dad wanted to keep me used to constant work so that I wouldn't get out of the habit.

My parents did not socialize with Harry Lavin at all. They would speak to him. But we didn't visit at all. In fact, Harry had his own group of people. Harry Lavin was probably fifty, about the same age as my father. Besides being a very accomplished blacksmith, he was also a very good squawman. That made a big impression on me. It would on anyone.

A squawman is a man that has Indian ladies living with him. Not married to him.

Harry's first wife (who was white) kind of kept him under control. Whenever he would get drunk up a little bit, she would get the gun out and chase Harry around the house. Just as Harry would get around the corner of the house, she would shoot.

At one time Harry Lavin went to Grand Forks on the Queen's

birthday. He took his wife and Agnes Seymour, who was a big, younger Indian gal. Took them to Grand Forks, rented rooms at the hotel, and farmed them out for prostitution. He had Agnes Seymour as a Spanish gal and I don't know what he had his wife named as.

Ann Bush, she was much younger than most of Harry's women. She went to Greenwood, B. C. with two fellas and they robbed a liquor store. The Mounties shot one fella. Ann Bush drug him into the car and beat the Mounties across the line.

They never did catch her.

Harry made homebrew all the time but they very seldom got any of it bottled because they drank it before. . . . They had a dipper hanging on the crock and they would just drink that baby out. They had one or two ten-gallon crocks of beer going all the time, but they never had time to bottle any whiskey. By the time it was supposed to be bottled, they had it all drank up and had another batch going.

There were quite a few Indians at Curlew when we moved there in 1928. I was twelve years old. Actually the Indians and the kids got along fantastically well. But a lot of the white people that moved in later, it was kind of frowned on that their daughters went with the Indian boys. Now the Indians are quite extinct around there.

Harry Lavin's bunch wasn't the general run of the Curlew people, white or Indian. It was just some of the sideshow part, more or less. There were a lot of respectable Indian women around.

But this one particular time, Ann Bush was living with Harry Lavin and they had been drunk for a month or so. Harry was laying on the cot taking a nap. Annie Bush she goes out and finds herself a two-by-four and she comes in and puts it right across the bridge of Harry Lavin's nose. She throwed the two-by-four down, runs into the kitchen and grabs this butcher knife and comes at him with this butcher knife. He says, "I just opened my eyes enough that I could see that butcher knife coming at me and I grabbed it and she pulled it through my hand. She came at me again with that knife and I grabbed it again, and she pulled the knife right through my hand again and cut me clear to the bone. By that time I was starting to sober up, so I knocked her flat on her ass."

Ann Bush, Humpie Agnes, and Big Agnes Seymour were all

around together quite a bit. Big Agnes lived up on the hill about a half mile above the school.

Several years later, Dutch Tonasket hung around down there quite a bit, too.

Harry was quite thrifty. He had lots of food for them. He butchered pigs and cured his own meat and everything. He was quite. . . . That was probably the reason they were hanging around, because the food was so good.

Harry also had at least two houses besides his own house, that he rented out right on the bank of the river. This one particular time there was some other fellas, Indians and white guys both, down there. Harry Lavin was pretty well drunk up and he thought these people were stealing his meat. So he went out trying to protect his stuff. Ann Bush and Big Agnes Seymour knocked him down out in the yard and took clubs and just beat him till he was almost coal black. Then they ran in the house and got the kerosene lamp and poured the kerosene on him and set him afire. So he had scars that were over an inch thick on his neck. It took him a long time to get healed up from that.

They did play pretty rough around there.

One time he had Ann Bush put in jail up in Republic. She wasn't up there overnight hardly and he was up there bailing her out. Plus he got a ticket for standing on the sidewalk urinating in the street.

Humpy Agnes was very short and sort of humped over. She was a very small Indian lady. She first was married to Pelliken, who was probably an Italian from Spokane. They had very beautiful daughters, quite small but they were not humped, and at least two of the daughters went through nurses' training down here at Sacred Heart. That was many years ago.

Anyway, Humpy Agnes got tired of Pelliken, so one spring when the water was high she got the rest of the Indians to take and hogtie him, and they threw him in the Kettle River. So that was the end of Pelliken. That was just below the bridge up towards the Canadian line.

I'm sure that was very common knowledge but it was many, many years ago. As far as I know, nothing happened to Humpy Agnes for doing that.

Later she picked up with this Ed Couts. They were never married. They were just living together but they had several children.

Humpy's parents were Indian. They were very old and one of them was totally blind and the other almost totally blind. One time they had been celebrating on their little ranch up in the mountains. Humpy and Ed Couts heard that they had been drinking for two or three weeks at least. Ed and Humpy went up there to take care of the animals a bit. While Ed was separating the milk Humpy took this butcher knife, about a two-foot blade, and stuck it through one side of Ed's chest and the end of the blade came out of the other side of his chest.

As far as I can remember, Humpy was in jail two weeks for that little escapade.

All the guys liked Humpy Agnes. In later years, she had a child after Ed Couts died. The welfare people were up checking her and she happened to be at my sister's house, and they said, "Your husband has been dead for eight or nine years now?"

She says, "That is correct."

They said, "Your son is seven years old and his name is Couts?"

She says, "Yes."

They said, "How can that be?"

She said, "I did not say I was dead, did I?"

Humpy Agnes spread her favors around the community quite a little. Ernie Bowman always claimed that she did not mind making love with him if he just promised to only do it one time.

These things were common knowledge in Curlew. That was about all the entertainment there was in Ferry County.

There was no money in Ferry County during the Depression. There still isn't.

I think the second year that Alice and I were married. . . . She was a new teacher, living at the Ansorge Hotel. We had met at one of the local dances, at the Malo Grange Hall or at the Woodman Lodge Hall in Curlew in 1935. I liked her dark eyes and she thought I was very friendly. There was quite a chivaree for us after we got married. The first year we rented a house in Curlew while I built a rough lumber house for us up on Deer Creek. I walked five miles every morning to saw logs.

The winter my son Bill was born, 1938, we lived on canned food, frozen carrots, and venison. Bill was born in Spokane, December

7, 1938. I think the doctor and hospital bill was forty dollars. We paid cash and so we only had twenty dollars left to get through the winter.

I had been trying to farm. I had farmed my folks' land for free of charge. After I got my dad's crop in, I could use the equipment to harvest what little grain I had. But it was too late by that time and we didn't get much crop anyway. It was pretty desperate. So boxing seemed like a pretty good way to make a little money.

I had done a lot of fighting and my brothers were fighters. One time in 1933 when I had been seventeen, Bill Helphrey, Vern Cotton, and I were up at Republic and wanted to get some beer. Prohibition had just ended but the drinking age was twenty-one. Bill had money because his family owned the general store. We went to the Bailey Hotel.[1] I went in and bought the beer because I looked older. We proceeded to get drunk up a little bit. I was getting a little noisy and wouldn't shut up. So Bill says, "If you don't shut up, we are going to have to knock you out." Everybody fought anyway so there was nothing wrong with that. We were fooling around. Vern was standing off to the side and Bill kept telling Vern to hit me. I looked around and Bill hit me and cracked my jaw and I wasn't able to work for a day or so after that.

After that my dad insisted that Bill and I have a blood fight. Bill and I had been real good friends all that time, but my dad insisted that we were going to fight, regardless. So to please him we fought at the smoker up at Republic that winter.

After I was married and had a baby boy, and was poor as the dickens, I fought once to get some money. Dean Neidifer, he was the light heavyweight champ of the Navy. He come up to Curlew and he wanted to fight in the smoker. None of the fellas in Republic, none of the tough miners or nobody would box him.

So I said, "Well, I am not in your class at all but if everybody is yellow, I will take you on for a short time until I got my money's worth." So Ed Nelson ran and got the principal, Mr. Slaughter, to say that he had a good main event fixed up. He, the principal, wanted to know how much I wanted. I was walking five miles up in the mountains to saw logs for two or three dollars a day. So I said that I would fight for ten or fifteen bucks.

[1]The Bailey Hotel was later owned by Sam Cassel. See page 54.

They talked to Neidifer and he said he would fight for three or four bucks. He just wanted to fight. Anyway, they decided that would be a pretty good main event. I used to box in the smokers at school. Some, but not much. They decided that they would give us seven and a half apiece.

So early in the evening Dean Neidifer was down at the beer parlor trying to bet his money that he was going to knock me out before the end of the second round.

Just before we got in the ring he came over and he said, "Bill, there is no reason for anybody to get hurt. Let's just go in there and box for exhibition."

I says, "Neidifer, if you are in no better shape than I am, no one is going to get hurt too badly. Besides that, somebody always gets hurt in those exhibitions. Let's just go in there and beat the hell out of one another. With anybody of your caliber, I won't be able to put up much of a fight anyway. When I have had my money's worth, I will just sit down in the ring and tell them that I have had my money's worth."

He was the only person that I had ever boxed with, with rubber gums. My brother had had some old boxing shoes and I went down to the folks and got those old boxing shoes that Andy had left up there.

So when it came time for the fight, when the bell rang old Neidifer just came storming at me like a wild man.

I was never hit in the whole fight. I hit him with a left jab and a right cross and his rubber gums went flying across the gym. Then I beat the hell out of him.

The next day down in the tavern he said, "Hottell, I am going to kick the shit out of you yet."

I said "Neidifer, right now is a good time to do it. You had me whipped badly before we got in the ring last night. Three or four guys like you couldn't whip me today."

He just set down, he didn't make any more brags at all after then. My dad died in 1948.

In 1941 Alice and I moved to Spokane where I eventually found work painting houses. I never saw Harry Lavin again, but I continued to hear about him from my brother-in-law Evan Brown.

In later years after we had left Curlew, Harry got in pretty bad shape. His testicles swelled up just like a football or a basketball.

He got Evan to take him up to Republic to see Dr. May. Evan said that on the washboardy roads Harry held his balls in his hands and cried all the way up there. Then when Evan picked Harry up to come home, Evan says, "Well, Harry, what did Doc May say was wrong with you?"

He said, "The dirty ole son-of-a-bitch said I had syphilis."

He was in a hell of a shape, I'll tell you. But he didn't die until long after that, in his eighties or nineties. After all his escapades, fighting the young guys and squaws and everything, Harry finally died at quite a ripe old age.

Every night he would go down to Curlew to the tavern and get himself a quart of beer. He lived right on the railroad track. The railroad track come right along the banks of the river. The town of Curlew was less than a quarter of a mile from Harry's house. Harry would get his quart of beer and walk back up the track home.

This one particular night in March the bottom come out of the sack and the beer slid down in the snow, down over the bank toward the river. Harry goes down the bank to retrieve his quart of beer. They found him drowned in less than an inch of water, face down in the river.

After going through all these exciting deals and so forth, it seems. . . . Well, I would just have wanted him to die on deck getting a piece of ass.

WALTER JACKSON: THE VIEW FROM A STUMP RANCH

Mendocino, CA

Born: 1888

Walter Jackson was born at the tail end of the Territorial period, a now almost legendary time when the Mosquito Fleet of ferries linked western Washington's many ports and when the primeval forests were yet uncut. His father was a demolition blasting expert, sheep rancher, and firewood cutter.

Walter Jackson left the Olympic Peninsula at the age of seven, but he can remember a time there that I would love to have seen.

There's been so many changes in my life, from steam to jets, from horses to gas. . . .

I came originally from Port Dungeness, Washington. That's where I was born and spent the first seven and a half years of my life.

Father and mother went up about eight miles due south of Port Dungeness and were raising twelve hundred or so sheep. From our place you could look over at the shores of British Columbia and you could see Mount Rainier.

We had a stump ranch in the hills near Sequim. Not SKWIM! The correct pronunciation is See-Quim. It's a two syllable word, not one. The later settlers came and instead of saying See-Quim, they called it SKWIM.

My father William Andrew Jackson used to put me on a ferryboat at Sequim. My uncle at that time was captain and he would drop me off at Seattle where my grandmother lived. She took care of me about half the time because Mother had a younger brother to raise. They raised him mostly. My grandmother had quite a lot of help in raising me, and she and the folks brought me up right.

A couple at their stump house, Snohomish County, 1907.
(Credit: Museum of History and Industry, Seattle, WA)

Grandmother Jackson! She was built just about like this table. Square shoulders like a heavyweight prize fighter. But she was a very nice lady and everybody liked her because she was always trying to help somebody out.

One of my uncles was a ferryboat captain, so he had a little more money. Another uncle was a fireman who fired the ferryboats with three-foot wood. People would saw the fir trees into three-foot wood and sell it at the ferryboat landings to supply fuel for the ferryboats. They'd cut big Douglas fir to make the firing bolts.

My father was about five foot ten inches. I guess he was about three or four inches wider than most across the shoulders. He was a powerful man. He would cut a Douglas fir up for firewood and take it down to Port Dungeness and sell it. I don't know how much he got for it but he made enough to keep us in clothes and food.

What is a stump ranch? There used to be a lot of stumps around after they had chopped down the forest with axes and handsaws.

They chopped the stumps very high. To clear the stumps (nobody will believe me but this is true), they would bore a hole from one side of the stump to the opposite side. Do you know what oakum is? Tarred rope. They would put tarred rope in there and light it from the top. By the time it got through the top to the bottom, the stump was afire.

The stump would burn up and leave a big hole. There was a lot of roadbuilding. They would go get dirt from the excavations and fill these stump holes. They always planted a fruit tree in the stump hole. So that's what they called a stump ranch!

Finally, my folks didn't like the snow in the winter, the flies in the summer, and the mosquitoes in the fall, so they disposed of their stump ranch and moved down to Bridgeport, California. But I remember that on a clear day you could see all the bays over in Canada from our stump ranch.

HAROLD "OLE" JOHNSON:

CUSTOMS BORDER PATROL

Colville, WA

Born: 1902

By 1919, when the Eighteenth Amendment was ratified, a majority of America's states had already had prohibition for some time. Washington had begun the "great experiment" in 1914, though some localities had already gone dry before that.

Prohibition, as Professor Norman H. Clark points out in *The Dry Years*, had always been part of a broader picture of class distinctions, nativist/ethnic mistrust, social reform, progressive sentiment, Protestant evangelism, and urban-rural conflict. But by the early 1930's a majority of Americans agreed that the "great experiment" had failed. Prohibition was repealed nationally and, except for die-hard dry areas, the country went "wet." Prohibition was replaced with the patchwork quilt of liquor control laws which Washington endures to this day.

Prohibition failed for many reasons, but as the following account by Ole Johnson makes clear, it failed because a large portion of the population practiced active resistance.

Ole Johnson's adventures as a Customs Border Patrol officer make for entertaining reading. His work on the "Dry Squad" meant that he had to put in long hours in all kinds of weather, using laughable cars, and suffering many indignities. Often the liquor smugglers, who otherwise were often ordinary locals, had the upper hand.

In 1924 Ole Johnson began liquor interdiction at Ferry, Washington on the Canadian border. In 1928 he was transferred to Tonasket, Washington and spent a total of eleven years patrolling the border, from 1924 to 1935, after which he went into regular

Customs work at Danville and Laurier, Washington, retiring at the end of 1965.

Behind the humorous, shoot-em-up facade of the rumrunners and their pursuers was an ongoing process of social change in Washington and the nation. Professor Norman Clark describes the evangelical fervor which marked the prohibition movement early in this century. Although this often verged on fanaticism and class hatred,

the prohibition movement also urged men and women to vote with their hearts and with their sometimes desperate hope that they could restore the lost purity of the great agrarian dream and make a better world. In the prohibition movement one can see an attempt of the "Age of Evangelism" to resist what Carl Bridenbaugh has called "the great mutation"—the change in American society from a natural environment to an artificial one, from a religious faith to a secular one. The age—and the movement—may end when the mutation is finally complete, when the symbol of "the country" has lost all of its reality. The dying flames of evangelism which one sees today may be, in fact, a true measure of this mutation. For when all the old Prohibs are dead—as so soon they will be—one may look in vain for the old America.[1]

I was stationed in Bellingham, Washington when I got orders that I was being transferred to Ferry, Washington. As I did not have a car, I had to go by railroad. It took four days. The train schedule called for a layover at night in Seattle, Wenatchee, and Oroville. I arrived in Ferry on November 4, 1924. There were six inches of snow on the ground and it was very cold.

There was no place to live in Ferry so I had to go over to Midway on the Canadian side of the border. There were two hotels. Only one served meals and they charged two-fifty a day for room and board. This was more than I thought I could afford, so I looked around and found a lady who was running a boarding house charging seven-fifty a week for board. I got a room at the other hotel for ten dollars a month. There was no heat in my room. When the

---

[1]Norman H. Clark, *The Dry Years: Prohibition and Social Change in Washington* (Seattle: University of Washington Press, 1988), p. 127.

Ole Johnson (second from right) and a 1920 Model T, Beaver Canyon,
Washington, 1925.

weather dropped to forty-five degrees below zero and I mentioned
to the proprietor that my room was kind of cold, he asked me what
I expected for ten dollars a month. He gave me another blanket
every time I mentioned the weather. By spring I had eight Hudson
Bay blankets on my bed and one over the headboard to keep the
wind and snow off.

The Customs Port of Ferry, as it was set up to handle traffic,
was a nightmare for the personnel. The railroad ran on one side
of the river and the main highway on the other side. To clear
with the U. S. Customs, a person had to cross the border into
Midway, as the Canadian Customs was in town, then cross the
river and go down to the United States Office. When cleared
there, he then had to come back through Midway and cross the
river to return to the U. S. Thus, if a person was inclined to
smuggle anything—Prohibition was in effect at that time—it was
quite easy to pick up liquor.

I worked some in the office but my main duty was patrolling. The
officer in charge, M. Romstead, and I were to work together, with
him furnishing the car. Mr. Romstead was a prince to work with,
but I worked a lot alone and on foot. Finally in 1926 I bought a
1925 Star touring car.

One evening while at the Customs House we saw the lights of a car running the line. Not reporting to us. Romstead and I, in his car, started after it. We finally caught up with it, but couldn't pass or stop it, so we decided the only way was to shoot a rear tire. Not being able to get our windshield open, I had to hang out of my side window. As I was doing this, someone in the car ahead knocked out the window of their back curtain and started to shoot. One shot came through our windshield and I almost jumped out of the car as it hit me in the seat of my pants!

I put my hand there to feel how much damage. It was nothing serious but it hurt and was a little bloody. After it was all over I had to pick out about six pieces of glass and lead, all about the size of matchheads. It was a slow job with a dull needle and a small mirror.

It was a long time before people stopped inquiring about my wound.

Back to the main story. When our car came to a halt, we found the radiator had several large holes in it. Also, when we lifted the hood of the gas tank, being on the dashboard, it had two holes in it and the gas was running out. As luck would have it, we were both chewing gum, so each plugged a hole. However, the radiator was dry, so that was that.

We found a spent bullet lying on the floor just in front of the driver. If it hadn't spent itself, it would have hit the driver in the stomach and if I had been sitting upright in the seat, I would have received the full blast of lead and glass from the shot through the windshield in my chest.

One day while in Midway, I picked up the information that a local smuggler had ordered two cases of liquor which he planned to bring across the border that night. I figured he would pack it down the main road just above the river across from my shack. I could get over the river on a swinging footbridge.

Just about dark, I left and headed for the bridge. By the time I got there it was quite dark and I had trouble finding the bridge through the brush, but I finally managed to do so. I didn't want to use a flashlight. I finally got located where I gambled he would come, and I stayed there all night.

But no one showed up.

Several days later, the party I had been waiting for came into the office. He said, "Ole, I thought you knew this country better than you do."

I said, "How come?"

He said, "I followed you down to the bridge the other night and had to wait until you found it."

After I had crossed and went up the road, he crossed and went *down* the road with his liquor.

There was never any animosity between any known runners and myself. When we came in contact with them, if they were clean, we visited as if nothing had ever happened.

One time I had a runner scout that I called my shadow. He seemed to be able to smell me a mile off. And after finding me he would sit and talk. As long as I was on the road, they wouldn't move anything, so he had as much time as I had. If I ever had a flat tire or was stalled and he came along, he would always stop and insist on helping me. I told him several times I might lose my temper and shoot him, but he said he would take the chance.

Occasionally there were some who carried a chip on their shoulder. If they wanted to play rough, I accommodated them to the best of my ability. When I came to Ferry, I was twenty-two years old and weighed about one hundred forty pounds. I didn't look my age. In Bellingham I had had trouble buying snuff as I didn't look old enough.

So some of them tried to be tough when I flagged them down. They would speed up and try to run me down as I jumped for the ditch. It wasn't long before I had to make up my mind that if I wanted to stay on the job, I would have to change my image.

I bought a .30–.30 carbine to back up my pistol, and the first car that tried to run me down I threw my rifle to my shoulder and shot. I had kept it out of sight until the last moment and I aimed it to just miss the car on the driver's side. He slammed on his brakes. I walked up to the car and asked him if he thought I had really tried to hit him. I also told him that if he ever tried to run me down again, he would find out if I could hit his car and to be sure and pass the word along. With this, and the previous shootout, my jumping into the ditch days seemed to fade into the distance.

In addition to the Customs Patrol, the Immigration Service had their patrol stationed along the border. During the summer of

1925, E. Lannigan and myself rented a shack at the mouth of Toroda Creek and Kettle River. He drove a Model-T Ford touring car. It was a good thing that I had three and a half years experience as a mechanic in a Model-T garage before I entered the Customs service. Between the car and our work, we had quite a summer.

Later, when I had my own car, I flagged down an old Ford T-model coming up Toroda Creek. Instead of stopping, it turned into an old road to an abandoned farm. I took off after it in my car. It went around an old barn and I thought I had him cornered but around we went out onto the main road again.

I couldn't get by him so I tried to bump him off the road on a turn. But he got back on the road up ahead. Since that hadn't worked, I tried to shoot a tire off. I got one before my gun jammed. I was having trouble keeping the windshield open. Every bump I hit, it would come down.

I finally got hold of my rifle and after several shots I got his other tire. He had me puzzled. Bumping along on two flat tires and not willing to jump and run!

I figured he must have help up the road somewhere. I could see the battery of his car and tried to hit it to put his lights out. But all I could hit was his muffler, which exploded in a cloud of soot.

I came around a corner just as he was getting out of his car. I called for him to stop or I would wing him. He stopped, but just as I came up to him he grabbed the barrel of my rifle. I hit his hand as hard as I could with my heavy flashlight and he let go in a hurry.

He was a big man and I didn't want him to get his mitts on me. I tossed him the handcuffs and told him to put them on. He put one on and all of a sudden he said, "Hell, I don't want them on" and put his hands in his pants pockets and just stood there.

His car was mostly loaded with beer. How to get him and his load back to the Customs House! I couldn't drive his car with the flats and bent rims.

I finally gave him the choice of putting on the cuffs, loading the liquor in my car or me putting him out of commission with my rifle. He decided to transfer the liquor, but very slowly! I kept jabbing him in the ribs with my rifle to speed him up as I was still expecting him to have help coming. His ribs must have been sore by the time he finished loading my car.

I ordered him to drive and as I had the car keys in my pocket, I told him to get in the car and as he did so I was able to slip the other cuff around the steering column. Boy, what a relief! I had him pinned down at last.

I couldn't leave his car blocking the road so with him cuffed to my car, I managed to get his off to the side. We finally got started with him driving. He drove very slowly, saying he wasn't in a hurry. I called his attention to the fact that I had the hammer of the rifle held down with my thumb and if he started any funny business, it was sure to slip and let the hammer go.

We finally arrived at a friend's place and I borrowed a handgun, which was easier to use than the rifle. We got the liquor to the Customs House and took the runner to the jail in Republic.

His trial was in the Federal Court in Spokane. The court appointed a young attorney to defend him. This attorney later became well-known in Spokane. On the stand the runner stated he was driving down the road when he noticed some flames and smoke off to the side of the road. He stopped to put the fire out and in so doing uncovered this beer and liquor. He picked it up and was looking for its owner when I happened on the scene.

During the intermission we kidded the attorney about his defense. He stated that that was the runner's story and that he couldn't get him to change it. The jury was out just a few minutes and brought back a verdict of guilty. On several occasions we brought up this defense when we met that attorney. He didn't seem to think it was as funny as we did.

The first part of February, in 1927, I was transferred to the patrol in Curlew. I was in charge and there were four of us. Curlew seemed to be the center of rum running for this part of Ferry County. The main road from the border crossed the river into Curlew and formed the main street. Just as you crossed the bridge on the left was a garage. On the right was a store and post office, and then a hotel. Going down the street on the left was a garage and on the corner another hotel. The street turned to the left around the hotel, crossed the railroad tracks and on toward Republic. The Dry Squad, as we were known, held sway at the lower part of the street and the runners on the upper part. Each had a garage and a hotel.

Before my time, there were about ten Prohibition agents working out of Curlew, besides the Customs and Immigration. While I was there we numbered four Customs and two Immigration. One day I counted twenty-four rum-running cars parked on the street.

A story going around at that time was about a shootout between the Prohibition agents and a runner car. The agents had flagged the car and a local man who was riding shotgun stuck his head and arm through the car curtain and shot the agent through the stomach. In return the other agent shot him through the neck and chin. The agent was taken to the hospital. The bullet had hit one side of the stomach and come out the other side without much damage, as it stayed in fat all of the way. The runner never even went to the doctor, even though the bullet went through his neck and nicked his chin, and he lived to a ripe old age at his home up Big Goosmus Creek.

The Customs boys at Ferry asked our help in catching a gang that was packing liquor across the hills west of Ferry. We spent a few days in the hills, decided the route they would take and that they would bring it into a ranch yard to load the cars. We picked a good spot to stop the cars on their way out. We arrived there about dark, and around ten P.M. we heard the pack string coming along the hillside above us. From where they were we knew they had to cross the road about a quarter mile above. So off we took and got there in time to meet them. There were two men and eight horses, a man on each end of the string. I crawled around the side trying to get to the tail end of the string before it reached my partner who would do the flagging, but I didn't make it. I was only about two-thirds of the way when he flagged the front man. My man got away as there was a fence between us. He took off as if he was shot out of a cannon. The front man ran too, but he ran into a low hanging limb of a tree that knocked him down. So we got him.

They had forty cases of liquor. Five cases to each horse.

In those days, liquor was packed for legal trade in wooden boxes. To make it easier for the runners, it was put in straw wrappers and sewn in twelve-bottle sacks. There was some kind of understanding that the Canadian government wouldn't export liquor to the United States, so each export house along the border had a man that signed the papers saying the liquor was bound for Mexico. This also meant that none was entering the Canadian market tax-free. But it seemed that anyone handling liquor had no knowledge of these regulations. I understood that you could buy liquor underground in Vancouver, B.C. cheaper than at the government liquor stores.

Back to the pack string. Huntley, my partner, took the liquor back to the Customs House in his car. I brought the horses in and was pretty sore after riding about twelve miles. The man in charge of the Ferry Customs put the horses in a field next to the Customs House. The following day or night, someone had cut the fence and we had no horses. Of course, we had a complete description of each horse as well as the brand. Huntley got the job of rounding up the horses. Knowing the names of the owners through the brands, it was easy to find them. However, each owner claimed their horses had been stolen. But the owners never filed charges against the man we held. And after Huntley had found all eight horses and we had sold them, they all went back to the original owners.

The man we caught was fined five hundred dollars and six months in jail.

The first time we saw him we kidded the party that had gotten away. Any man who could run up a steep hill covered with brush as fast as he did should go out for track, as he could break world records. During that part of Prohibition we could only prosecute for possession. As he'd gotten away, we couldn't prosecute him. But later the law changed and we could prosecute on conspiracy *anyone* that had been involved in a smuggling case.

It was a thankless job trying to enforce the Prohibition Act. We were always undermanned, with poor equipment, and with no support from the people. Our only cars were the ones we seized. The brass got first pick and we got what was left. Most of the runners had the best, fastest cars and plenty of help. They had pilot cars, scouts, and even help from the citizens. Many gangs wouldn't move until they knew where every officer was located at that particular time. And remember, there were no C.B.'s, radios, etc.

After I left Curlew and was working out of Tonasket, we knocked over a load of liquor. Several days later a runner came up to me and said, "Good for you, Ole. You knocked my boss over the other day." He said they had been laying low as they were getting pretty hot, meaning we had the country pretty well covered. Their boss told them to move it anyway, and to prove it was clear enough to do so he came up from Spokane without their knowing about it, got a load, and about five miles from the border got caught. It sure pleased his boys!

DWELLEY JONES: "BACK THERE SUCKING THE HIND TIT"
Walla Walla, WA
Born: 1916

Agriculture has always been a mainstay of Washington's economy. Think of, say, Idaho potatoes, many of which are grown right here. Or the Washington state red delicious apple. Or Walla Walla sweets. Or wheat from the Palouse, that loess-rich breadbasket of southeast Washington. For almost a half century, until 1985, wheat was the state's leading income-producing commodity.

Agriculture is like religion and politics. The wise person should shy away from it as a topic of conversation in polite company.

Well, meet Walla Walla wheat grower Dwelley Jones. He'll talk your ear off about wheat because he has seen so many of his farm friends go broke. And not just because the Palouse is blowing away in the wind or because of the catastrophic rate increase from the Bonneville Power Administration.

Dwelley Jones is a Walla Walla native whose grandfather was an 1849 California Argonaut and then a cattle-herding foreman headquartered in San Francisco. When he retired to Walla Walla, Washington he owned mining properties in Idaho and wheat ranches in the Palouse. Dwelley's father was an attorney and a farmland overseer until he acquired his own spreads. His wife, Verna Dwelley Jones, inherited farmlands near Walla Walla. The stage was set for young Dwelley to come onto the scene in 1916.

He symbolizes for me the complexity of modern Washington agriculture, which is as dependent on that other Washington back

East and on interdependent world markets as it is upon the weather.

Dwelley received his undergraduate degree in Political Science and Economics from Whitman College and then began life as a farmer. In 1956 he was a founder of the Washington Wheatgrowers Association, and was president in 1959. As a frequent lobbyist in Washington, D.C., he was a persistent spokesman for wheat interests.

I believe that the public image of these wheat farmers is that of the ultra-efficient producer of gigantic surpluses. That outmoded picture has blinded us to worldwide changes in wheat production. In recent years more than a dozen countries have suddenly become wheat exporters. As their productivity has increased geometrically, that of the Palouse has lagged far behind. With typical Palouse wheat production costs relatively high, Dwelley says, "There is no profitable market for our wheat, because we have not been keeping up with agricultural research."

This canny farmer from Walla Walla is outraged that we have been sabotaging our own agricultural future through policy blunders on every level, including U.S. government-subsidized research for foreign producers, which soon backfires on our own farmers in increased international competition.

I asked Dwelley my favorite question about who had most inspired him. "The bank," he said, only half joking. "It always wanted me to pay on my debts, so that was my best inspiration."

But as we talked it became apparent that he greatly admired a Washington State University agronomist named Professor Orville Vogel[1] because he had solved the problem of low yield by cross-breeding a semidwarf Japanese variety. "He called me up one night," said Dwelley, "and told me that he had a terrific new wheat, but that it was getting stolen as soon as he could plant it. Pretty soon he brought the only handful of it in the world down here and he asked if I had a rifle. I said, yes. And he said, 'Don't let anybody know that you've got this wheat or let anybody see it.' "

---

[1]Orville Vogel (born 1907) was a U.S.D.A. wheat breeder and a Washington State University professor from 1931 to 1973. He led a team of researchers which bred the revolutionary, semidwarf Gaines wheat, named for his mentor E.F. Gaines, 1930s W.S.U. cerealist.

"So we planted it about two miles from the closest public road. And I guarded that stuff.

"I let nobody onto that ranch!"

Prior to that Dwelley and his neighbors had been raising thirty-five bushels to the acre. But this experimental wheat produced one hundred to the acre!

Dwelley remembers storing his growing stockpile of the new wheat at his own granaries so that no one would learn of it at a public granary. "It took me five years of raising that wheat," he says, "to get enough to be able to release it to other people. Finally I had five years' worth harvested and I called Vogel and asked him what to do with it."

Dr. Vogel told me, "I sent Norm Borlaug some early semidwarf seed and he bred special strains for production in southern areas. Gaines and other Washington wheats mature too late for use in Mexico."

Mexico's Dr. Borlaug received the Nobel Prize for breeding new semidwarf varieties and for helping developing countries to grow them. In 1975 Professor Vogel received the National Medal of Science from President Ford for breeding the revolutionary Gaines wheat, a strain specially adapted to Washington's Palouse.

I have talked to a lot of Washington old-timers who planted by the seat of their pants or by the *Farmers' Almanac*. And to some Indians who planted according to native lore. Dwelley Jones has always tried to take advantage of the newest agricultural innovations. For instance, in 1948 he read an article in *Better Homes and Gardens* about a new chemical which would kill dandelions, but not harm a lawn. He immediately called the manufacturer and asked for a fifty-gallon drum. He was told that hardly any of what was later called 2-4-D existed "this side of the Mississippi River." Instead he was offered a pint. "What are you going to do with it?" the man asked. "You must have a terribly big lawn!"

Dwelley had stumbled onto the greatest agricultural weed killer the wheat fields had ever known.

Professor Orville Vogel says that Washington has increased its wheat yields through a combination of new varieties, better management (better weed control, disease control, fertilizer use), and more efficient planting equipment. But he says that foreign producers enjoy a subsidy advantage so that "they can grow wheat on their most productive land instead of on their poorer lands."

Genetics, markets, droughts, erosion, politics, plagues. Where does it all leave the Palouse farmer? As Dwelley puts it, "back there sucking the hind tit!"

I raise other crops besides wheat. I raise potatoes, peas, lima beans, snap beans, lentils, hay, and grass seeds. I raise everything that comes down the pike. But where do you go with it? If something looks good, everybody jumps on it. Then there is a glut of it.

My Welsh grandfather, Melzar Bailey Dwelley, came for the Gold Rush of '49. I was named after him. They came out to San Francisco and worked out in the mines until they got enough money together to buy a mule and a pack outfit and prospect on their own. I still have some little bottles of gold dust that he had, including some gold bars.

Grandfather began by digging for gold and ended by herding cattle to a San Francisco slaughterhouse that had been losing many animals to thieves. He prospered because he could shoot accurately at marauding Indians and at cowboy deserters. Grandfather lost fewer cattle on the way to the slaughterhouse than anyone ever had before. Soon he became the slaughterhouse's herding manager, running cattle from New Mexico to Pasco.

Walla Walla has great farmland. We don't have as much moisture as we'd like. Overall, the average in Walla Walla, the town, is seventeen inches a year. Over seventeen you can raise a crop of peas, and a crop of wheat the next.

I lived here for seventy years. Not in this house but in this area. I like it. That's why I am here. I haven't found any place I like better or as well. It's a nice valley with good temperature. You've got mountains and lakes up there. You can just walk out your door and you're looking at the mountains.

I grew up here and I was born here. Went through grade school, high school, and Whitman college. And have nice friends here. I wouldn't want to live anywhere else.

But a lot of wheat farmers have quit. There's a lot of land without tenants. A lot of land is being farmed and the landlord doesn't charge any rent. He wants to keep the weeds off it until things get better, or he wants to keep his base with the Agriculture Stabilization Department so that he can get some payments on it. Some of that is farmed for nothing. If you own your own land you can break even on wheat, though I don't think you can make any money.

If you've been doing it for thirty or forty years, then it's a little difficult to switch into something else. You just hope that things will get better.

The rainfall comes in cycles here. There's an eleven-year cycle and a twenty-two-year cycle. You can rely on that. We're going into the dry cycle. '88 was a drought year.

In '77 we didn't harvest our dryland crops. No harvest at all.

I have dryland farms up above this one, with eighteen-inch rainfall. We never had had a failure up there, but in '77 I was late trying to repair something and the combines went up there without me. Later I bustled over to the grain elevator so that they'd get the right labels on all my wheat because I have different landlords.

And I asked the grain elevator man, "Any wheat come in yet?"
"No."

"That's strange," I said, "They've been up there a couple of hours now."

Finally they came back and said, "There isn't any wheat up there."

So I took the combine, charged off into that field, and I cut some for a whole hour and there wasn't enough wheat there to put in your hat.

That was '77.

That year I had about a thousand head, which I used to take up into the mountains in the spring to some rented pasture. I and two neighbors pooled our cattle and put them out on the Magellan Ranch. But in '77 there wasn't enough there for a thousand cattle to eat. It was all sagebrush and rattlesnakes. More rattlesnakes than I've ever seen in my life.

Farmers are always hoping the prices we get for our beef and wheat will go up, and they would, too, if the government would get out of financing the rest of the world.

I try to diversify out of wheat. In 1986 a third of my land was in garbanzo beans but we had to drop out of that lucrative market because the U.S. government had subsidized Turkey's garbanzo production.

I try.

I was going to grow potatoes. I'd done well in them thirty, twenty years ago. Before I even got them planted, the bottom fell out of the market and they were bringing fifty percent less than the year before.

It makes me pretty sad to see my friends go under. I stay OK because I do my own research but if this keeps up, I'll go broke too. At a hundred bushels to the acre, it costs four dollars and fifty cents to raise a bushel of wheat under irrigation.

But you can't usually sell it for that much.

So you lose your ass.

Sometimes in farming, the more you sell, the quicker you go broke.

JOE KRUPA:

WILLAPA HARBOR

HUCK FINN

Raymond, WA

Born: 1911

Joe Krupa led a Huck Finn boyhood fishing the sloughs and lagoons off the Willapa River in southwest Washington. But today's Joe Krupa is a fish raiser rather than a fish catcher.

This is the story of a man who mourns the lost abundance of Nature. He mourns the giant trees whose wealth fueled Raymond, Washington's twenty mills and provided employment for a thriving community of Polish immigrants.

Today's Raymond, Washington is a pretty tame place. The lumber mills have closed, the Willapa River has silted up, and the ships no longer call to pick up wood products and to discharge randy sailors. Floods no longer threaten businesses and homes. Downtown's sloughs have been filled in and children no longer fall off sidewalks into the water. The rich bouillabaisse of ethnicity is only a memory.

Raymond in the old days before flood control was a city built on tideland stilts. Fabulous bass, trout, steelhead, salmon, and other delicacies were often no farther away than the nearest sidewalk railing.

Joe Krupa says of nearby Willapa Bay, "People really have a prize here if they would just appreciate it." He is referring to Willapa Bay's traditionally having been one of the least polluted estuaries in the United States. But increased pollution, development, and uncontrolled logging have decimated fish populations.

Now Joe Krupa, the old sports fisherman, is helping to repair damaged streambeds and to restore salmon and steelhead runs.

What he can never revive is the Polish culture in which he grew up. The last of the two hundred fifty or so immigrants are dying, and the Polish hall has been converted into a theater. Joe himself is now the president of the Polish Club of Willapa Harbor. The club is down to twelve members.

But this is not a sad story, because the old fisherman has lived to see the restoration of some of the original fish runs. In fact, in mid-October, 1986 he said, "Boy, this year they're spawning in the lower reaches of the Willapa River. That's real unusual. In fact, today is the first day I've seen salmon spawn in a riffle where I used to see it fifty years ago. That gives me hope."

That's my sister Jenny on the left. Then me when I was about twelve or thirteen years old. Ed Hudziak and Al Hudziak. We must have went to church because see how we're dressed up in these knee pants?

When I was about ten years old my mother, who was a husky woman, could pick me up with one arm and just slap me across the face a half a dozen times with no problem at all.

I didn't really get very many beatings, but across the street there was a family named Paul Sharek, just like the fish only not spelled that way. Them four boys were the most hyper boys that you ever seen in your life. Their mother was a little tiny bitty woman. She wasn't big like my mother at all. I don't think she weighed a hundred pounds. But she'd whale the tar out of them kids and you could hear 'em screaming and hollering at any hour of the day. She was continually beating them poor kids. I used to really feel sorry for 'em.

The Polish mothers were all strict. They sure were! But they would get things for you that were beyond their means to pay for. I remember that my mother bought me an amethyst birthstone ring that was a terrific cost. I picked out the ring and she said, "If that's what you want, that's what you're going to get."

If I wanted to go fishing and I wanted some hooks, why she gave me the money to take and do it. All of the Polish mothers were good to their kids in that way. Kids meant a lot to 'em but, like I say, they were really strict. You toed the line.

We Polish kids had the reputation of being devils. But that was not true. There were non-Polish kids that we looked up to and *they* got us into a lot of trouble. We weren't asking for trouble, but we went along with the gang and we got involved. Naturally we paid the price when we got caught.

My Aunt Elizabeth and my Uncles Joe and John Hamerla came from Poland. My mother operated a boardinghouse in Raymond when I was a boy. She came over here when she was twenty-five years old and she picked up English real readily. My dad didn't. My dad was a bookbinder and a musician. He made wonderful books for the schools, the papers, professors. He'd take magazines or newspapers and you wouldn't believe what it would look like when he got through binding them.

He settled in Raymond because he had heard of "the land of plenty where the streets are paved with gold."

And it *was* really good here. I'd say that at one time there was two hundred fifty immigrants from Poland right between South Bend, Raymond, and the valley. There used to be a sawmill called Quinault Lumber Company. My dad worked for that outfit for thirty-five years before they run out of resource.

Some of the Poles picked up English faster than others. I remember my dad telling me that the new immigrants in the mills and the logging camps would have sore muscles at the end of the day until they got used to the job. Before they went to bed they'd rub each other down with liniment. My dad was working at a mill up the line here about twenty-five miles when he had just come over from Poland. He and the others had sore muscles and Dad was asked to go to town to get some liniment. He said, "Well, I don't know how to say that." Finally they thought that one particular fellow said it correctly. So they sent him to town.

He came back with a lemon. He went to the drugstore to get liniment and he came back with a lemon. [laughter] The druggist probably couldn't understand him at all.

It was really hilarious at times. I used to laugh myself sick, them fellas when they got together and they started talkin' in English. [laughter] They murdered the English language!

When I started school I remember the teacher told me to get up in front of the class and say my ABC's. So I started out, Aah, Bah, Sah, Dah. . . . That's the way my dad talked. And all the kids started laughing. So after school I picked out the boys who had laughed at me and I just beat the tar out of them.

But it didn't take me long to learn English.

Raymond is filled in now but in the olden days it was built on tidelands, up on stilts from five to six, all the way up to twelve, maybe twenty feet high. As the tide came in, I could see the suckers and trout. This flat where the town has been filled in was a paradise for fish. And for otters, mink, muskrats, ducks.

The sidewalks had railings so that kids and drunks wouldn't fall in the slough.

I started fishing from the sidewalks when I was five years old. My parents had no interest in fishing. None whatsoever. But one of our boarders bought me a fishing pole. He was a sport fisherman who had come from Krakowa, a beautiful old city about one hundred seventy-five miles from the little community of Harta in Poland where my folks had lived. His name was Roman Wrona. Wrona in Polish means raven. He was a pretty good-sized man who finally married. Our other boarders were all Polish, too, and they never did marry. Here's a 1915 picture of him with me on the back porch of our house.

Roman had a real good education. He came over from Poland and worked in our mills here for the rest of his life. He had sport-fished in Poland and he had brought his gear with him to America. The Pole had a fishpole, let's put it that way! [laughter] And it was made out of cane and it came in sections that were two feet long. He put 'em together and he had this reel, a single-action deal, and he'd bring fish home. Suckers—there was fish all over then. I don't care where you went, you could get fish. It was that good!

When we lived in houses on stilts over these sloughs, we'd fish off the streets. Roman was the one that taught me what a bite was, what bait to use, and how to fish in the lagoons and sloughs around here. He'd take me fishing so that in case I fell in, he could rescue me.

It was an incredible thing that when somebody fell in, that splash in the water, if they fell in when the tide was in, you could tell from the sound if it was garbage thrown over the side or if it was a person who had fallen in. If it sounded like a body, everyone started running looking for these kids. I remember the time that I was leaning against the rail fishing and it gave way on me and I fell in. Well, I didn't know how to swim. I was thrashing around down there, and lo and behold somebody jumped in and picked me up and put me back up on the boarded walk.

Once Roman rescued my sister Jenny. She was floating upside down and I tried to get to her but the water was too deep. It was up as far as my arms and I was yelling bloody murder. Roman was asleep but he heard me. He worked nights in the mill. He ran down in his underwear and he seen me down in there. He said, "What's wrong?"

I said, "Jenny's floatin' underneath the house."

She was floating on her back just as peacefully as could be. Not even moving a muscle. So Roman jumped in and pulled her out.

Quite a number of little tots drowned there. I remember two or three that drowned right around our place. But Roman never did take me out on the river. Whether he was afraid that I might drown or fall in, I don't know. So I took it upon myself to take and sneak away and go to the river and fish. And it was fantastic fishing, too, right in the tidewaters here in town. You bet!

I remember when I was ten years old getting a Dolly Varden that weighed nine pounds. At first I didn't realize how big the fish was. A fellow helped me land it. I don't think I could have done it myself. But he helped me and he held onto the pole after the fish was so played out that it laid on its side. He said, "Now you wade out there and grab ahold of that fish underneath the gills and don't you let go 'cause you got a prize."

So I did. I went out there and when I clamped onto that fish, I think I was something short of a vise. That fish would have drowned me before I ever let it go.

He was a baker, and he said, "Let's take it down to the bakery and I'll weigh it on the scale because that's the biggest Dolly Varden I've ever seen."

He had two trout that were pretty good size. So we weighed my fish and it was nine pounds. And he says, "How would you like to have two fish instead of one?" And so I traded him that nine-pound Dolly Varden for two big trout. It didn't make any difference to me. But then he went around bragging that he'd caught the nine-pounder!

But that river has changed so that you can make about three jumps and you are acrosst it. It used to be just loaded with fish.

I caught that big one where I learned to swim on the South Fork of the Willapa River. We'd do our chores in the morning, milking cows, picking strawberries, weeding and so on, and when it got too hot, why we'd go swimming out at my cousin's place in our birthday suits. My cousins—there was two girls and two boys. And we had another Polish boy and myself. Six of us all speaking Polish. We did that for quite a few years. I don't remember who killed it, but somewhere down the line they made us wear bathing suits.

In 1929 I was a senior in high school when a whole bargeload of whiskey came into Willapa Harbor. A barge about forty feet wide and possibly seventy feet long. There was one hundred seventy-five thousand dollars of Canadian whiskey on board this barge. But it looked empty.

It was towed in by one of the local tugboats and was put into a pretty good-size lagoon up here called Alexander Slough. But somebody tipped the federals off and they confiscated this barge and they tied it up here at what we called The Island (because it was surrounded by tide flats). Then they hired some of us high school kids to break up the bottles with sledgehammers.

The whiskey bottles were in burlap sacks. While we were hitting the sacks with sledgehammers, the whiskey was pouring off the top of the barge into the water. Finally one man couldn't stand it anymore. He put his hat under that whiskey that was pouring out and he got half a quart. Boy, was he loaded when he finished that! He couldn't make it off the dock. We had to help him onto dry land.

The federals didn't like how we were doing the work, so they decided to tow the barge out into the river and to dump the burlap sacks in the water. That way they finally got rid of the whiskey.

Of course, we kids knew where most of it had been sunk. Other people started dragging a pipe with hooks on it up and down the river with hooks attached to snag any whiskey sacks out there. But we had two Hawaiian exchange students at our school. They taught us how to hold our breath and to burp in order to get more oxygen out of our stomachs. We'd dive overboard holding onto a rope with a rock attached. I expected everyone to be drowned, but no one was and we got a lot of the whiskey.

I don't know how many bottles of this stuff I had. But pretty soon I started bootlegging it for a dollar and a half a bottle. I had it stashed under the street near my house. Like I said, the town was up on stilts. Anytime anyone wanted a bottle, I'd tell them to go down a couple of blocks to meet me 'cause I didn't want anyone to see where I had it stashed away. At the last of it I was getting ten dollars a bottle because it was getting rare.

During the Depression things were pretty hard here. We bartered a lot, by working for somebody for so many hours to get credit at the grocery store. And Raymond had fake money called Oyster Money. There was two bits, four bits, and a dollar that they made that stuff in and it worked real good.

Raymond never got so wild that they vandalized or anything like that. But they had a good time. It was a good town to have a good time in. It was a cosmopolitan town, with Poles, Irish, and Scandinavians. Loggers, mill workers, and sailors off the many ships in the harbor. Most of them were bachelors and they never married. I was a taxi driver, 1929 to 1930, and I used to get quite a lot of money from these people when I took them to the beaches, the taverns, and the whorehouses.

Raymond's whorehouses helped the town's economy quite a bit. There was a payoff for the police and there was a payoff for the prosecuting attorney.

The taxi company was owned by a Polish fellow by the name of Louis Sittko. He had a garage here in town that him and I operated. We took turns, each working twenty-four hours on and twenty-four hours off doing this here taxi deal, and parking, steam cleaning, storage, gasoline and oil, and some auto repair. All you needed in them days was a hammer, a screwdriver, a pair of pliers, plus some ingenuity, and you could fix about any car.

We had two Model-A Ford sedans and a huge green seven-passenger touring car. We had no taxi signs on them. They looked just like any other cars.

We used them between South Bend, Aberdeen, and Raymond to take men to the whorehouses. We had one, two, three, four hotels in the late '20s. And all the fellas had to do was ask the desk clerk where to get a bottle of whiskey, a woman, or a taxi. When they got into my car, they'd ask me, "Where's the best place to go?"

I didn't have a favorite place to recommend, but there was no place that I would not have recommended. On the outside they looked like dilapidated buildings, but inside they were actually castles.

I used to find out what the cathouses were like inside because I often went there to pick up drunks. What they did at first before they did anything else, they did a lot of drinking. Sometimes they did too much drinking and they never got to the point where they got to do what they wanted to do. So I'd have to drag 'em to the taxi and take 'em back to their ship or to their logging camp.

They had beautiful girls. I was often surprised. I remember a fellow who was well-liked in town. He was actually a pimp, just in plain words. But he didn't call himself that. I was a car salesman for a while and he bought a car from me and he paid me in cash.

He kept his girls not over a year and then he'd trade them off with someone else. My friend Georgie, a madam, also did a lot of trading to get new girls in. Georgie was from Idaho. She was the last madam that closed up shop. That was 1957. She was really a doll.

I never patronized the whorehouses, because I didn't want to and I didn't believe in it. But the girls were very courteous. They were not the type to give any guff. They never raised any hell.

Raymond woke up at ten at night and went until about five in the morning. It was a serious blow for Raymond when the cathouses were closed in 1957. A lot of sailors came, not only off ships here in Willapa Harbor but also from other ports, too. From Aberdeen. That helped a lot. And a lot of people from inland, too. Chehalis. Centralia. Maybe farther.

It was a wide open town. Say we had a dance hall that had music but no liquor license. If they knew you, you could get a drink, whether it was beer, wine, or homemade whiskey. Raymond was a place to go to have what sailors called fun. After Prohibition there were at least twenty legal taverns. Some that were hidden and were whorehouses. We didn't call them that. We called them cathouses. That's a nice name for them.

I used to know where they all were because I used to deliver sailors to them off the ships in the harbor. We used to have a lot of ships because we had twenty mills. The export from this town was something terrific. Especially to California, the Orient, and Australia. When they stopped dredging the Willapa River the ships couldn't come into Raymond anymore. It's too shallow now. In fact, Willapa means shallow water in Indian.

So I used to deliver these sailors to the different places of fun in town. I knew a lot of the girls personally and they were really nice people. Better than some of the people that would walk in the streets and were supposed to be straitlaced. They didn't want to create any problems for anybody because prostitution was against the law.

It was up to the prosecuting attorney to say if they could operate. Back in 1955 I was one of the city commissioners. The prosecuting attorney told us, "I will give you fellows ninety days to move all the girls out of town."

Well, we had twenty lumber mills but suddenly we had to close down the twenty or so cathouses. I'm not going to name anybody, but the prosecuting attorney wanted a payoff. And we city councilmen didn't realize it until it was too late. But that's neither here nor there. It's gone by the wayside. We had never realized until we got tipped off that if we would have used our heads and paid him, say twenty-five thousand dollars, why those cathouses would still have been in operation.

I continued sport fishing as often as I could throughout the Depression. By the late '30s I had a family to feed, and my wife canned a lot of fish.

In 1941 there was commercial fishing on the Columbia River but there wasn't any sport fishing. So another fellow and I got together and he says, "You know, as long as we can't catch fish up this river, let's go down to the Columbia River and see if this gear that we use here for sport fishing would work down there."

Anyhow we went down there and, oh boy, was it fabulous! You just wouldn't believe what it was like. I don't think that we got a Chinook that weighed less than twenty-five pounds. One time there was three of us in the boat. That's when the limit was three fish apiece. And we had three hundred sixty pounds of fish in this boat, so you divide nine into three hundred and sixty and every fish had to average forty pounds!

My wife Berniece and I used to spend our vacations down there. We would get a cabin on the Columbia River at Chinook and be on that river from daylight to dark. I thought that was a big deal!

But that was the wrong thing to have done! As time went along, you could see the decline. The fish got smaller and there wasn't as many of them. It was harder to catch 'em.

I think in 1941 that the commercial season opened the first of July and ended when there was just no more fish in the river. Now, it's a different story. The state only allows them so many days to fish, because it takes a vast number of spawning salmon to get that run in future years. Without it, there are a lot of streams, even in Alaska, that are absolutely dead.

On this huge river there'd be three thousand commercial fisherman at night and some of their nets were a thousand feet long. You get that many fishermen on the Columbia and the fish didn't have a chance.

We used to go out from our cabin at night and it was just a din and roar of boats going back and forth making their drifts. The current on the Columbia River is about twelve miles an hour. That's really moving, and by the time that you take and make one drift, you're down the river five miles and you're gonna be out in the ocean in no time at all. So they'd pick up and they'd go back upriver and put their nets back in and they'd make another drift. They'd sweep the river clean.

I'm telling you that we sport fished above 'em, never in among 'em, because we'd have to go parallel to their nets or we couldn't fish. So we'd fish above 'em and not get anything.

Their nets would just pick up everything! And they'd drag the bottom. A lot of times a chinook salmon, to rest from fighting the current, will get down into a hole. A whole mass of 'em will rest in a hole together. Well, these fishermen would put a lot of weight on the bottom of their nets and they'd drag through that hole and pick up these fish. The fish just didn't have a chance.

I quit fishing in 1981 because I thought I had had enough. Something was wrong and I felt that I was not adding anything. I was taking away. When I was young it was nothing unusual to catch a forty-pound fish. A big fish now is twenty-five pounds. Fishermen don't even know what they are talking about now when they say a "big" fish. I remember two boom men that worked at a huge mill a quarter mile up from Aberdeen. During their noon hour while they were eating their lunch they take and cast their Colorado spinners right off the boom and catch salmon that weighed seventy, seventy-five pounds.

So I got into the business of raising fish instead of catching fish. What alarms me is that we're not leaving anything for the future generations. I've got a son and two daughters and a granddaughter, and so has somebody else got sons and daughters and grandkids, too.

We've got to leave something for them. We are using our resources too fast. I think this world is God-given and for us to take care of.

Roman Wrona would have understood that!

JUDGE JOHN LANGENBACH:

LOGGER POET

Olympia, WA

Born: 1893

Washington, unlike say, Maryland, has no official poet laureate to celebrate its grand occasions, such as the opening of geoduck season or the dedication of a new bridge to replace the last one washed away by a "hundred year" storm. So I hereby propose Judge John Langenbach of Olympia, Washington for the job.

A Supreme Court judge in Olympia from 1965 to 1968, Judge Langenbach was known from his earliest days on the bench (1949, Superior Court of Pacific and Wahkiakum Counties) as a stickler for fairness, an important qualification for poet laureates. A Raymond, Washington admirer, Joe Krupa, remembers:

It didn't make any difference to him whether you were the mayor or you were a ditchdigger. You got the same treatment. Right was right and wrong was wrong. There was no partiality.

Sometimes I went to the court just for the novelty of seeing someone who was so fair.

John Langenbach is usually described as a "logger poet" because he worked in the woods as a young man (1913–1917) to pay his way through college. But he is a true poet for any occasion and many of his commemorative verses have appeared in the *Timber Cutter,* Aberdeen *Daily World,* and other leading poetry journals.

His verses graced the dedication in May, 1932 of a marker (on the Washington shore opposite Astoria, Oregon) commemorating Captain Robert Gray's discovery of the Columbia River:

> Proud the sturdy ship Columbia rides full-rigged into
>   the west
> For her tasks were well accomplished, sailed the ocean
>   of the blessed.

Abandoned by his parents as a tot, John Langenbach grew up with his grandparents in southwest Washington at a time and place rhapsodized in John's "McCleary Nineteen Hundred Two."

> Ensconced within the verdant circling hills
>   Whose crests were cedar, hemlock, spruce, and fir,
> The village lay. The babbling, gurgling rills
>   Raced noisily while drooping willows stir
> On reed-draped banks. A cedar-puncheon span
>   A yoke of oxen yarded into place
> A bridge. A lumber mill, steam-powered, ran
>   Employing villagers. Adjoining space
> A whining shingle mill completely filled. . . .
>   Fed bolts erupting from a V-shaped flume
> To fan into a spreading, holding boom. . . .
>   Surrounded by the shingles, freshly milled.

John had just begun school in 1902 when a catastrophic forest fire burned unchecked, encircling the town. "McCleary was in a kind of depression," says John. "The fire was all the way around it. People thought the world was coming to an end."

> A sullen, sultry haze rimmed 'round the dale.
> The village was an isle 'neath smoking veil.

The town was saved and so, even more miraculously, was the abandoned boy's chance at an education. First, an aunt inspired him to love learning. Then a steam donkey driver taught him the beauty of verse (bawdy logger ballads). And finally a University of Washington professor turned the budding poet in the direction of a college education.

The only occasion John Langenbach ever spoke with his father was just before going off to Seattle to enroll at the U.W. His father asked where John had obtained money for college. "College students don't amount to very much," said his father contemptuously.

The boy who rose from abandonment and homelessness to sit

on the state Supreme Court is, it is true, a logger poet and a poet laureate manqué. But his greatest ballad has been his own life. This picture was taken in 1900. We used to go from McCleary down on the train to Hoquiam where we would stop at the Recep-

John Langenbach writing poetry.

John Langenbach (far right) as a boy with his family.

tion Saloon. The Hay's (my mother and her second husband) lived over the saloon. And then we would take our luggage and tent and go on the Harbor Belle from Hoquiam down to Westport. This photo was taken at the Westport GAR Campground. My sister Lizzie and I are by the Hay's. Uncle Will, Aunt Cora, Aunt Ellen, and our grandmother are the others.

My mother was called Susan Hay after she married William Harold Hay, a bartender down in Hoquiam who owned the Reception Saloon. When my sister and I were living with our grandmother, Will and Susie Hay used to come up to Elma on the Northern Pacific, get a buggy, and come out to Grandma's home with a box of old clothes which we would always say, "Will and Susie are coming and bringing some clothes!"

My Aunt Cora and grandmother would make them over for us kids. We sure thought Susie and Will were good friends! We always knew them as Will and Susie. I never called her Mother.

My sister and I weren't adopted. We never lived with our father. He was a farmer/logger and raised a second family.

When I was about two or three years old my mother Susie took us to McCleary and left us there with a letter for her mother Sarah Langenbach. "Here's Johnny and Lizzie. If you want them, keep them. If not, turn them out to grass."

That's just the way it was. She said she was going to jump in the lake or something. Oh gosh, later she was married four or five times! The second time to the Hoquiam saloonkeeper, William H. Hay, a fine man.[1]

My Aunt Cora started me off. She and my grandmother are really responsible for me. My grandmother didn't want me to "work for a living." Her sons and my grandfather all worked in the mills. You worked when the mill worked. If they didn't work, you didn't work. She didn't want me to do that day labor.

My Aunt Cora taught me poetry before I went to school. I remember one poem was about as long as your arm. I was kind of stocky and I wore a blouse with a ruffle on the front and short pants. With curly hair I looked more like a girl than a boy. But Aunt

[1]In 1914 my mother abandoned Will Hay and their tiny daughter and ran off with the hired man.

Cora got me to recite that poem for Christmas when I was about four years old. That developed my memory and I appreciate it now.

Aunt Cora and my grandmother were always interested in seeing me in school. They often drove a buggy down to Montesano High School to watch my performances as an actor or athlete. My mother never went to see me do anything. All she ever did for me was to sign my report card, which the school required.

If you are going to be anything, you have to have the gleam inside you. But you can't start out by yourself. You have to be inspired. I had only a few teachers that way. In the fourth grade I had a teacher named Stella Smith whose husband was a logger. She was an outstanding, inspiring teacher. When I took the eighth grade exam in the next district (where she was then teaching), she helped me review the past four years of studies and I passed with high marks. Stella Smith knew what was coming and she just lifted me up. I never forgot her. She was inspiring! She got me started, and once I got started I couldn't stop. She got me interested in poetry. I guess that is how I got started to write a few poems.

In 1909 when I was in the eighth grade at the Mox Chehalis Creek School, Prof. Eldridge Wheeler, the superintendent of schools of Grays Harbor County, came out to where we were living on Mox Chehalis Creek (after we had moved from nearby McCleary). We had a farm down there and my grandfather was clerk of the Mox Chehalis district school board and Prof. Wheeler wanted to see him about some business. He asked me where I was going to attend high school that fall.

Few people went to high school in those days. There was no high school near enough to our farm, and anyway I had no money to attend any place and was earning nothing on our farm. I said, "I am going to work in the woods." Some neighbor boys named Mannie Boling and Charlie Lund had quit school, and were working for Vance Logging Company right over the hill. They were logging and I could make two and a half a day, which was money!

Mr. Wheeler said, "I can get you a place to live in Montesano for your board and room." He sometimes helped bright students find work and he wanted me as a student on account of my grades. Well, that opened things up and it began to look like I could get an education!

Then my stepfather, Will Hay, sold out his Hoquiam saloon and bought a farm two miles east of Montesano towards Elma. I decided to live there and to help out on the farm after school.

So, thanks to Stella Smith and Mr. Wheeler I was able to attend Montesano High School. Naturally I was quite relieved when Professor Wheeler told me. My grandmother and Aunt Cora also approved. Besides, Will Hay had sold the Reception Saloon in Hoquiam and had bought a small farm east of Montesano. My folks believed that my mother would not object to me living there and going to school. So pieces of the puzzle of my education were slowly falling into place.

I used to walk two and a half miles to high school in Montesano along the railroad tracks. I would be writing poems and reciting them as I walked along. Sometimes people would come along. I wouldn't be paying attention and they would look at me like I was a nut.

Funny, the habits you get!

I saw a lot of hoboes[2] along the railroad track. They would have a fire and a camp alongside the track where there was water. Those fellas were smart. I'd ask them, "Where are you from, where are you going, and what experiences have you had?"

In the summers I stayed at my grandfather's new farm near Malone and worked in the woods at various jobs.

I got through high school in 1913 and went to work for Joe Vance in the woods. I worked from noon, New Year's Day to September fifteenth and saved seven hundred fifty dollars to go to the University of Washington later that month.

A teacher named Leo Baisden from the University of Washington had told me it didn't cost very much to go to the university. He told me I could go for about three hundred dollars a year. Well, my seven hundred fifty dollars would get me started.

So Leo Baisden fired me up! I had to sling hash at a fraternity but I finally got through the university. Then it was six years of law school. Two years of prepping and four years of law.

---

[2]See page 123 for Judge Langenbach's poem "Hoboes' Convention."

After I got out of the Navy in the spring of 1919 I finished up law school and went to Ilwaco, Washington, down near the mouth of the Columbia River. I practiced law there until 1923, when I received a letter from Pacific County Superior Court Judge Henry Ward Beecher Hewen. He asked me to come to the county seat, South Bend, because the two lawyers there were ill.

So I moved to Raymond in the fall of 1923 and remained there until recently. I didn't want to go to Raymond, because I had gotten married in Ilwaco. My wife was working for the power company and I was trying to get a little ahead. I got on the boat at Nahcotta and went to see Judge Hewen at South Bend at the courthouse. I did want to better my law practice and he said, "If you want to come to the courthouse, now is the time. The deputy prosecutor is sick and is moving to Spokane."

I said, "I'm not ready to come."

He said, "It is like setting a hen. You have to set her when she wants to be set."

It was right in the middle of winter, but I moved to Raymond. I felt that the judge knew best and that he was friendly to me and so that was the thing to do!

I had been writing poems all through my years practicing law. Always it was the old logging days that I liked to write about most. I can remember at McCleary when they logged with oxen and when the people built a bridge there in 1900 with oxen. Yokes of oxen hauled pieces of split cedar logs to use as planks across a little creek. That bridge became part of a puncheon skid road for hauling logs with oxen down to the mill pond.

When I started to work in the woods in 1913 as a spool tender on a steam donkey, they had a line horse to haul back the cable to the woods. They didn't have a haulback line then, only a horse to haul that cable out into the woods to where a log could be attached to it. Hauling logs that way required a skid road. My Uncle Frank was the skid greaser. He would go ahead of the horses and grease the skids so that the logs would slide easily.

Later I became a drumtender for Vance Logging Company at Malone. This was not a hard job, but it required more skill to handle the logs and to load them on cars. At the end of the donkey engine's main shaft there was a drum about eight or ten inches wide and a handle that pressed it against some blocks. The drum had a line on it which ran out to a ginpole at the railroad siding. That line had hooks for lifting logs onto flat railroad cars.

Logs were placed in a row on the bunks on flatcars, depending on the sizes of the logs. Usually four on the lower row. Then the other rows were narrowed into a rough pyramid. Small blocks were often used to make the logs level and secure so that they would ride safely and securely to the mill pond where they were dumped to be sawn into lumber.

I started out first as the fireman for a roader donkey when Dutch Joe was the drumtender. One day Dutch Joe got drunk. He got a gallon of liquor and went into his cabin and stayed there until it was gone.

So they fired him and gave his job to me. When he sobered up he came looking for his job. When he found me there he didn't like it. But he couldn't do anything. The boss told him that he couldn't work just so long and then take a week off to get drunk. He had to have somebody more reliable.

Loading logs at a landing in those days required a ginpole. It was placed on the opposite side of the landing with a lean over the middle of the tracks. The loading line ran from a drum on the end of the donkey's main shaft through a lead-in block up to a block hanging over the middle of the tracks. Then the line came back in a fork with a hook on each end. These were placed in the ends of the logs and the logs were lifted and stacked on the cars.

My job was to place the log properly on the car so that it would stay there during the ride down the hill to the mill.

It isn't everybody who can handle those logs. If you are lifting them up for loading on cars, you have a man at each end of the log and you put a block under there, and put it so that it will stay and not fall down. You can't drop it down too hard or it will bounce off and hurt a man or something.

One man got tangled up in the cable, not with me, but another drumtender. He threw his hook when he was standing in the bight of the line and it knocked his foot out from under him. He got tangled up in the cable and he broke his leg.

Lawrence Kennedy was our donkey engineer and he was smart as he could be. He was a high-class engineer. In fact, he was the one that got me started with my logging poems. He didn't like to be called Lawrence. We called him L. C. and loggers would write him letters addressed to "Elsie." I don't know as he ever drank, but he was certainly quite a character.

He didn't write any of his own poetry, but when we weren't busy bringing in a log he would recite off-color poems by the yard. He would recite one of them and I would say, "Can you recite it again?" I concentrated so that I could pick up most of it and then piece it in afterwards. Lawrence Kennedy had a pleasant personality, a ready smile, and he was full of the dickens for a good time.

My years as a logger were always exciting and I met a great many fine men. L. C. was typical. He had roamed into camp looking for a job and had rapidly qualified as a competent engineer. He always kept his donkey in perfect order. He did not seem to have any family, and he left camp as quietly as he had come.

Life has always seemed like a maze or a great puzzle and much depends on the quirks and turns which one meets. Little things occur which vitally affect our lives. Who knows where I might have landed had my family not disintegrated at its inception. My father had a second family of three girls and two boys, only one of whom rose above his environment so that he might say, "Life was a success."

Education comes from the Latin "e-duco, to lead out." It is intended to develop the inherent qualities of a person's innermost emotions and ambitions. I was urged at an early age to seek the other side of the hill. I have retained that urge ever since.

I am intensely interested in the young people who have entered my life. I dream with them their dreams about what they might accomplish. They look forward to the morrow. And so do I.

> Let us then be up and doing—
>   With a heart for any fate;
> Still achieving, still pursuing—
>   Learn to labor and to wait.

Cheerio and good luck,
JJL
February 2, 1989

DAVE AND MARGE LESLIE: SMALL RANCHERS, WORKING OUT

Chesaw, WA

Born: 1916 and 1923

Though Washington is only a century old as a state, many areas have already gone through at least three waves of migration to the land. Yet the lure of country living remains as strong today as ever. As Chesaw rancher Marge Leslie said, "Seattle people come in by the droves."

The reality for a large percentage of back-to-the-landers, however, is eventual failure to sustain the dream. And for many the road back to the city must be longer than the way out.

The greatest fantasy of young back-to-the-landers is that they will become totally "self-sufficient." The phrase is almost a talisman of faith. I remember hearing it in 1978 from twenty-four-year-old Bob Mathews, an Arizona newcomer to an untamed piece of backwoods Pend Oreille County. The future fish ponds (where Bob was to harvest his "protein") failed. The cement plant broom-pushing job was not big enough for his fantasy world. Within a few short years Bob had died in a police shootout, the Götter-dämerung of his vision of a whites-only "Aryan" Northwest.

Bob Mathews was the craziest person I have ever known in the Evergreen State, but he had originally attempted the common goal of balancing a salaried job with the independence of homestead life.

Marge and Dave Leslie have spent a lifetime building up their four-hundred-acre spread and making that dream succeed. But when I visited them in 1986 they were quick to tell me that they approached rural living from a very different base of experience than the urban back-to-the-landers. Both Marge and Dave grew up in homestead families and were accustomed to the rigors of mixing economically marginal, but full-time ranching with "working out."

When I arrived at the Leslie ranch, Dave had just come in from fixing a cattle trough, and he and Marge were completing the job of preparing a bunch of chickens for freezing.

MARGE: We are in the process of putting them in the deep freeze. We scalded them in hot water and pulled the feathers off. They come off real easy. And then we scalded them and cleaned out all the pin feathers, just black blobs in the skin that would be feathers eventually. You pull or scrape them out.

We buy a hundred baby chicks. After they grow, we get our hens for eggs and the others go into the freezer. [laughter] The roosters have to die!

I raise my own chickens. And then we have the milk cows and we sell some milk. Not a great lot now. We used to milk ten or twelve cows and sell the cream. That was 1941 to 1958 when the creameries bought it. We just took the cans of cream to the post office in Chesaw and got back our empties. The mail drivers took it to Oroville and I don't know how it got to the creamery in Spokane from there. By the time it got there, it was probably pretty sour.

But country people wouldn't buy whole milk, because everyone had a milk cow. So we separated our cream and fed the skim milk to our calves. We had what we called skim milk calves. If we started them out on a bit of grain and if we gave them enough milk, why they got nice and fat.

My mother's name was Pearl Hirst. She was number one of fourteen kids. And she lived up on Strawberry Mountain. She was born in Grandma Walker's house in Molson. She was one of the first children born in the area after the North Half of the Indian reservation was opened to homesteaders in 1900. She rode horseback quite a few miles to school. There were no fences in those days and she could just go across anywhere.

My life is much different today than when my parents or grand-

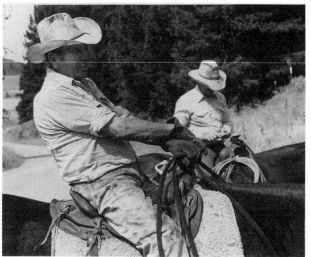

Dave
Leslie

Marge
Leslie

parents were growing up. That was a pretty rough life for them. Washing clothes on the washboard. Actually electricity only came here in 1951 and I even scrubbed diapers on the washboard.

So I don't want to go back to the good old days. I am not like a lot of these new people that are moving in now who want to revert back to the pioneer days. No way! I like my electricity and I like my water. I like my comfortable house. And not freezing to death in the wintertime like we used to.

Dave and I built this house in 1960 after our first house burnt in '59. It was down in town, across the creek on the other road. It was a comfortable house, but it wasn't insulated, because in that day and age there was no insulation unless you'd put sawdust in the walls.

When the R.E.A. finally brought in electricity in 1951 it didn't make any difference in farming. There wasn't anybody who ever got electric milkers around here. The only thing it made a difference in was that we had running water in our house and we could take a bath without having to heat the water on the stove. And on a summer day, we could cook a decent meal without having to suffocate inside the house.

But as far as the farming went. . . . Oh, in '59 we put in irrigation when we finally got enough money together for a sprinkler system. We had to have electricity for that. Before us, the people that had homesteaded this place, they had had rill irrigation, water down by ditches from way up the creek and they had spent their time out here maintaining ditches and whatnot. Our new sprinklers were hard work, though. Changing them after supper. And getting up early and changing them.

It really is a good life, though, cause you're your own boss. Of course, at a lot of places, the bank is the real boss. But not at this place, thank goodness. We have been real careful and we haven't owed that bank any amount of money for a long, long time.

Dave: For the last twenty years I have been working out on Copper Mountain, mostly for farmers that have their cattle on the Forest Service summer range. I'm a modern cowboy. I come home every night.

Every summer I go to the same range and I dig water holes and move cows from one area to another. If the grass is getting real short in one place, you move the cows over to another area where the grass is better.

Damn tough work. Did you ever take a mud hole out? Did you ever chase cows when they don't want to go in the direction you want?

MARGE: It's dirty. The dust is rolling. It's hot. It's miserable. And you are chasing this bunch of cows and they all bunch up in the brush someplace and you can't get them out. And you fight and fight and fight to get those cows out of there and down the road where you want them to go.

I've been there lots of times.

DAVE: She is the one that does the cussing. Have you ever heard a cowboy cuss?

MARGE: Well, the reason I do that is because his dogs won't go with me. And so long as Dave has his dogs with him, why, he can make the cows go, 'cause the dogs will go out and beat them out of the brush. But the cows that I've got back here someplace, why, they know there's no dogs around so they brush up, and then I can't do anything about it.

Up there on that range there is so much brush that you can't get through it. But the cows can get into it and then just stop when they can't go any further. And that is what we call "brushing up."

If I get off my horse and go in there and start chasing them, I'll get one going in one direction and pretty soon there will go the other one in the other direction.

That is why I swear!

DAVE: I have two cow dogs, Spade and Old Joe. Spade hasn't been taught anything yet and I'm not sure I can teach him anything. He's not too smart.

But when Joe was a pup I took him along with an older dog which was a good cow dog. And I think Joe must have had enough smarts to learn what he learned from that dog.

And I just worked the heck out of him. If I told him to go way around, he went way around and headed the cows off.

MARGE: Maybe you could teach him how to dig out those mud holes?

DAVE: He's got to have them to sleep in when he's hot.

Cowboying runs into work.

MARGE: But it is nice! Yes. You get up there and there are no people. Nothing around. You see a deer once in a while and maybe you'll see a bear.

I love the outdoors.

DAVE: It's a nice life. It really is. I like it.

MARGE: There's days that aren't bad when the cows move real good and you don't have any problems. But there are days that it *is* bad.

There is always lots of hard work on our ranch but I am my own boss. That's what I like. If I don't want to get up at six in the morning, I can sleep in till seven—if I don't have too much work to do. But *most of the time* we have too much work to do.

I was born in Molson in 1923. I left the homestead ranch about two miles south of Chesaw when I was six so that I could start school and not have to ride horseback. My parents owned and operated Plunkett's General Store in Chesaw for many years. So I lived in town until I was seventeen and Dave and I were married in 1941. That's when I moved to this ranch and became a real rancher.

My dad, Bub, (his real name was Lester) had worked out all the time driving a school bus and driving a grain truck and things like that. I had been kinda like a city girl. We had milked cows and had had chickens, but that's all. Of course, I helped like in harvest time from about the time that I was twelve. Why I'd go around and help the women cook for thrashers. That would be twelve to fourteen, maybe eighteen, men that we'd cook for. I got initiated there. I would make enough money to buy my clothes to go to school in the fall.

DAVE: My parents were born in Scotland and were married in Greenwood, B.C. in 1906. They had eight children, one girl and seven boys, and I am the youngest. I was born between here and Molson on the place my parents had bought as a relinquishment in 1905. I haven't left the area yet.

MARGE: I think it was about 1959 that you went to Seattle for the first time, when Steve was over there and we went for Thanksgiving.

DAVE: Oh, we went to Moses Lake for a year and a half and farmed down there. But Seattle is the farthest away I've been.

MARGE: Oh no, you have done some rodeo over in Montana.

DAVE: Oh, I been there.

MARGE: I can't hardly move you. I can't go anywhere because you like it right here.

DAVE: I don't know what it is about this area.

MARGE: Beautiful country. I could not hardly stand the year and a half that we were in Moses Lake. I just wanted to get home to see the hills and the green trees. It was just one of those things. I was used to this. I couldn't stand that flat, treeless country.

My dad passed away in '56 and if he could come back today he would get a shock seeing the changes in this part of Okanogan County. But Mom has only been gone about eight years, so not much difference. A few more hippies!

This is what bothers us old-timers, is all these new people coming in. We've met some real nice people, but the hippies have been dumber than the original pioneers. A lot of them, sure. Why we knew lots of the original people that had come in to homestead. But these new people, they have had a different idea of how to go about things. For instance, they think that they can go out and get water any place there is a tree growing. And then they always build on *top* of the mountain.

A lot of these people that we call hippies that moved in north of town, now they are moving off. They've had enough of this no water and no electricity. And can't get to their place in the wintertime. Things like that.

But we still have piles of them coming in because these real estate people bought up these ranches and they are selling forty-acre lots cheap. So Seattle people come in by the droves.

It's been difficult for Dave and me. We've had to work out. For many years, if he wasn't working out, I was.

And I'm *still* working out!

But yeah, that's how we keep the farm going. Like I packed apples for several years and I went to town and worked in a tavern and in cocktail lounges. On sale days I clerk at the Okanogan Livestock Market.[1] Since 1949 I have been drivin' the mail route as a substitute. And Dave works out herding cows.

---

[1] In 1942 Marjorie Leslie was one of the founders of the Chesaw Fourth of July Rodeo. She was Rodeo secretary for many years and often trucked rodeo stock.

We had two boys. Neither one of them wanted to be farmers. One was a cowboy. That's all he could think about. But he drowned in the Kettle River back in 1966. And the other one, all he could think about was trucks and he became a long-haul truck driver.

So it's up to Dave and me to keep farming.[2]

---

[2]Marjorie Leslie died of an aneurism of the brain in 1987.

Dave is still cowboying. He says he has the cleanest goddamn fingernails in Chesaw from dishwashing. Now he has a monthly Social Security check. In March, 1988 he had a successful knee replacement operation in Wenatchee and by May 1 he was back on his horse. "If the weather had been better," he said, "I would have been back in the saddle sooner!"

JIMELLA LUCAS: CREATING GOURMET MEALS FROM NORTHWEST FOODS
Nahcotta, WA
Born: 1943

Jimella Lucas grew up in a Portland, Oregon Italian family where food was valued for both enjoyment and employment. Then at age eighteen she began a three-year apprenticeship with a German master chef at the Waverly Country Club. Next, she and a partner built a fishing boat and fished it from Canada to Mexico, 1968 to the end of 1973. For someone who was to become one of the most widely-heralded Washington chefs of the late 1980s, this was a priceless combination of experiences.

Fishing gave me an eye for quality. The knowledge to know how I want my product handled. Good simple taste for right-on-the-nose quality fish. It really helps me out when I deal with some purveyors that say, "Aw, that woman, she doesn't know what she wants." Many of those walk right out the back door with the product that they walked in with!

If there is truly a "Northwest cuisine" (of the chef-cooked variety, not merely logger breakfasts and ranch feeds), its hallmark is freshness. Jimella, for instance, works as closely as possible with purveyors to obtain exactly the seafood she wants for the Ark Restaurant she and her partner operate in Nahcotta, Washington.

Jimella says, "That way I can contract the size and quality of the oysters I want people to eat cooked and the ones I want them to eat raw."

What I like best about Jimella Lucas is her commitment to local producers of fine foods. She repays their efforts in part by profiling them in her folksy cookbook, where a recipe for the Ark's Salmon Lucas might appear fin-to-fin with a description of how Ernie Soule brings in his catch of Dungeness crab or Willapa Bay sturgeon.

"Sharing is what food is all about," says Chef Lucas. "Seeing the other person at our table enjoying our food." She responds to that challenge with creativity, part of which has meant participation in public events such as Ilwaco's Cranberry Festival. Her cookbook tells us that when Lewis and Clark came through the country, they celebrated Thanksgiving at Chinook with local cranberries. (Jimella herself celebrates Turkey Day with gobblers decked out with oyster dressing made with local oysters.)

Jimella, as a hard-core Italian, created a Northwest Garlic Festival in 1981. I photographed her beside a boat called the Aioli, where she told me that garlic doesn't create that much of a stink and that the effect depends on your own body chemistry.

I love garlic. I eat fifteen to twenty raw cloves a day. I'm addicted to it. Raw cloves. This has been publicized on local television and I have had people walk into the restaurant and say, "Let me smell your breath."

Jimella Lucas and her partner Nanci Main are quick to agree with the old adage that a woman's place is in the kitchen—"if you own it."

Jimella says that, "There is nothing wrong with nurturing. I mean it has always been the woman's role to do that. Of course, you best do that by cooking and by sharing a meal. By bringing people happiness."

I love food. I like the way it makes me feel. There is nothing in the world that smells as wonderful cooking as a spring chinook salmon around the end of February. And there is nothing more exciting than getting my first small lettuce out of the garden in the end of May. And parsley, you can't beat it. I drink the juice, too.

We chop it and then my prep person squeezes it. We've made some special Bloody Marys for people, with parsley juice.

I am a recovering alcoholic. You betcha! It's been five years. I think you reach a point in any addiction where you are forced to be honest. There are no other alternatives. The wall is behind your back and it is too dark to fall on your face.

Every once in a while all the old patterns come back. I get tired when I run my mouth a lot when I'm training the staff, or just standing at the stove a long time dealing with the food. It is hard work and I think about a drink.

Stopping drinking is a commitment and it is a very personal one. And when you make it, you are at a very honest state. You don't make things for pretend. When you make that commitment, it goes a lot deeper than the wonderful fine wines that I've certainly enjoyed in my time. And that I still enjoy. I create five-course dinners around our wonderful Northwest wines and I do that with my nose, with no cheating allowed. I don't put it in my mouth and kind of swirl it around and spit it out. I know a lot of people, recovering alcoholics, friends of mine, that do that kind of thing. I don't take any raw alcohol into my body knowingly. I don't drink anything at all.

I apprenticed when I was eighteen years old in Portland, Oregon at a very exclusive country club under a master German chef. There is not a day that goes by that I ever regret the fact that he was pretty hard-nosed about what he expected from me during those three years.

Al Kuester was from Germany and at that time European chefs dominated the culinary field. He let me apprentice with him only because I was damn persistent. I used to take the bus to the end of the line and walk two miles down a railroad track to get to that country club. I did that for two months before he finally decided to take me on.

I went to a Catholic high school. That cost money so I needed to find ways to work. I'm Italian and grew up in the Italian community in Portland. Outside of being Mafia-oriented, Italians have always had very famous produce. So I would work in a produce warehouse packing delivery trucks. One of the people, Menduini, that I worked for said, "You ought to go out and apply at the country club. If you are going to learn, you ought to learn the best."

I said, "Ah, OK." So I drove out with him one morning and I put in an application. It was sort of dealt with like, "Oh, OK, we have to do these things." I was pretty much in awe. It was a European-style kitchen where all your different stations and prep areas are laid out from bakery to pantry. It just fascinated me.

In the middle of the kitchen was this huge steam table called a Bain-marie. You could have taken two people, three people, four people and given them a bath in that baby. A Bain-marie is regulated by steam and has water in it. That is where you coddle eggs for Caesar salads or it has all your sauces in it. In the old European kitchens, they used to have big steam tables for all their hot sauces. The history behind Bain-marie is that in a big kitchen in France there was a woman who cleaned up in the wee hours of the night.

Marie always had a particular way that she would clean the entire kitchen and when she was done she would take a bath in this wonderful steam table. One morning one of the chefs came in early and here was Marie taking a bath. That's the reason they call it a Bain-marie, the bath of Marie.

I am grateful for the foundations that Al Kuester gave me as far as my techniques and my food procedures. I apprenticed with him for three years and then I fished for five years. When I was fishing, there was a part of me that was lonesome for the kitchen. That was one of the reasons that after five years of fishing I decided to get back home, so to speak.

Being from the Portland area, I've always followed James Beard. Because I've been exposed to him as long as I've been exposed to food. Years ago, there were things that I didn't agree with, because I thought that they were a bit pompous. In his later years, I really enjoyed dealing more personally with Mr. James Beard. He thought about food the same way I do, very simply, and with elegant but simple touches so that the flavors were not destroyed or distorted.

I place a strong emphasis on seafood, of course, because that is what I like. I get as much as possible of my fish directly from the fisherman so that I can regulate the time, the quality, the area. The same thing with having our own garden produce grown for us. We deal with our own herbs.

The bay produces a lot of wonderful things, sturgeon, being one, and, of course, oysters, our local industry.

We have to call it something so we call it Pacific Northwest cuisine. The emphasis is on Northwest products. They may come to you the way I want to serve it, with Dijon cream sauce and capers as a complement. Or it may simply come to you grilled or pan-fried. There is quite a variety in the Pacific Northwest, but in my opinion, Northwest Cuisine is just a style, using our abundant bounty of the Pacific Northwest.

I am fairly well-respected as far as the culinary field is concerned and I have people that approach me on different levels for advice. I encourage them to get away from purveyors and brokers, and to go out more independently and deal with individuals. There are a lot of wonderful people out there on a smaller independent scale that need to stay alive and not get sucked up by large companies.

At my restaurant I have certain people who provide me with wild blackberries. I contract for ninety or a hundred gallons. I deal with it from that point. Or when chanterelles are coming out I have certain people that I buy from. I buy everything that they have. Or when one of the fisherman goes out and gets twelve hundred pounds of sturgeon, I buy that. And I process it myself because I know what I am going to do with it. And some things we'll freeze.

I have a great time. I get to operate my restaurant the way I believe that it should be operated. Regionally and seasonally.

Right now our clientele is primarily out of Seattle. This area had always been supported by Portland because it was a summer resort for people out of Portland. But right now the trend in food and for our restaurant is basically out of Seattle.

Of course, in the summer people come from all over the United States. I've had a couple come back to eat the traditional Ark oysterfeed to celebrate their fiftieth wedding anniversary. They had come here thirty-five years ago when the Ark was first being established by Lucille Wilson, a local person.

I had two young women the other night who asked my partner's bakery apprentice to see a menu. They looked at the prices and I think the prices were a little out of line for them. They asked the young lady behind the counter, "Can you recommend another restaurant that wouldn't be quite as expensive but would be as good as this?"

So Karen, our young apprentice, came up to the kitchen and told me that. My reaction was, "Let me go talk to those young women right now." I walked around the corner and I looked at them and I said, "So you think you want to go eat someplace that doesn't have as much of a price tag on it, huh?"

"Well, we've heard about this restaurant, but we really can't afford to spend that much money."

I said, "Did you look at the light fare? Look, you can eat fish and chips made with local fresh sturgeon. Pasta, great pasta, with my own Roma tomatoes out of Oregon, done with pesto that I did myself. Laced with a little bit of cream and served with garlic bread.

Check these prices out. Where are you going to go? It doesn't make any difference what you eat here. The quality is the same from the highest-priced item on the menu to the lowest.

"The waitress won't get mad at us if we go in and eat the cheapest thing?" they said.

"Just tell her Jimella sent you, OK!"

ED MARROY:

COAL MINER

Bellingham, WA

Born: 1891

The century from 1850 to 1950 was the heyday of Washington's once-flourishing deep-mine coal industry. Rich underground seams kept places like Bellingham, Carbonado, and Black Diamond humming until the advent of cheap oil destroyed demand.

Ed Marroy was a Belgian-born miner who spent much of his life underground, eventually retiring in 1944 as boss of the Bellingham Coal Mines, a quarter-mile-deep, eleven-level operation. The most sophisticated of Bellingham's mines, it had begun in about 1918 as an energy supplier to a cement plant in Concrete, Washington and had finally folded in 1953 (though there was still an abundance of coal beneath downtown Bellingham).

Despite grueling working conditions, ever present danger, and the threat of black lung disease, Ed Marroy late in his life spoke nostalgically of coal mining.

I would like to have discussed it with the miners' silent partners, the horses and mules who literally spent their lives underground "until they were finished."[1]

Once they went down, they stayed mostly till they were finished. Although we had one, name of Jack, who was a very fine mule and was just as intelligent as a human being. *Him,* I know they retired. In fact, I was foreman yet when they retired him. He had been down in the mine at least ten years. At least! Between ten and fourteen years, that I know.

---

[1] Ed Marroy described their lot to Bellingham historian Galen Biery on May 24, 1970.

You'd take Jack on a run pulling coal up to one of these entries. He'd be wet from sweating. He pulled five or six cars on a thirty-six-inch-wide track, and each car had two tons of coal plus the weight of the car. But the next time that Jack went there, he knew exactly where to pull and when he could slack off. He was the smartest mule that I ever seen. He would pull steady. When he got to a little up-grade, he knew it was coming and he'd start out. There was no getting stuck with him at all. He'd just keep on going.

We had about half-and-half horses and mules. About sixteen altogether. At times mules were better than horses. Only, they were more stubborn. But they could stand much more punishment. They could stand more abuse. I don't mean beating them or anything like that. But at rough work they were much better than a horse.

And another thing, they'd know when to quit eating. You'd put a lot of oats and hay in their box, and they'd just eat so much and quit. Only a horse would eat everything he had in his manger. They had the best of food. No doubt about that! The best fresh grain and hay would go in every day. And fresh water from the surface. There was a man that done nothing but clean 'em when they came off at night. Brush 'em off. Feed 'em.

When they came in from working, they were turned loose in the man-way. What I mean by a man-way, that's a place that's on the same pitch as a slope, only about two hundred and fifty feet from the slope [a rail car tunnel between levels]. They'd be turned loose there and they'd go right on up to the barn. The barn at that time was between the second and the third level. They'd go right up in there. They knew that everything was in their manger because this man was there right ahead of them and he had everything all fixed up.

They never came out of the mine.

Sometimes people would say how mean we were to those horses and mules. Well, that was wrong! That was wrong because, you know, you take them drivers, they thought as much of their mule as they did of some of their kids. And sometimes some of them drivers would come to their mule and give 'em a chew of tobacco.

And that mule looked for that chew of tobacco every day or, by gum, he wouldn't get out of that stall.

Another driver would bring some candy.

So you see, they thought a lot of their mules.

They don't call them miners; they call them drivers. And the same driver would always have the same animal all the time. You take a stranger. . . . For an example, if you was driving Jack and you wasn't working today, well, I'd have to get another man to put in your place. Well, now that mule knew right away and he just wouldn't function.

ED "DUTCH" MONAGHAN: "WE ASK GRANDFATHER TO CLEAN OUR MINDS"
Keller, WA
Born: 1917

Dutch Monaghan grew up at Keller, Washington on the Columbia River. Rejected by his white father, he idolized his maternal grandfather, Chief Jim James of the Colville Indian Reservation. well-known as a Colville leader. But despite the fact that his mentor, Chief James, was a teetotaler, Dutch Monaghan began drinking liquor by the age of twelve.

Alcohol has been a Northwest Indian scourge ever since 1820s fur traders began giving a free dram of rum each time they bought furs. That and European diseases soon devastated the region's once-proud native cultures.

Today the tragedy continues. Old patterns die hard among people accustomed to the inertia and despair of joblessness, isolation, and heavy drinking. For Dutch Monaghan it was only the threat of his thirteen children's becoming orphans that broke the long pattern of slow self-destruction.

We should teach our children, our people, everybody, how to love and respect one another. How to share and to help ones that are sick. Because if you see a drunken man staggering around, he's saying, "Come here somebody and look at me. Somebody come. I need some help. I need your guidance." That's what a drunken man does. He doesn't come asking. *But when we see him stagger-*

ing around, he's saying, "Somebody help me, please. I don't want to do this."

Grandfather Jim James never drank. He was a church leader. He was a great big man. He had a heart for all the people. He was the greatest person on earth.

In the mid-20s my grandfather was an Indian prayer leader and he would go to Nespelem and anywhere as far as Montana where people needed his prayers. Sometimes he rode a buggy. He never had no cars.

He would marry people in the four seasons according to the Indian ways. But he told people to go get married according to the white man's way as soon as they could. He taught people how to pray, how to be together. How for people to get along. How not to fight and not to kill.

He took a strong stand not to do anything bad or to hate anyone. Everybody, young and old, used to come a great distance to hear him pray. He would say a prayer for anybody, any time, any place to help them feel better.

When I was a little boy, I used to be dark, dark, dark, dark. And my Dad, he was pretty much on the white man's side and he did not care for me because I was the darkest of the family.

There were seven of us in the family. I was the darkest. He would say to people, "I'm not Dutch's dad. Look at that kid, see how black he is. Look at the other kids. *They* are my kids. They are my children." I felt bad. That's why I went to stay with my grandpa. I learnt all his ways. He taught me the good things. I stayed with him and I was taught by his wife Nellie James. I was her favorite.

One thing I did not care for, Jim James had two wives. I learned that that was wrong. Also, we used to have square dances around here every week. Young girls would say, "Jim, give a dollar and see me over behind the old jail." She was going to pay him for his dollar. And he'd say, "O.K."

That was one part I didn't care for. Yet I liked him a lot. He never drank. He taught me to ride and to live the Indian way out in Nature. We didn't have to take food to be out in the hills. We'd be out for a weekend or a week, hunting deer or bear.

Before we started hunting, we said a prayer to the deer. That helped the deer to be less afraid and they were closer to the humans. In them days when we killed a deer, every piece of meat on that deer (head, legs, feet) was used. Hides were tanned into buckskin. And the bones were either buried or tied up in a bundle up in a tree so that no dogs would ever play with them. My grandfather respected the deer by doing it that way.

Jim died quite a few years ago when I was forty-five. When he left us, he left with cancer. His house had always been full of friends from Inchelium and Nespelem and Omak. People walked or rode horseback to visit him and to fish.

Keller was the place where everybody came in the summertime because we had Chinook salmon. They stayed all summer long. Right from the first week of May to the late part of October. People would catch all they could with nets and spears and gaff hooks and they would dry it. Nothing was wasted, not even the heads and the fins and the tails. Everything was dried. People would have camps all the fifty miles up the San Poil to West Fork. They'd fish up and down. The older salmon weren't so fat and they kept longer. The people preferred the old fish.

I refused to ride horses. I'd see other boys gallop their horses. They'd get so sweaty. It would look like soap was forming on their body. I'd tell my mom that I would never ride horses. No use to run a horse and abuse it.

So I walked everywhere around Keller. As I'd walk, I'd see bottles of home brew cached. A few of the older guys made it. I knew just what that would do to a person. I'd look around and look around and I'd pick up the bottle. Oftentimes it would be full. Next thing I knew I was hooked on the stuff.

I was about ten or twelve when I started.

My grandpa liked me so well that he wanted to see me be happy, because I helped him in every way that I knew. Even after I grew up and moved away from him, I'd cut his wood. When we took the water out of the spring, my job was to get the coldest water for his drinking. When I saw him come, I'd grab a canteen or a bucket and get him a drink from the spring.

After I grew up, I'd give him money and I'd buy him food. He liked his pop. In turn, he'd do anything for me. Once in a while he'd watch guys caching a bottle and he'd say, "I'll take this for Dutch." What he found was mine. This was when Indians couldn't buy alcohol. Them days we'd drink anything.

Jim never did take a drink. He'd say, "Here, I found this for you." He'd tell us not to drink but he'd turn around and give it to me.

We had white friends up in Republic who were always around liquor. Somebody always knew how to treat Indians. "Want me to get you a drink?"

"Yeah." We'd give him money to buy a bottle for us and enough to give himself a bottle.

In 1940 Grand Coulee Dam flooded Keller and we had to move about twelve miles up a creek. But before that when I wanted a drink, our next-door neighbor (who was a white man) took me to town and bought me a drink of moonshine. The old-timers used to pour a little on the ground and light it with a match. If it burned with a blue flame, it was safe to drink.

H. Bacon was a tall bootlegger and a real good guy. Everybody knew him on the river. He taught me how to be a Democrat.

"You're a working man," he said. "You're not rich. The best thing for you is to be an honest Democrat. You should always vote Democratic, even if your friends are running as Republicans." When I was twenty-one, I registered Democratic. I have always voted a straight ticket.

As time passed, there were times I didn't drink. Nobody ever saw me drunk until I came back from World War II. Before I was in the service I got drunk once a year on homemade wine which my friend H. Bacon and I had made. Once a year, I'd tell my mother, "I want to get drunk, Ma. I'll be in the cellar and don't you tell anybody where I am."

She'd say, "Take care, now."

I'd go in the cellar and tell her to tell people that I wasn't home. I didn't want anyone to see me.

When I came back from the South Pacific, I went to drink here at my friend's house. I could hear all the old ladies saying, "Look at Dutch Monaghan. He's staggering drunk. Look at what the Army taught him how to do. Made him drink."

I sold cattle in Keller when I got back.

When I was working driving a logging truck, I never took a drink. But the moment I turned that ignition switch off, I had a drink waiting for me. Sometimes I'd drink all night. I'd go to work the next morning without having slept at all.

By 1971 I had cirrhosis of the liver. I weighed two hundred twenty pounds. I was sick and I knew it was from the alcohol.

I went in the hospital in Republic in 1971 because I was feeling sick and tired. Our family doctor, Dr. Thornton, said, "Dutch, I found out your problem. You're sick from alcoholism. You'll either have to quit or you will die from it and the state will give your children away to different people and different homes. Maybe they'll see each other, and again maybe they never will. But if you quit drinking and continue working for your family and throw that bottle away, then you'll live a happier and better life."

I said, "Doctor, being as you told me this way, I'll quit drinking. Just for my family, I'll do it."

When they let me out that Monday afternoon, he gave me some medication to take. I said, "Doctor, what is that for?"

He said, "It will help you stay away from liquor."

I said, "Doctor, what you have told me has struck me at heart and it is going to stay there. I don't need any help. I need my family together in one house."

I never took that medication. If I had not stopped drinking, I would have died. I was that bad off. So I quit, and Dr. Thorton would come down and check on me once a week. He said, "If you need help, don't be afraid or scared to call on me and I'll come down."

After I quit, my friends would come to me and say, "Come on and have a drink. You'll feel better".

"No, I gave my word. I'll never take another drink. I don't care to drink. I found myself and I am living the way our Lord wants us to live."

I had Doctor Thornton as one of my best buddies.

It wasn't long after that I got a job. I got better. I graduated from a short course in how to be an alcoholism counselor. Without liquor I was able to do my work. I enjoyed working with my friends and our people. On the other hand, I kept thinking, "What if my Grandpa were alive?" He would have objected to my taking these classes and learning white man's ways. He was strictly for helping people in *our* ways.

I began counseling every day and I was able to help many people stop drinking. My buddies tell me, "We would rather come to you, Dutch, than go through the alcohol program."

Us Indian people, we have a tendency to stick together and walk together and do things together. We have many different ways. Our old medication that we get from these herbs helps us greatly in many, many ways. We use the herbs to help kick the alcohol. We cannot get everyone to walk away from liquor.

I make a sweat lodge because people would rather go there than to a treatment center. I use that sweat lodge to tell people what the herbs will do.

We heat rocks and throw water on the rocks. The steam makes us sweat and when we are sweating in the sweat lodge our Grandfather is helping us to go straight. According to Indian belief the sweat lodge is our Grandfather.

You can make a sweat lodge as hot as you want. We cut willows and stick them in the ground and make an arch about three feet high. We take and put a cover over the willows. We put a door on the sweat lodge. Put hot rocks in there and go in and throw water on them while we are asking for help and guidance from our Grandfather.

When the Lord made this Earth, He made the people. He made the animals. He made the Nature. When He made the red-skinned spiritual people, why He told them, "You are to practice your medicine to take care of sick people. The black race and the yellow race are the same as the red race, all human beings."

He told us to stand up and have medicine men and use herbs. We have herbs right out here that will take out any kind of soreness you have. I give medications that will take away a stiff neck. We have stuff that I can give you that will clean your insides out. What we use is always powerful.

We get in the sweat lodge and we talk to Grandfather as if he was our Lord. We ask for help. We ask for guidance. When we first get in, we say a short prayer.

We ask Grandfather to clean our minds.

SILVER MOON: HEALER AMONG THE HILL PEOPLE

White Mountain, Curlew, WA

Born: 1945

Silver Moon grew up south of Seattle, but most of her adult life has been spent among the Hill People of northeastern Washington. Hill People, whether young or middle-aged, maintain a 1960s "counterculture" lifestyle. Aside from leaders like Skeeter and Gray Owl, who have organized past Barter Fairs, Silver Moon is probably the best known of the Hill People.[1] She is a holdout from a time when yurts, dugouts, and tepees were the Okanogan dwellings with the best karma and when bongs, boddhisattvas, and beads were as common as knapweed.

But the communes folded, lovers split the scene, and the faith grew dim. Silver Moon's faith, too, has wavered. By necessity, her three children have had a lot to do with that because children can quickly lead to things which a subsistence, moneyless, living-off-the-land lifestyle can't provide. Formal education. Medical care. The wider world. The consumer lifestyle.

I had known Silver Moon for a long time when I met her again by accident at a "Nuclear Free Okanogan" rally and dance on a remote homestead in the Aeneas Valley. Later I visited her at her White Mountain wickiup for a chappatti dinner and a talk about healing.

---

[1]See *Going The Distance*, which describes the 1979 Barter Fair.

Silver Moon and her children cooking dinner at their wickiup.

Right now I have these warts or moles which are getting bigger. They are from impurities in my body that are reacting with the sunlight. So, recently I just really felt that I would like to brew up some knapweed roots to cleanse away the warts. I wasn't really clear on which part of the knapweed to use. I ended up with the roots. I brewed that up into a strong syrup and poured it on these moles. I treated them very frequently for days. There has been no change in the moles, but the knapweed intrigues me. I am not clear on its usage yet.

Not long ago my daughter got impetigo, a kind of skin disease, after I got her some kind of inoculation in a mobile clinic van. I remember when I was in there not wanting to touch anything. And she got that impetigo. I wanted something that would help her, because her skin was hurting from drying and crusting. Some way that she wouldn't have scars because there were these pits all over her face.

For some reason I didn't feel real comfortable taking her back down to the doctor and putting antiseptic on it.

What matters is not the name of it, but what you are going to do about it. How can I help the healing which is happening? How could I help that wound to be soft and healing? How could I help that scar?

I walked through the woods looking for something. There were wildflowers, trees, grasses, berries, mosses, and clay. An old, dried puffball drew my attention. I was not really clear that the puffball powder did it. But what was really exciting was that something was needed and that I could go out and that there was some gift out there that would help.

We need to look around and think about it. We don't trust ourselves anymore. We've learned not to. We trust the big guy who earns all the money because he's read all the books. We need to reach some kind of understanding that now there are no leaders.

Everybody is now reaching that point of understanding. Just like that meal we just had. It works real well for us. It's shared. The salad is from our garden and the olive oil and the tamari came a long ways.

I remember trying for a long time to figure out how to eat these garden vegetables. We tried stew and dumplings on them but that didn't fill us. Bread made us tired.

About the same time that we figured out the salad and chappattis, we went somewhere else and they were eating the same thing. It fills you and makes you strong. It works. It tastes real good to me. You reach that point where you eat because your body wants it. The taste is much more minor than that your body is saying, "I want *that.*"

Chappattis do taste good though!

Actually we have been eating them since the '60s but we changed it recently by adding the yeast. And we've started to leaven our bread to make the zinc available. Other cultures have had this problem with zinc shortage when they didn't use leavening. My friend John is one step ahead of us. He uses a natural yeast in the air.

I am disappointed that we Hill People couldn't have learned our lessons faster, learned more about sharing, and couldn't have learned faster all those commandments. What are they? I don't even know them. They have to do with loving and sharing and compassion and not judging. Apparently it must take a long time to learn them. We can't really live in communities very well until we learn those things. You have to have those things to allow people to be themselves.

It was probably better that we weren't successful in creating our own little villages in the Sinlahekin, because those villages could have become ingrown. Instead I think we all realize that we are part of the world.

And as for the bomb consciousness. . . . One thing about the bombs is that they have made us all understand that there are no more corners for hiding. That we all have to work as a whole and that each one of us has to change.

A long time ago the idea was that something could be created that would be a viable alternative. Another way of life. On a social level we all started out with certain ideals. Of course, everybody was different and we had to work a lot on ourselves. We got together and what happened was that we were just tiptoeing around each other. And that only worked for a while. Then you had to work through things that were inside of you.

A lot of us are doing that.

I think one thing that is happening is that our families are very weak. We've been torn and ravaged by doubt and confusion. And I think that the family unit is trying to find ways to be strong as our children grow up.

My family unit hasn't worked out. And many people's haven't worked out. But in the process maybe we've learned the value of having a strong family unit. We've each improved things that were preventing our relationship from happening. And maybe our families might take shape in unique ways, too.

I've watched our children heal up to some degree. I don't like to see anything in terms of dead ends and mistakes. I don't think that is necessary. Doesn't it just seem like we are small parts of mankind? We are part of the learning, the failing and the triumph, and the sadness and the joy.

There are so many different levels of life. Sometimes I kind of wonder why we are up here on this mountain when that makes us spend all our time in the car traveling to a school and other places many, many miles away.

Before coming to the Okanogan, I went all over to other countries. I was pretty much into people. I had majored in psychology. I wanted to find out more about life. I chose psychology as a path. The University of Washington was very weird. They wanted to make it a science. Very experimental and objective. It was different than what I was looking for. And everywhere I walked I was surrounded by big buildings.

I always remember that poem, "Tiger, tiger, burning bright." It's all about who we are and what we are doing on this earth.

I ended up working as a psychiatric aide and housemother and counselor. I worked with children and adults and generally saw very little improvement in them. Drugs weren't used as much back then. You'd send a depressed lady or an angry man right back to their work or to his unloving wife. I'd say to my boss, "Gosh, you send people back to these worlds that aren't very human. But maybe another way would be to change these worlds around."

So then I said to myself, "Well, what's wrong with me? Why do I think this way and other people don't seem to?" So I went to other places and I saw people that were human in ways that I could understand. I saw people who had energy, who had beauty and vitality deep within them. I saw old ladies who still had enough energy to chase the giraffe when it got out of the zoo in West Africa. I saw women who were more like I wanted to be.

I'm not a Barbie doll.

Those women were strong. They had feelings. They expressed them. I saw that they were full-blooded, beautiful women. Maybe I could try that direction rather than fitting my feet into tiny slippers.

We hitchhiked across the desert of West Africa. This guy took us out on some camels. There were footprints everywhere but we didn't see a soul.

So I returned with a little more faith to find a way.

Also, after I got out of the UW with my degree, I remember walking into the big grocery store in the U-District. You know the one. I remember getting through the door and thinking, "If this door shuts, I'm going to be the first one starved, degree or no degree."

So I decided to go and find a way. It was difficult. Up here we tried to do what seemed right. We tried to live our ideas. We became hippies.

But, in a way, I'm not made to be a black sheep. I have wondered all my life, as my mother does, "Why doesn't she wear make-up, nice earrings, and look pretty and try to attract some decent guys?"

I wonder why we are so different. I went to the coast last Christmas. Everybody had infections, sore throats, and runny noses. Later on, I realized that the smog had been hanging in the air for weeks. One lady took her kid to the doctor six times. A nurse told me, "Aw, their throats hurt. Give them ice cream."

And I said, "Wait a minute. Here's this registered nurse and she wants to give my kid ice cream. My child is full of mucus. What is happening in this world!"

I knew that I was supposed to travel here from Seattle because long ago my family used to travel Highway 97 on vacations. By the time I was twenty-seven, I knew that if I did not follow my heart, I would forget what it had been telling me.

Highway 97 didn't look like much at first. I traveled up to Okanogan to pick apples to make some money. I remember sleeping in a shed. It was pouring rain, almost snowing. "Gosh, if I just had some hot coffee," I thought.

At that moment there was a man above me with toast and coffee saying, "My wife and I saw you sneaking in there last night and we thought we'd wait till morning and maybe this will help you."

At that moment I felt, "Maybe there are other realities if we just leave ourselves open to them."

Many of us get jobs and try to pay our way every second. Maybe there are other ways. Money means a lot to all of us. This year my kids are going to be teenagers. Do they need that corner drugstore? They need plenty of stimuli in their lives. That wasn't what I needed, but this summer I was thinking about moving, to fill my teenagers' needs.

But here we can grow gardens and I can take my daughter down to Midway where my friend has a pottery shop. Or I can see if my friend John will give a gymnastics workshop. We don't need to go anywhere else. We can create what we need.

These kids have people who love them. They have brothers who play with them or show them a microscope or take them to the fair. Or sisters who show them beadwork or how to make moccasins or ask them to help out with their baby.

If my kids were unsuccessful or unhappy, and if this place was not giving them what they needed, then I'd move on. But if we moved somewhere else, it would be a whole different set of variables. Like how to pay my medical insurance, get my kids to school at seven, and get to work at eight.

You have to live so much on faith. And follow your heart.

MINNIE PETERSON:
OLYMPIC MOUNTAINS
OUTFITTER
Hoh River Valley, WA
Born: 1897

Minnie Peterson was one of those legendary figures who loom larger than life. She emerged as a celebrity backcountry outfitter from a pioneer girlhood. She was the first white child born on the upper Hoko River, was often the only child in her school, and was a person as at ease sleeping out under a tarp as she had originally been patrolling her childhood trapline.

What interests me more than the details of her upbringing and packing career is the legacy of shared love of the out-of-doors she left to her many friends and admirers. One of those was a young woman named Sandra Patton, who was a twenty-one-year-old University of Washington student when she first met Minnie Peterson on an Olympic College pack trip in 1963. Two years later, when Sandra had moved to Forks to teach, she renewed her acquaintance with Minnie. Because the young teacher and the seventy-year-old woman had the Olympic Mountains in common, they spent long hours at Minnie's Hoh River ranch comparing backcountry experiences, with Minnie recounting tales of her Hoko River childhood, her packer husband, Oscar, and her favorite horses.

Then Sandra slipped into helping. Eleven summers of helping! Minnie's out-of-the-saddle mobility was restricted by a horse-kicked knee. Sandra started staking out and saddling up the pack strings "and doing a lot of the footwork." She learned the Peterson methods and idiosyncracies.

After Minnie's death in 1989 I asked Sandra Patton for examples of life with Minnie on Olympic Mountains trails.

Minnie had a lot of nice qualities. We'd be out packing for days at a time and if we hit a streak of rain, my feet would get wet and I'd finally go through all my socks [laughter]. I'd say, "Minnie, do you have an extra dry pair of socks?" And I tell ya, she always had an extra dry pair of socks and she'd let me use them. Oh, that felt so good just to put on a dry pair of socks!

She'd share a dry pair of socks with me. If you have been there, you can appreciate what a kindness that is.

Minnie used to roll up at night in the tarps we used to pack the horses. Do you know the tarps I mean? OK, you put the alforjas[1] on the pack saddles, then a top pack, and then before you put the diamond hitch on, you'd throw a tarp over the boxes to protect everything, because if you went where there were bushes or branches, the packs could be snagged. The tarps not only helped to protect the loads from moisture, but also they helped keep the horses warm. If I came into camp late, I knew my sleeping bag would be warm from having absorbed the horse's heat all day.

Minnie never slept in a tent until she was almost eighty. We always put a pack box tarp on the ground and put a sleeping bag on it and then just put another tarp on top.

Minnie didn't like cooking, so I did it. Her favorite was a dinner of freshly-caught mountain trout, especially if her grandson caught them. She would admire the length and coloring of each fish and find out how it had been hooked, and then comment that her dad had been a good provider too.

When I first started going out into the high country with her, she did a lot of the work. Oh, she had such strong arms! I remember one trip we were on, we had this one horse Robin who was just immense. He had been used to pulling logs over rough ground for people who made log houses. He wasn't even used to being on a trail and following in line.

See, the horses eventually get used to following one another. Minnie would always spend time figuring out who should be be-

---

[1]panniers

hind who, because there was one horse who kicked and so would have to go at the end of the string. Depending how many horses she had, she had to figure out who would be in what string. Minnie always liked to lead this one horse, Nancy, that she'd raised from a foal. So, Minnie would be on Rats and she'd lead Nancy and then, depending on how many horses we needed and who she was going to be using, she'd figure up her strings. Like who worked well behind who. Who liked to drag and who liked to bite.

Rats was the head horse. If you caught Rats, the other horses wouldn't be far away. Some horses could graze without being staked because they wouldn't go far away from other horses. But you always had to be sure that Rats was tied up tight because she'd take off down the trail. . . .

Minnie liked it when horses rolled after packing and then being staked out. She'd say, "You can always tell how valuable a horse is by how many times it rolls over." So everybody would be watching and counting to see how many times a horse would roll.

Certain horses would get along better with certain other horses. Anyway, we were on a steep slide slope and this logging horse, Robin, backed right off the trail, and me and another of Minnie's helpers couldn't pull Robin up. It was hard to get below him and push because the slope was so steep and because he was in such an awkward position. Anyway, Minnie took ahold of the lead rope and she just pulled—and she didn't give up!

If it wasn't for her, that horse would have gone overboard.

She had a lot of arm strength. One time we had boxes that were eighty pounds, but she was so strong that she could lift them. I'm a very slight person (five-ten, and she was probably five-four), but at the end of that summer I could lift those boxes, too!

Minnie never liked to pack her horses over a hundred and fifty pounds if they were working every day, because she said it was too hard on their backs. She'd say, "I can always get another packer, but it's hard to get good packhorses." [laughter] So that always kept us in our places. [laughter]

She always said, "The horses live for their food." And she made sure that they were well taken care of. At the end of the summer they were in good shape. I've heard ranchers who saw her cattle *at the end of the winter say, "Minnie's cows look good. She's fed them well."*

You judge a person a lot by how their stock looks. And Minnie's horses were always well-fed on the trips. We'd bring in extra food so we could grain them. She'd stake them out twice a day so they could get their grass: real early in the morning and then in the evening after packing. Then tie them up short at night.

Because the horses were so important to her we'd camp in places where the horses could get their food. If we had a party that wanted to camp in a place without grazing, we'd unload their gear and then maybe move up a little ways to where the horses would have good food.

Minnie would say, "Each horse has its good points and its bad points" and she would work around the bad points. Minnie could pack horses that would bite and kick. She'd work around that and utilize their good points.

She did that with people, too. People were always sending her young boys to straighten out. She'd say, "Maybe this will make a difference later on. Maybe they're at a crossroads and if I can just help 'em, maybe it will make a difference for the rest of their lives."

She'd go out of her way to be nice to people and to be helpful. One example was that if someone was lost or hurt in the mountains, she'd always haul them out and she'd never accept any money for it. She'd never charge anybody for emergencies, because that would be taking advantage of their misfortune.

I just never thought of her as old. I never even thought about why most people her age weren't doing what she was doing.

It was nice for me to be out in the woods having a job to do. Getting the goods through. Getting the scientists' gear up. And then seeing the people that we knew. People from Olympic College in Bremerton that we'd grown to like.

Since Minnie died, I probably won't ever again be able to keep in touch with all these people that I had nothing else in common with except that they knew Minnie. She kept track of them. I'd call her and say, "Well, how's this person and how's that person? What have you heard?"

You see, all of these people liked the out-of-doors. She was the center of a network of people. She didn't travel a lot and we all thought of her as being there. And everybody eventually would drive a long way to go up to see her and talk. [laughter]

Minnie was just the type of person that people liked to keep in contact with. Oh, if I could look out my window now and see Minnie riding up on Rats and saying, "Come on, I have a contract to haul some stuff up to the glacier. Let's go!"

There's a lot of us that would drop anything to go on a pack trip with her.

When I visited Minnie not long ago at her Hoh River ranch, she was dressed in an old sweatshirt and looked as if she was ready to head up into the hills. She greeted my news about the Pacific Northwest Trail with rapt attention and offered her support for the all-volunteer trail-building project. That led to many yarns about the trail crew supply trips she had made, such as up to the High Divide.

Minnie was very proud of her potato patch and as she showed me the luxuriant plants, I asked her to tell me what it takes to operate a high country pack outfit.

I always like to have fun when I'm out. Who doesn't?

But you have no idea how much work that I do on a trip. Nobody knows the amount of work that there is to taking care of a bunch of horses and guiding people. They have absolutely no idea.

First, there is the know-how. You and the horses have to be capable. People don't know how to pack a horse. They put the packs on so uneven and get the horses' backs so sore. They don't see to it that the horse has food. "Oh well, he can do without food for a few days." They just don't care. What can you do? The horse has already been mistreated.

Like this Jeffreys that went up to the top of the mountain and fell in a crevasse. He wanted a horse to take him up on the Divide. Then he was going to come down through the Seven Lakes. I told him, "Now don't take that horse down through the Seven Lakes. The snowfields down there won't hold up a person, and the horses fall through and get all skinned up and get broken legs."

"I know how to handle a horse," he says.

Well, what did he do? When he came back the horse's legs were all blood. He'd taken the Seven Lakes route over the snowfields and the horse had fallen through. I couldn't use the horse for several months because it took that long for all the gouges from the rocks to heal up.

Besides know-how, then you have to be out in all kinds of conditions, favorable and unfavorable, rain or shine. You can be so cold you just wonder if you're going to live or not. Just sopping wet to the skin.

The horses have to be taken care of before you even think of giving yourself any care. Lots of people don't do that and that's why they don't have a business. Your horses come first.

Sometimes you sleep. Sometimes you don't. I've gone without a lot of sleep because I've been so cold and wet that I just could not sleep. Like up there on the Little Divide. I came from Hyak before it was added to Olympic National Park. I had taken in some hunters, and cutting back, I got caught in a regular blizzard. I got off my horse on top of the Little Divide and I tailed my pack horses to my riding horses and I *walked* all the way down to Sol Duc. About five miles. I was that cold!

Oh, I tell you it snowed! But lots of people will sit on the horse and shiver.

Boy, after that we had snow for a couple of days.

We have a lot of rain. When you're up in the mountains, sometimes you can have real bad wind, too, and thunder and lightning. I don't remember what year it was but once we had so much lightning! Oh, we really had it. I had told a group that I was booked up and that I could take them into Sol Duc Park a week later than they had wanted. If I had taken them on their original date, they would have all gotten electrocuted, because lightning hit the shelter where they were going to camp. We found a great big doe about three feet from the shelter with burned patches on her body. It burned the shelter completely.

It's a shame that the Park Service is burning the shelters. That's one of the worst things that can be done. Because I tell you the hikers can sometimes be caught, tired and wandering in a storm. How wonderful any little shelter is to get into.

It beats a tent. In a heavy rain a tent can collapse. Boy, I've seen people huddled together in some of these shelters!

I didn't carry a tent. Just slept out. For years I didn't even have a sleeping bag. I used a canvas tarp to keep the packs dry on the horses and I could cover myself up pretty good with one of those. I'd take an extra one along for my bed. I just lay it underneath my blanket. Then I put a couple of tarps on top of my blanket and partly covered my head. And if I slept, OK, and if I didn't, that was OK. 'Cause morning would come sooner or later. No worry about that. It will come.

If you are tired enough, you can sleep any place.

You always try to ride the same saddle horse that will obey all kinds of orders and will go ahead and take the lead. Lots of horses, if they are not accustomed to trails, you just can't get them across the bridges and different places. Once the Silver Spurs from Bremerton came up there and they couldn't get some of their horses across the bridge at Sol Duc Falls. Sometimes when the water hits the log down below in the falls, it forms a spray right over the bridge. Those horses were scared to death of that. Real nice saddle horses, but they wouldn't cross.

You have to train your horse and your horse has to get confidence. You have to be careful, for instance, not to get out on a real steep bank where your horse gets scared. The biggest danger is that your horse might back overboard with you.

Say you are in a bad place like the cliff on one side of Glacier Meadows. I tell you it's quite a job taking horses around there. But you never want to take and turn the horse around with his head towards the wall. Always out. Always out, because a horse can then look down and turn.

I might have yelled at a person to do it right if that person was dumb enough to try to back a horse around a steep place. But I tell you, a person just has to learn!

They used to always talk about city people. Well, I tell you I'd rather take a person that doesn't know the first thing about a horse if they'll follow directions. Now this Sandra Patton, we packed together for eleven years. She's a teacher and was born and raised there in Seattle. She helped me before and after she got married. I told Sandra, I says, "You follow directions and you won't have one bit of trouble." I said, "I'll show you exactly how to tie up a horse, how I want 'em tied up, and how we're going to pack everything." And I says, "I'll give you a horse. I'll give you Sparky. If you can manage him, you'll do alright. He'll try to manage you, but you just follow directions and you'll do alright and we'll get along."

She's a tall, slender girl and quite an athlete. To mount him was a job in itself but she could do it.

To this day I'll trust her with any horse. She knows how to pack just as well as I do.

HELEN PETERSON:
1962 WORLD'S FAIR
INDIAN VILLAGE HOSTESS
Neah Bay, WA
Born: 1905

We have had three grand expositions during the century of Washington statehood: the Seattle Alaska-Yukon-Pacific Exposition of 1909, the 1962 Seattle World's Fair, and the 1974 Spokane Expo. Well, let me add a fourth, the Vancouver, B.C. Expo 86 extravaganza to which almost everyone in Washington went and where there was a major Washington pavilion.

Helen Peterson is a Makah Indian who was a representative of the Makah Tribe at the 1962 Fair, most remembered today for the Space Needle and the Seattle Center. She reminded me that the goal of increased cross-cultural understanding is not easily achieved, even by expensive fairs.

Coming to know another person's culture requires a commitment which costs no money. It leaves no legacy of opera houses and manicured grounds.

As Helen Peterson says, "We have to understand each other more because we are a lot different. We think a lot different. I don't really think that the World's Fair helped in this kind of understanding."

I had a very happy childhood. Both my parents were Christians. My father used to interpret for our first missionary, Helen Clark, after whom I was named. My father used to read to us from the Bible, making it so easy to understand and so beautiful. Through

Helen and
Susan
Peterson.

this I grew up with a love for reading. My father also had a wonderful library with a lot of good books with good illustrations. We had a beautiful and happy home.

Both my parents followed their Indian traditions because they were both from prominent chieftain families and they had certain cultural responsibilities. Nevertheless, they worked together to get ahead in the white man's culture and customs.

As a child I was very secure, being exposed to both cultures, and so I was at ease in both of them. I feel that the Christian and Indian training from my grandmother, Maryann, and from other relatives was of tremendous influence. I remember my grandparents as well-bred, with great personal stature, self-respect, and integrity.

My great-grandmother was a chief's daughter at Port Renfrew. She came to Neah Bay to marry Chief Claplanhoo to make peace with the Makahs here because they were always fighting.

My grandfather on my mother's side, James Claplanhoo, married my grandmother, Maryann George Claplanhoo. They had six children. My mother, Minnie Claplanhoo, was the oldest of those six children. She and my father married around 1886.

My father, Chestoque Peterson, was the son of Chief Peter and Che-chahtl-quah-ukts. His mother's name means "One That Wears the Dentalium." My father was a teacher in the local school. He owned three or four sealing schooners which he operated in the Bering Sea. He was a building contractor for the Presbyterian church and for the government houses. In 1902 he owned his own store. Later he had his own fishing boat. He and his son were lost at sea in April 1920.

If I had it to do all over, I would work at the World's Fair again. I enjoyed every bit of it. We could dance. We could sing. I showed people how to make necklaces out of olive shells. The Spanish called it olivilla. I guess it was always used to decorate our Indian necklaces. Olive shells were used for trade a lot.

I like to meet people. I like people.

Of course, at the World's Fair, people asked funny questions. We had our blanket on display on a railing and one woman said, "Oh, are you airing your blankets out?" I think that most questions that were asked were kind of nonsense questions.

I always wished that we could make the people understand Indians more because we are all not alike.

I have heard a lot of people say that they are tired of the Indians' rights to this and that. I say, "Look here. You haven't had to fight for your rights. We have had to fight for our rights all the way." We had to spend a lot of our money to get what we have left.

We spent a lot of money to hold Ozette. They were going to take that away from us. We had to go to court for it. And we had to fight for Hoko so that we could continue to fish in the Hoko River. That was our fishing place.

For a lot of things we have to go to court and fight for it. Like my father. At one time they said that this reservation was a rich place. People used to say the Makahs had gold in their pockets because when they would go to the Bering Sea and get seals in their schooners, they made a lot of money. But the government made them stop. They said that we were going to get some money because that is how our people had been making their money. But we didn't have it in writing. Two of my father's schooners were in the Bering Sea when the government put an end to that fishery. The revenue cutters seized one of my father's schooners, but his fast boat, the Columbia, sailed away and they couldn't catch it. My father was in a case against the government for our schooner, but it took years and years before we won it. We had to spend a lot of money on lawyers.

Both my mother and father were taught by their parents to further their education and to know as much or more than the white people. Their byword was, "This is the way the white people do it." So my father taught school and had a store. And he used to go to the Bering Sea to hunt seals in his schooners.

But it is a weird thing to say: to do something because the white people do it that way. That used to irritate my grandnephew a lot, because he didn't think that the white people's way was the only way. I have found that out, too, for myself. I pick out the best of what the white people do and the best of our culture.

We have to understand each other more because we are a lot different. We think a lot different. I don't really think that the World's Fair helped in this kind of understanding.

People have to understand more of the things that we get. *They* are not giving it to us. It is our right! We gave away a lot of land. Our old people when they signed their treaty, they said, "We want education for our children. We want doctors. And we want to fish and hunt wherever we have always hunted. And you can have the land."

To increase the understanding between groups, they should talk together and see what our thoughts are. And try to iron things out somehow or another.

I have many very true white friends. A lot of white people do understand Indians. But there are a lot of them that don't.

Right now there is a lot of hard feelings about fishing. One of our chiefs, my grandfather's brother, said, "I am not going to sign that treaty because the white people will never keep their word."

Well, it is so now that I am afraid of what is going to happen if we don't all get together, the friends of the Makahs, and see that we don't lose out.

At the World's Fair, I gave away a lot of things that I made. The most enjoyable thing for us is when we have something to give. I don't know why we enjoy giving. It has always been that that is what Indians love to do. To give away.

My mother and grandmother always loved to give something.

Roy Rogers was at the World's Fair and we gave him a paddle.

I will tell you a funny incident. My cousin Susan Johnson and my sister Mabel Robertson were supposed to entertain Roy Rogers and Dale Evans and dance for their group. So my sister said, "Susan and I will sing and you will dance."

So I put on the wolf mask and a cape to dance. Roy Rogers was sitting there. I thought, "Oh, I am going to dance like a boy and he will not be able to tell the difference." I had watched my nephew learning how to dance. So I got out there like he always did, and my sister and my cousin laughed. They just laughed away, because there is a certain way that a lady is supposed to dance. Always slow and kind of graceful. But a boy dances different. On his toes more and faster, and with more verve and energy. So my sister and my cousin had a hard time trying to straighten their faces.

Roy Rogers didn't know what the joke was about.

The Indian Village was a separate part of the World's Fair. One corner was fenced off where we had an exhibit of Makah things. Other people had exhibits at the Indian Village too, and I liked to meet and talk with them.

The Warm Springs, Oregon people had an exhibit of a wooden horse with all its beaded blankets, decorated saddle, and everything that they use for parades. The Warm Springs people used to keep all their valuable costumes in an old, old trunk. One time the Indian Village got robbed. They even took the horse and threw it over the fence. But they overlooked that old trunk. I guess they didn't think it had anything valuable in it.

We Makahs used to get together with other tribes in their tepees. One time a Warm Springs woman had a relative in Oregon, a young boy, who was kicked by a horse and killed instantly. And she gathered us all together in her tepee where she told us about her relative and about his death. She gave each one of us something to remember that boy with. I got a Scottish shawl with fringe all the way around it. I wear it a lot, it's so light and soft and warm. I prize it very much.

My sister went with that woman to her country, to Warm

Springs, and she got in on a ceremony that they have after the death of somebody that they love. My sister had met the woman during the Fair, but it is our custom to comfort someone in sorrow. We do whatever we can to help. We don't leave any person standing alone with their troubles, sorrows, or losses. We share whatever we have in time or resources without counting the cost.

I remember we went to the World's Fair in April. The very opening of it was a thrilling moment because they let loose a lot of balloons. Beautiful! The sky was just full of these balloons of different colors. The first day was very special. There were Germans on a trapeze wire walking across the Center. And we were all invited to have breakfast at the Space Needle.

Everything there was interesting. Everything imaginable was represented from different countries. But I enjoyed the Hawaiian Pavilion best because I have always wanted to go to Hawaii. We could go into any place free if we had on our Indian costumes. I went to the Hawaiian Pavilion a lot.

I liked to taste the different foreign dishes like Mexican dishes, Japanese food. I always went to eat a different kind of food every time at the special building for foods. Spanish, Mexican, Japanese, Chinese food. Or I would have hot scones with jelly inside or oyster soup.

I spent almost a year in Seattle. But we could tell that the Indian Village was going broke because we had a hard time cashing our wage checks. My sister suspected that something was wrong. She said, "We had better get home before the Indian Village goes bankrupt."

So we did. And we weren't home very long when we found out that it did go bankrupt.

I had lived in a city before. I had a sister that was married in Ballard. She married a Swede and she had little ones very close together, so my mother sent me over there to help her with her children. I guess I spent two or three years with her around 1924, going to school in Seattle.

I enjoyed Ballard because I never came across any prejudice there, because those Norwegian and Swedish fishermen were used to native people in Alaska. I enjoyed the time I lived in Ballard. I got acquainted with a Swedish girl named Ellen Lund. She and I went everywhere together. My brother-in-law belonged to the Eagles and we would go to the Eagles' hall and play cards and dance. I can truthfully say that I never encountered any prejudice in Ballard.

I learned their dancing, the Swedish dances. I liked those fast dances, especially the hambo. And the Swedish waltz, too. I could really dance their own dances better than they could. I enjoyed every bit of it.

It was nice to spend 1962 at the World's Fair because it was a treat for us to be in the city where we could go on the monorail and get down to the city and shop. Or we would have dinner in downtown.

We stayed with a relative at Crown Hill, so every night we would walk across from our Village to the other end of the fairgrounds to take our bus. I wasn't used to walking. I would be so tired! But every night it was easier for me to walk.

One time as we were going home, we heard, "Plunk! Plunk!" Somebody had fallen into that fountain. He hadn't seen it and had walked right in. We didn't stop. We couldn't see anything. But we heard this person sitting in the fountain, laughing.

GORDON "THE HORSE HEAVEN KID" POSTON: FOURTEEN-YEAR-OLD RUNAWAY

Spokane, WA

Born: 1898

In recent years urban Washingtonians have experienced many dramas of missing children and runaway kids. Gordon Poston's adventures in escaping from his father's onion patch in 1912 take us back to a different type of family crisis.

Young Gordon's father was a tall, no-nonsense figure from Quebec, whose Spokane store (where the Davenport Hotel is now) had gone broke when the bookkeeper absconded with the assets. Income from a second store in the small railroad town of Cliffs was augmented with the ranch work of the Poston sons. Gordon Poston finally ran away from that stoop labor at the age of fourteen and enjoyed the open air life of a Columbia River cowboy. During his summer on the range he helped to round up wild horses for World War I at Moses Lake.

That summer chasing bands of cayuses at Moses Lake and Othello was followed by high school at Pendleton, Oregon, where Gordon's sister was a teacher. In 1913 he was a grandstand usher, a race horse exerciser, and a trick mule rider at the Pendleton Roundup. A successful ranching career followed.

Gordon is proud of making a polo pony out of Cyclone, a bucking horse that had bucked off a 1920s Pendleton champion. Cyclone joined Gordon on Spokane's first polo team in 1927.

In the early 1950s the former runaway had accumulated over twenty thousand acres of grazing and wheat land, thirty-five miles south of Lewiston, Idaho up the Snake River. The Grand Coulee Dam's newly available water opened up rich opportunities. He sold his ranches and co-founded what became the then-largest irrigation pipe company in the United States.

Gordon Poston's father, Albert "A.H." Poston used to say, "Get out and do something. Don't just sit there. Do something even if it's wrong." Gordon's success at cowboying, ranching, and manufacturing irrigation equipment shows that he learned that lesson well.

He also learned how to shoot. In World War I, training at Fort Lewis, an officer told Private Poston,

"Can't figure you out, kid. You make a better score of rapid fire standing up than you do laying with your gun over a sandbag."

I said, "Well, where I come from, you don't crawl around on your belly in the cactus. You stand up to shoot grouse and running jackrabbits."

The captain said, "When you get over to France, you'll be glad to be behind the sandbag."

But, you know, the Kaiser heard I was coming and he quit!

It was my last year in grade school and Dad had a farm store down there in Cliffs, on the Columbia River. Dad said, "Well, we made pretty good money on the onions last year." He raised those onions and sold them at his Cliffs Mercantile. He said, "We will put in twice as many this year."

And I said, "Who's going to take care of them?"

He said, "You did a good job last year. You can do it again this year."

Well, my brothers were both bigger than I was and they did the haying and the heavier work. All the tools I had was a rake and a hoe and my fingers. I had to crawl up and down these rows of onions, and it got as hot as one hundred fourteen in the shade and there is no shade in an onion patch.

I didn't say anything.

I must have been about fourteen. I was in the eighth grade. I

Gordon Poston riding
Golden Slippers, 1935.

didn't say anything because Dad was six feet four and I didn't
argue with him. He was very strict. *Very strict!*

So school was out in a few days and I said to my brother—we
were milking cows after supper, and I said, "I am leaving tonight."

And he said, "You are? Where the hell are you going?"

And I said, "I don't know, but there's something better in this
world than weeding onions by hand." I said, "Don't say anything
to the folks until tomorrow morning and then you can tell them
that I am gone."

So that night after about ten, everybody had gone to bed. I went
into the pantry. In those days we had a pantry instead of a refriger-
ator. I took a flour sack and I went in and I got some bread and
some cheese and a little cold meat. And I got a blanket off the bed,
and I had an Indian pony that I had bought from the Indians for
five dollars and broke. I had no saddle. I got on my pony, it was
moonlight, and I rode all night and all the next day. I was afraid
Dad would come after me.

That evening I stopped at a farmhouse. I did a few chores and
they gave me supper and let me sleep there and have breakfast.
Then I went up the Columbia River towards Pasco, only I didn't
go into Pasco. I went up Horse Heaven Hills. That's what it was
called in those days. Horse Heaven Hills. It was all open range.
There weren't any ranches at all up there then.

I knew which way to go there because we had run horses on the Horse Heaven Hills and I knew that country pretty well. My idea was to get away from home fast, so I rode east and north on the Horse Heaven Hills and I crossed the Columbia River at North Pasco.

I had no money, but the ferryman said that if I would wait until a team came along, he would cross me for nothing. So he let me cross on his old-fashioned scow, pushed by a gasoline launch. After I got across the river, I relaxed when I realized that I had gotten away from Father.

I rode up into the Saddle Mountain wildlife range. I continued until about moonlight to put more distance between me and home. Finally I tethered my pony out and slept without any supper. Along about daylight a coyote howled and I came standing up, straight up. I got on my pony and I rode farther north through the Saddle Mountain hills west of the Columbia River.

About six that morning, I was getting up near Vantage Ferry, two to four miles above where the I-90 bridge is now. But I was up in the hills and I saw a fella rounding up saddle horses. I went over and I asked him for a job and he said, "I'm not the boss." He said, "Come on into camp and talk to the boss."

So we went on up above Vantage Ferry about five miles, up into that canyon. If I had a map I could show ya. There was a trail along the river and we followed it into camp in that canyon. There had never been automobiles yet in that part of the country.

The boss, we called him Chuck, said, "Have you had your breakfast?"

I said, "No." I didn't tell him I hadn't had any lunch or dinner either.

"Sit down," he says. "Sit down and have something to eat."

So I put away a stack of hotcakes and bacon and eggs and I told him I wanted a job.

And he says, "Can you ride?"

I said, "Sure, I can ride anything." (I thought I could, anyhow.)

So he said, "Take that saddle horse and bust him out through the sagebrush there."

So I did.

And he says, "I will give you a job herding saddle horses."

Now he was rounding up wild horses for the First World War,

and he would go clear up to Moses Lake, starting out about six in the morning with, let's see, five riders. Sometimes more. At Moses Lake they waited for wild horses to come in to drink. If they took after the horses before the horses had had a drink, the horses could outrun them.

The wild horses, they come in about every other day and they'd run out into Moses Lake or Crab Creek and you could just see 'em take on the brown water. Then they couldn't run near as fast. Chuck said he'd wait until a band or two would come in and then he and his riders would take after them and drive them down twenty or twenty-five miles to where he had corrals and a spring, about five miles up from Vantage Ferry in that canyon.

Some of the horses had Indian brands on them and some were branded by white men. But a lot of them weren't branded at all.

Each rider had two or three saddle horses to ride, because it was about a fifty-mile round trip up to Moses Lake and back. Each day a man would ride a fresh horse. My job was to herd all those saddle horses.

After I had been doing that for about a week, one of the riders got sick, so the boss asked me if I had ever chased wild horses. I said, "Yes, my brother and I rounded up Dad's horses and the neighbors' horses."

So he said, "Come on," and he put me on a good horse.

There were five riders, one fellow behind and two on each side of a band of cayuses. We'd have about fifty head at a run. We'd come across Frenchman Hills near where George, Washington is now. Because I only weighed seventy-five pounds, it was my job to ride in the lead and to keep them from going up over the hill, 'cause if they got up over the hill, they could outrun you going downhill, but they couldn't along on the level. That was my job. I rode in the lead on the Frenchman Hills.

I just rode beside the leaders and yelled and waved at them and headed them down. But as my horse was galloping along at full speed, he fell. You take a range-raised horse, they won't step in a badger hole. But sometimes a badger plays a dirty trick on you. He digs down after a squirrel and then he will dig along underneath about a foot underground.

Well, I was going along there at a pretty good gallop and my horse broke through a badger burrow and fell with me. I rolled away. It didn't hurt me. My horse got up and he was dragging his front leg because it was sprained.

The boss was coming along behind me and he said, "Get your saddle off, Kid." So I pulled my saddle off and he roped a wild one. One of the other boys front-footed it, and they threw it, and they put my saddle on and my hackamore.

And now the boss says, "It's ten miles to camp. Kid, are you going to ride or walk?"

I said, "Let him up. I'm going to ride." I pulled down my hat and I took a grip on the saddle horn and they let the horse go.

I learned that a wild horse don't buck near as hard as a horse that has been ridden a few times and bucked, like at Pandleton Roundup or something like that. I stayed with him and the men chased him along with the rest of the bunch. If I'd sit still, he wouldn't buck. But if I'd raise my hand to pull my hat down or move my legs or anything like that, why he would buck a little bit. But he couldn't buck very hard when he was running in a bunch like that.

They ran me into the corral and pulled me off and I was alright.

I rode with them all summer and in September he says, "Well, Kid. . . ." They called me "The Horse Heaven Kid." I hadn't told them what my name was and they hadn't asked me. I was "The Horse Heaven Kid." So he said, "Well, Kid, it's time for school. Better go home." He said, "Would you like a horse?"

I said, "Sure."

"Well, take your pick." I was getting a dollar a day wages and board. He said, "Take your pick."

So, like a kid, I picked out a pinto, a pretty good-sized pinto.

There was a fellow that was half Indian. I think his name was Joe. The boss says, "I'll have Joe break him for you."

I said, "Oh, I can ride."

"No," he says, "He breaks mine." So Joe broke it for me.

They put me up a sack of lunch and I had my new horse. Oh, he'd gotten me a ten-dollar saddle from over at Ellensburg. So I started home riding my pinto with the new saddle and leading my little old cayuse.

I timed it about right. I was kinda afraid of Dad, but I timed it at about supper time.

In those days, all the country homes had a porch and I rode to within twenty feet and whistled, and my sister came out and called to Mother, "Gordon's home." And Dad walked out with a cane. He'd busted his leg, but I stayed on my horse 'cause I knew I could outrun him on horseback and I couldn't on foot. I'd tried it before.

Dad looked at me and said, "Well, son, that's a pretty good-looking outfit you got there. You better come in and have some supper. Put your horse in the barn." He was very strict. We always had to take care of our horse first.

"Put your horse in the barn and come in and have some supper."

So I did.

Anyhow, I went to school at Pendleton, Oregon, and the next year we didn't raise onions.

ELLEN RAINEY:

COLLEGE GRADUATE

Lester, WA

Born: 1919

Washington is such a beautiful state that it would be easy to forget that many people here do not have beautiful lives. Ellen Rainey grew up as a persecuted minority, a victim of a forgotten kind of discrimination. Almost all of her adult life was spent in or near logging camps in the Lester, Washington area of extreme southeast King County. Lester was a railroad and logging town in the city of Tacoma's watershed, and gradually the City of Destiny bought out almost all of the Lesterites. When I first visited Ellen Rainey there in 1978, she was the sheriff because she had inherited the job from her deceased husband, Roscoe. But she was also the postmaster of her living room post office and front gate mailbox. Those duties did not keep her from also running the town library and teaching crafts at the Lester school. But most of all she was the soul of vanishing Lester.

My visits to the isolated Green River Valley town were permitted by the Tacoma authorities because I needed to pass through the watershed to meet a local person. When the metal gate swung open at the lower end of the Depression-era CCC road, I felt that I was entering alien territory.

Fortunately, there was nothing standoffish about Ellen Rainey, though she was suspicious, she said, of college graduates. "Sure I went to college," she said, "the college of hard knocks. Darn tootin!"

Ellen was sad because her husband Roscoe had died and because she knew she was fighting a losing battle against Tacoma's take-over. She knew that Lester would soon become a ghost town and that its chances were "not worth a whoop in hell." She knew that the Scott Paper logging camp, the last or next to last old-fashioned bunkhouse-style camp in the state, was about to close. She knew that one by one her friends and neighbors were dying or leaving for the outside. For instance, a man I knew named Joe Melch was later found dead and boiled in the valley's hot spring.

The lifeblood was draining away from Lester. The number of schoolchildren would soon fall below the number needed to keep the school going. The post office would close when the postmaster was gone.

In January 1979 when I had breakfast with her, I think Ellen Rainey may also have known that she was dying. She passed away March 11, 1985 of heart failure. But our January breakfast was a cheery occasion. Though outside my breath had steamed in the mountain air, inside I was warm and toasty from the heat of Ellen's wood cook stove. She bustled about fixing me a classic logger breakfast, the highpoint of which was three huge trout, borrowed on the sly from Tacoma's river.

In recent years the city of Tacoma finally succeeded in bulldozing the logging camp, the elementary school, and the remaining houses. The town of Lester has disappeared into history.

We've got bacon, hash browns, three trout, eggs, pancakes, toast, raspberry jam. I'm serving you on paper plates unless you want to wash dishes. To hell with the fancy bullshit around here. I can't go for it.

Damn. I broke the yolk. Oh hell, you don't like the yolk anyway. I'll bring you some fish. Some jam? Strawberry?

I don't get up until seven and then I piss and moan around here until noon.

My mother had a saying for everything. She'd say 'em in Swede or English. For instance, "If food drops, a lady friend is coming."

My father, Herman Manicke, and my mother, Hilda, homesteaded here in 1912.

Here, have some more of these trout. We used to fry the milk of the male trout. And one time we saved the eggs to make caviar, but our dog sucked every one of them up, just like a vacuum cleaner. [laughter]

My mother used to go out in the chicken coop and break an egg and suck it. Her parents and some of her sisters and brothers came from Sweden.

My father, Herman Manicke, was naturalized, from Germany. He and Mother (who was from Sweden) homesteaded at the hot springs in 1912. Back in the mountains there was a cave about as long as this kitchen. The water just boiled out like it came out of a fountain. There was a natural bench there where you could sit and let that water fall on your back.

Of course, in those days the farther back in the cave you went, the hotter the water got. It was one hundred thirty degrees Fahrenheit. Really hot!

They had a concrete abutment so that the water would be deeper and then they could drain it and clean it. But Tacoma blew that up. I have pictures of the porch outside the cave where there were benches to sit on. It really stayed hot!

My mother was one of the ones that was always making curtains out of old gunny sacks to put across the front. 'Cause women and men and everybody went down there for years. When the curtain was drawn, someone was there. When the curtain was threw back, you knew there was nobody in it.

When you came out, it was a courtesy to draw the curtain back. In those days people weren't like they are now. They had more thought and feeling for the neighbor than they do now. Now nobody thinks about anybody else.

In those days you didn't have to lock your door. Would you leave and not lock your door? No, I didn't think so. We never locked doors for weeks or months and nobody would bother a thing.

When I was growing up I was taught to respect other people's property and to keep my dirty little fingers off of it. And now people don't.

This is my honest opinion. I think that people don't care. Just so it don't bother them. They're so damned busy trying to get something better than what Mrs. Jones has and vice versa down the line. They are too worried about what their neighbors have. People are going nuts with a standard that they set.

It's a class distinction. Were there class distinctions in Lester? You're damn right there were class distinctions in Lester! Engineers were at the top. I remember the railroad superintendents here. And the bosses in the roundhouse. Three or four men. Night and afternoon and day foremen.

At a logging camp they have one superintendent and he is over all the foremen. He should know what the foremen are doing, how they are conducting themselves and so forth. If superintendents did that, it would save a lot of problems. But they don't care to know it. They've got their nose so far up in the air, up their ass, that they can't see, anyway. I remember some wife-swapping among the bosses. The way I found out about it was from two of their little teenage girls. The one, she didn't like the way her mother and father drank. And the other one said that her mother was going to run off with this other guy and that her dad was going to go with that man's wife. Sometimes that girl felt like she didn't want to go with either of her parents. But if she had to make a choice, she'd go with her dad.

So I talked to them a long time so that they didn't run away. That would have been awful, because kids raised up here and then all

238 • WHISTLEPUNKS AND GEODUCKS

of a sudden taking off and running away, I don't think they are as knowledgeable as a girl that grows up in those town schools. One of those girls went away from home really young. She wasn't through school yet. About sixteen. That's sad! They're still just babies to me at sixteen. They don't know what life is all about but they do it.

My childhood. . . . When I was born, I was so tiny that my father built an incubator of warmed bricks for me. They didn't expect me to live. We were all preemies except my youngest brother. He's the only one she carried full time and that's because she left home to live in the city and have Tony in a hospital where she had good care. All the rest of us, somebody scared out of her, I guess.

When I was little, most of my life was staying home. Even though I was born in 1919, there was still a terrible discrimination against anybody of German descent. My mother was not German, but my father was. Mother was discriminated against just as bad. So the best way to stay out of trouble was to hide the kids behind an eight-foot fence. I remember one old lady that used to sling coal at us and cuss us and call us nice names. "Huns" and whatnot. She'd chase us with a stick. Anything to scare us.

So my folks just put this barricade up. If we played out of it, we couldn't play with the white children. We had to go up in a field east of our home. We played there mostly by ourselves. We didn't mingle with the white kids till school started. My next to oldest brother, Dutch, kids beat him up so bad he couldn't go to school the first year. My folks were afraid he'd get killed.

I wasn't born yet, but that hatred stayed on in this valley a long, long time. I was born in '19. The war ended in '18. I still remember certain families that did all kinds of things to us.

That's about the size of my childhood. I'd never want to live it over again.

In the early days this country was all burned off. They just let the fires burn in those days. After the fires it was all domestic sheep up here. Sheepherders used to drive the sheep up here from Yakima or Ellensburg along the highways to trails over Williams Pass and Kelly Butte and onto Williams Basin, just the back side of the hills here, until they came down into Grass Mountain. It was a long ways. Then in the fall the sheep were loaded onto railroad cars at loading pens in Lester to go to market.

But the city of Tacoma stopped all that.

During the Thirties it was all railroading here. Then in 1946 Soundview Pulp started logging second growth for pulp. And Scott Paper came in.

My husband, Roscoe Rainey, was in the Wobblies. He fought for the unions. He was one of the first ones that proved that the logger did work in the wintertime. That was when the state wouldn't give loggers unemployment benefits because they said that loggers did not work during the winter. Roscoe happened to have saved his check stubs. Him and another fellow. So the union used those.

See, Roscoe used to be a ranger for the state. When that would close down in the fall he would go back to work in the woods in the wintertime. When he lived down around Buckley before he met me, he was drinking and fighting, just like all loggers. He did a lot of that. But he didn't get into half as much trouble after he met me. I had a calming influence on him.

We met when I worked in the logging camps. They were the best place to work. Them days you made more money just being a plain old waitress in a logging camp than you did in a restaurant. You made good money. That was after I had to quit work at Boeing's because of allergies and I went back to work in the logging camps.

When my two kids were growing up, Lester had a lot of kids in school. Almost all the social life was carried on up at the school. And still is to this day. You can't have liquor there, but the building is free gratis to you. The lights, warmth, and whatever it has to offer. If you wanted to have a party or a gathering, you could talk to Mr. Eaton and he'd check his schedule to see if it was a night that somebody else had already spoken for.

The school is a community center. They don't bar anybody. Anything within reason—if Joe Melch would expose himself they would call the police—you could do up there right in the school. It's used for the church and everything. If you want to have a movie, they have a projector. If you want to have a potluck, you can have that. Ladies Club. Scott Paper used the school. Election time. Lots of dances. And when Tacoma started condemning, Lester people used the school for fundraising affairs.

As far as I can remember, it's always been a good community town. But, of course, they had their cliques in the old days, too, even in Lester.

An engineer and a fireman wouldn't be as low as a greaser or an oiler or a call boy. See what I mean? The greaser or the oiler are all important to the jobs, but still the wage and the classification put them on a lower level. I mean they have just as much responsibility, because without them, say the oilers, that engine wouldn't run. The callers, if they didn't call the men, nobody would go to work. So who could you say is the most valuable?

Roscoe and I were wealthy people because we had a double-holer backhouse. One hole was for her and one hole was for him. No partition between the sides.

Why should there be?

Roscoe and I were sitting out there one time and this guy came by and handed a picture of his girlfriend in for me to look at. I passed it over to Roscoe so he could look at it, too.

What the hell! It was our toilet we were sittin' on. It wasn't my fault the damn fool fell in love. [laughter]

I still am sheriff and am in charge of the library. But they cut the library way down when the Scott Paper camp closed because there were not so many to check out books. At the school, I work as a teacher's aide and I keep their library up. I teach ceramic classes to adults on Tuesday nights. But mostly crafts to little kids. I hope somebody else can do the post office. I hate it!

The only job I don't do, I'm not a qualified teacher.

I don't have a college education, but I'm just as good as you are. Or do you think that you are better than me?

We are both struggling for a living. You may have a better education, but it don't put you any better than I am. Anybody can educate theirselves. You don't have to go to college to do that, except say a doctor. I wouldn't know how to cut your appendix out, but I don't believe that anybody is better than I am just because they've gone to college. So many young people today think you are far beneath them if you haven't gone to college, and I could kick 'em in the ass!

See, I get rubbed into that a lot because I work at school. Sure, I went to college. The college of hard knocks. Darn tootin!

Your guess is as good as mine what will become of Lester. Maybe they'll bring the oil line from Alaska through here. Wouldn't that be nice!

Here's a picture of me clear up on top of Huckleberry Mountain. I used to ramble all over. I still am doing it. I went up in the brush yesterday all by myself. Way up. I always do that and then I talk to myself. I tell myself what a great old bitch I am. I get up there and I just pat myself. Just really carry on something terrible.

Anybody came around, I'd scare them away. Especially a flatlander!

NEVA HOWARD ROBERTS:

NIGHTRIDERS VERSUS

CLAIMJUMPERS

Montesano, WA

Born: 1897

It wasn't long ago in western Washington that great wealth was available free or almost free from the government. All you had to do was file a claim.

Just imagine if you could do that today!

There were two types of claims relevant to the following story, homestead claims (requiring a certain value of annual improvements over a set period) and timber claims (requiring a nominal fee). In places like Pacific County, where the old growth forests were almost unimaginably rich, this giveaway attracted many happy homesteaders. It also attracted claimjumpers such as Mrs. Margaret Ross and her sons Earl (26) and Frank (24).

Neva Howard, later Neva Roberts, is long-retired from farm life, but she still maintains a magnificent garden (including forty-five "triple hills of corn") at her home at Montesano, Washington. As a child, her mother's hard work was her model. "She was so good, long-suffering, and never knew that she had it rough," says Neva. "Washing to do by hand and get it dried in the house. Great big family. There were ten of us, including two babies that died."

This is a story about claimjumpers, but it was actually much more common for claimholders to lose their lands because the Northern Pacific Railroad finally persuaded Congress to allow it to trade equal amounts of desert land for valuable timbered properties.

My parents always referred to that Lieu Land Act as the Lieu Land Fraud. The railroad could come and select the finest timber claims and trade even-up for desert land that nobody wanted at all. We knew lots of people that lost their timber claims or homesteads. Next to our place was the Walker place. Their house was just a half a mile from ours. They had one of the best-improved places in the whole valley. They had built a four-room log house and they had built a good-sized barn at some expense, chicken house, hog pens, and a bearing orchard that I can remember. (Mrs. Walker was with my mother when I was born.) They put in ten years of hard work on the place. When the railroad men came there and nailed the script up on the door saying that was preempted, that they had taken it in lieu of other land, the Walkers believed them. It looked so official and what they said looked so true. They moved out and never told anybody where they were going. It could have been contested.

Many timber claims settlers lost their claims to the railroad company, which immediately sold out to Weyerhaeuser. That's how Weyerhaeuser got its start.

However, in the following story the good ranchers outwit the bad claimjumpers. The nightriders run the baddies out of the county and eventually Mrs. Vanderpool receives the patent to her land.

Because so much of the story involves young Neva and her neighbor Claude Vanderpool, I was hoping that the story would end with their marriage. However, it was Neva's sister Lena who married Claude in 1916. (Claude was to be a druggist in Montesano for over thirty years.) Neva herself married Earl Roberts of Salem, Oregon in 1915, when she was eighteen. In 1923 she moved back with her husband to her family's ranch and farmed there for forty years.

Neva Roberts's life was always that of a traditional Washington farm woman except for that one night, January 8, 1914 when she became a Pacific County heroine.

I never thought of such a thing as women being involved as nightriders. But it was pitch black dark when I rode down from Mrs. Vanderpool's cabin to alert everyone. It was so dark that you couldn't see a thing. The horse was trying to keep out of the muddy trail and he scraped me real bad on the cut-off end of a log. Skirting around the edge of a mud hole he crushed me between the saddle and the end of that log. I was a nightrider when I rode that horse down home that night!

I was born in Brooklyn on North River. Did you ever hear of North River? It comes into Willapa Bay from the north.

My parents were homesteaders. They came there in January of 1895 because my father was interested in timber. In fact, he owned a sawmill in California. He lost a leg in his own mill when he was only twenty-nine. It didn't make a cripple of him, although that leg was always stiff because he had lost it at the knee.

My dad had a good claim, with seven million board feet of marketable timber on it. That doesn't count downed cedar or hardwoods such as maple. Or even hemlock in those days.

After our place was all proved up on we had the government patent which is the government deed to it. A half mile away another place had been surveyed and became available to a homestead or a timber claim. A Mrs. Vanderpool moved there and had a good cabin built. Three rooms plus a cellar or basement. It was good for a cabin.

Three years later she had made all of the necessary improvements, her son had cleared quite a lot of land, but she had not been on the land long enough to get her patent deed. She went away to work, which you are allowed to do just as long as you spend the required amount of time on your claim. While she was away at work, her claim was jumped.

Late one evening, we saw a wagonload of household goods go by our place and we knew that somebody's claim was being jumped.

Our neighbor Mr. Mike Hanrahan, who was also a claimholder, followed the wagon, keeping out of sight, and saw it turn in at the Vanderpool place. So he hurried up to Mr. Al Bradley, who had been more or less of a caretaker for Mrs. Vanderpool.

Mr. Bradley came down early the next morning and found that the Rosses had knocked the hasp off the back door of Mrs. Vanderpool's cabin and had laid two mattresses in there. And the mother and two grown sons were in there sleeping!

Neva
Roberts

A 1915 photo of the alleged nightriders of Brooklyn. *Standing from left to right:*
Earl Timmons, Joe Axford, Virgil Dolan, Homer Blaine, John Norman
Howard (Neva's father), and Claude Vanderpool. *Front row:* Enoch Dillard
(Neva's brother-in-law), Trent Tidwell, Ernest Burke, Walter Burke, and
Ralph Howard (Neva's brother).

Well, Mr. Bradley was a gentle old soul. He wouldn't make trouble for anybody. But he was outraged. He said, "I can't keep you from jumping her claim but, by golly, you can't stay in her place while you're doing it."

It was midsummer and that day he worked for my dad in the hay. He went home when it was getting dusk. A couple of people jumped out of the brush and knocked him down and beat him awfully bad. Of course, we all knew who it was. Nobody else it could be but those two that he had antagonized that morning.

They beat him so bad that he couldn't drag himself up to the Vanderpool's. By that time the Vanderpools had been called and they were back at their cabin. But they didn't know that Mr. Bradley had been attacked.

The next morning Claude Vanderpool found Mr. Bradley lying on the trail. I saw him two days after. His face looked just like a plum. He was cut through on the eyebrows and below the eyes. The whole face was battered up.

But he hadn't seen the Rosses. He couldn't identify them.

Claude got Mr. Bradley up to his house and took care of him there. Mr. Bradley was so badly beaten that he was in bed about a week before he was able to sit up at all. Then the Rosses commenced making themselves very obnoxious to Mrs. Vanderpool. Throwing wood against her house and all sorts of things like that.

About Christmastime Mrs. Vanderpool was sick in bed and her twenty-year-old son Claude rode through a storm and swam his horse across the rivers to go to South Bend to ask the courts for a restraining order. The Rosses had been very obnoxious. If Mrs. Vanderpool went outside to work, they would have target practice over her head. They let a big log roll down against her house and startle her real badly. Anything to be annoying. But the court considered it a neighborhood quarrel and wouldn't do anything about it.

We heard a story later that Mrs. Martin in Aberdeen who had been a friend of Mrs. Vanderpool's had encouraged the Rosses to locate on the Vanderpool place as claimjumpers. The Rosses came from Aberdeen. They were from South Dakota or Nebraska. Mrs. Martin had the best timber claim in western Washington. It had sixteen million board feet of timber! I've seen the cruise on it, right from those who cruised the place. Sixteen million board feet! (My dad had a good claim but it only had seven million.)

It is speculation about Mrs. Martin sending the Rosses. That's a side story in itself. We guessed that she and Mrs. Vanderpool had had some difficulty and so she sent this other woman to jump Mrs. Vanderpool's claim.

There was some claimjumping back then, but it was mostly the lumber company preempting our claims through the Lieu Land Act. You had to stay on your land six or seven years to get your deed.

Mrs. Vanderpool's claim was a quarter section, one hundred sixty acres, the usual size.

Neither Mrs. Vanderpool nor Mrs. Ross had husbands. A woman couldn't take a claim in her own name so I think they were conveniently divorced. I know Mrs. Martin was.

Anyway, the Rosses immediately built a cabin. Just a little nine by twelve room. And an attic above where the sons could sleep. They used the land which Mrs. Vanderpool's son had laboriously cleared for a raspberry patch. They just preempted the place and used it for themselves.

We didn't like the Rosses and we were all angry at them but we were unable to do anything about it. We all called Mrs. Ross a hellcat, but not to her face.

Claude didn't have any luck at all appealing to the Pacific County court to restrain the Rosses and when he got back his mother was quite ill. But she wouldn't leave the place, because she said, "That's just what they are trying to get me to do." They were throwing chunks against the house and shooting over her head. Things like that.

So she stayed right there and one of us Howards, there was a big lot of us, you know, we would go up every day and relieve the one who was up there and stay overnight. Mother went and stayed sometimes. My sister Lena was out of high school so she would stay more than any of us.

One evening about the eighth of January, I was making myself a sandwich and getting ready to take the mail up and stay overnight. Mother had just come back from spending twenty-four hours up there. And she said, "Oh Neva, I hate to have you go.

Those awful Ross boys are cutting on that big tree on the steep hill above the house and every little while they yell 'timber.' And you never know whether they are faking it or if it really will come down."

Earl Ross was twenty-six and Frank Ross was twenty-four. They had that big tree undercut as if to fall away somewhat but since it was right above the house, it was a worry.

That evening about seven, I had cooked some supper for Claude and Mrs. Vanderpool, and had washed the dishes. Mrs. Vanderpool was in bed. Then we heard the wedging. A steel sledgehammer striking a steel wedge to direct the fall of that enormous tree.

Claude said, "By golly, I'm going to go up and see what they are up to."

It had already been dark for two or three hours and Claude had just gotten up to get a lantern. He didn't have it lighted yet and we heard the tree breaking. They were still wedging and down came the tree. What a thundering and crashing and the tree all breaking to pieces!

Naturally we thought, "This is it."

Part of it came through the roof. The ceiling was sagging down. Branches came into the room, and one of them knocked over a kerosene lamp that was on the table with the day's paper that I had brought up. The lantern set the papers afire.

There wasn't anything to do but just grab up everything, lamp and all, in this heavy cover that was on the table. I just took it up by the corners and ran out the door and gave it a little toss down the hill away from the house. Then back to the house to see if Mrs. Vanderpool was all right.

Her bed was in the living room. For a cabin, it had a rather large living room. Her bed was in the corner. She was real sick with a heart condition, even though she was probably not yet even forty years old. She was married real young and Claude had been born when she was sixteen.

They say that kinetic force caused that tree to break. It was standing high, but the slope was so steep that it gained a terrific force in falling and pulled itself apart. After it passed ninety degrees there was a terrific pull on the fibers in the tree. It broke into eleven pieces. There were nine big pieces of that tree scattered around the cabin. There was about a thirty-five-foot tip that went through the roof. There was a big trunk that lay on the hillside and pushed the side of Mrs. Vanderpool's cabin in. Tipped her china closet over with all of her nice things in it. The tree angled, or it would have gone right across Mrs. Vanderpool's bed. It would have if it hadn't broken. It would have went directly across her bed.

The Rosses couldn't have planned it that good.

I was right there. I remember both of us running towards Mrs. Vanderpool. Then I saw the table was on fire and I stopped and grabbed the things off that. When I came back in, the crashing had ended and Mrs. Vanderpool was lying in bed, moaning and moaning so we knew she wasn't injured but was terribly, awfully shocked. She had quite a bad heart condition.

Claude went down to saddle his horse so that I could ride down and tell my folks. It was pitch dark. He came up with a lantern and he said, "Neva, I want you to see something." I went down with him to the barn which was only a little way down the hill. A hundred feet maybe. That tree tip that had gone through the house's ceiling had also gone through the corner of the barn and had just barely missed the horse. It took the corner of the barn out, flew on down the hill, and stuck into the canyon as we saw later.

That Douglas fir was six feet across the stump the largest way. A little less the smallest way. That's a big tree! The sheriff came and they made a map right on the stump to show where Mrs. Vanderpool's house was. The Ross's had wedged it directly onto the house. They had used a crosscut saw. They put an undercut in first and that indicates where it is to fall. Then they sawed it with a saw. They had worked on it about three nights until it finally came down. They had worked at it after dark.

The Rosses purposely did it but we knew the court wasn't going to do anything about it.

Nobody went to the Ross's directly about it that day. But that next night, January 9, many local farmers went up there with bandannas tied across their faces. They went up there and fired guns into the air. Scared the dickens out of the Rosses. I don't know what time of night but they had apparently gone to bed.

The farmers ordered the Rosses to come out. Gee, with their guilty consciences, they didn't know what was going to happen.

They were terribly frightened. The farmers herded the mother and boys off down the road. They had an extra horse with them for Mrs. Ross to ride, because after all, she was a woman.

When they got down to our place, they banged on the wall and with masks still on ordered my dad to come out. Great surprise! Ordered him to come out and hitch up a team and put a mattress in the wagon for Mrs. Ross and take them down over the county line. Because it was a cold night (it wasn't freezing, but it was cold), they said, "Could you get some wool socks and wool gloves for Mrs. Ross?" We couldn't find any wool gloves but found another pair of wool socks that she could put on her hands, a cover, and a pillow to make her as comfortable as possible.

The masked riders took the Rosses clear down to the McCormick place which was about seven miles from our place. That took quite awhile, at night with a work team and wagon on dirt roads and these masked men riding along with these Ross boys.

My dad, of course, knew all the voices. He said that one of them took a loop off his saddle at the bridge. It had an arched metal over it, you know, the inner county bridge at Brooklyn. He just said, kind of unwinding this rope, "I guess this is as good a place as any."

The Ross boys commenced to beg for dear life. The riders let them believe for a while that they were going to hang.

But the farmers drove the Rosses out of Pacific County and left them at Mrs. McCormick's place. They said to her, "We brought you a friend." Mrs. McCormick didn't know a thing about what was going on. She lived seven or eight miles from us and had been friendly with Mrs. Martin, who was hand in glove with Mrs. Ross. Anyway we considered her friendly to the Rosses so that is where they took them.

Then the farmers turned around and came back home.

The Rosses later told the sheriff that there were nine riders, which was probably true. But they didn't know who it had been because they hadn't met people in the community at all. So the Rosses just had *everybody* arrested.

The Rosses claimed that they could recognize everyone because it had been bright moonlight. We had good lawyers who weren't going to let that go by. All they did was produce an almanac and show that it had been just as absolutely dark as it could be.

The Rosses had a hard time identifying anybody, but they brought them through court after court on everything they could think of. It was a terrific expense for us. The Rosses were paid for all their trips and their witnessing because they were witnesses for the county, the state, and the nation.

The last trial was at our federal courthouse in Tacoma. None of the accused went on the stand themselves. They entered a plea of not guilty and it was up to the Rosses to prove their charges. I and the other family members testified that as far as we knew our husbands and brothers had been home safe in bed.

The Rosses couldn't prove anything.

[The *Tacoma Daily News* of December 23, 1916 declared, "Night-riders Not Guilty. North River Ranchers Win. On All Four Counts Jurors Clear Twelve Men Accused of Conspiracy . . . Wives of Defendants Visibly Affected and Announce That They Will Speed Home at Once."]

Our judge was Aaron Cushman. In private, he put his arms around my brothers' shoulders and he said, "You boys go home now and behave yourselves. I want to tell you that we couldn't have found a jury in the state of Washington to convict you after they heard the whole story."

BABE RUSSELL:
HORSE PACKER
Entiat, WA
Born: 1913

Babe Russell's father had a great influence on his son even though he died before Babe had a chance to know him. The elder Russell, a horse logger, had been a horse packer when the Entiat River country was being resurveyed in 1913 and 1915. Babe grew up around horse packing and what he couldn't learn from old-timers, he figured out for himself.

The pack string is one of the most romantic parts of the Old West for onlookers, but for the wrangler whose hours are long and tiring the reward has to come not so much from image as from self-identity.

Although with the creation of artificially-restricted wildernesses horse packing has enjoyed something of a resurgence lately, they don't make packers like Babe Russell anymore. Babe grew up at a time when pack strings were still *the* way to get things into the backcountry. He grew up, too, with a set of attitudes about work, horses, bureaucrats, and game laws that are no longer in fashion. His answer to the disappearance of plentiful game is to hold an open season hunt on Game Department officials, the rascals whom he holds accountable. And although the old-time Forest Service men, according to Babe, had some common sense, the new breed are likely to spend all their time riding around in pick-ups, letting little lightning strikes get out of control and flare up into monster fires, like the Entiat burn of 1970.

Horses were Babe's great love, whether he was packing construction materials up to a mountaintop lookout cabin or trailing dudes into the backcountry for an autumn hunt. For Babe, the

horse was more than just a way of getting someplace. It was a tradition. A lifestyle. Everything else just wasn't his "ball of wax."

I was born on the Entiat River, February 6, 1913, about four miles from here. When I was born, no one seemed to know what to call me, so they started to call me Babe.

My grandparents on my mother's side came here in July, 1889 and filed on a homestead. My grandad, D.M. [David Morgan] Farris, had a big meadow right on the river. In 1904 my grandad and his family sold out of there, moved downstream and started an orchard and built a store. They founded the town of Farris, Washington. I think I'm the only resident left with Farris, Washington on his birth certificate.

There is nothing now at Farris but an orchard. The store burned down and Grandad never rebuilt it. We moved to town in 1916. I lived down in Entiat till March, 1958, when the Rocky Reach Dam forced us out of there.

The first packing that I did, some of us kids would go up to the head of Mad River and go fishing, and I had to do the packing because the other guys didn't know how.

Then in 1929 after I had been going up to the head of Mad River for a couple of years, I killed a big deer up in 25-Mile Creek near Mount Chelan. The old packer that usually packed up in there had said that I was too young to pack a horse and that if I got a deer, I would not be able to pack it out.

But I had learned packing from old-timers and I did pack that deer out. You gotta know what you are doing. If you can't tie those diamond hitches, then you can't pack a horse. I grew up naturally around it and I figured out a lot of it on my own.

I really didn't know my father. He was a horseman who had logging teams. He packed hunters and surveying crews. He had hunters who came from the East who were hunting trophy deer and he made lots of money off of it. More than he did off of the local people, since they didn't have money for that. He died in 1918 with the flu epidemic.

I had friends, older fellows, who if I asked 'em, they'd show me. There were a lot of guys around the country who knew how to pack because they had had to pack over to Ellensburg which had been the nearest place to get supplies.

In 1933 I joined a CCC[1] camp in Mills Canyon. I didn't like being in the three C's. There were twenty-five guys in our camp. One black guy from Chicago. They fed us and gave us thirty dollars a month and Army clothes. It was like being in the Army, but they weren't quite as rough on us. If we wanted to, we could go home at night and on weekends.

The Chicago men were dumb about the West but they were nice guys. They made a camp sergeant out of a black guy who had never been out of the alleys of Chicago before in his life. And he was really going to whip us guys into line. I mean we had to be working eight hours a day building a road in Mills Canyon on the Entiat forest. He didn't even let us sit down to smoke a cigarette. I started calling him "Sarge." I said, "Sarge, you had better cut it out. You had better leave these guys alone or you're gonna wind up on the wrong end of the stick."

---

[1]Civilian Conservation Corps

One night I and another guy came in late for supper because we had been hooking up an emergency telephone line. We had moved camp and had to have a telephone. I had caught me a great big rattlesnake and I had tied a piece of telephone wire around its neck and I had come dragging that snake into camp.

And I mean there was twenty-five guys from Chicago and some local boys that left camp right then. And this old black Sarge, he didn't smart off no more after that.

We were building roads and I was doing a lot of crosscut sawing, felling trees. I didn't like that and when one time the cook got sick, I made a deal. I did the cooking for ten days for fifty-five people. I never had any trouble with it because my mother had run a boardinghouse up at Entiat for years and whenever she had been sick, I had done the cooking.

But the CCC and roadbuilding wasn't my ball of wax. I wanted to go back to horses. It was born in me.

In 1934 I began to pack horses for the Forest Service in the Entiat River drainage. I remember packing stuff up Cougar Mountain when they built the lookout cabin up there. I packed sixteen four-by-fours. It was the silliest-looking outfit you've ever seen going up the trail. We made up our own sling ropes for those loads.

We used diamond hitches. Pack saddles have a fork that you hook stuff to. They are not like riding saddles. There is a round ring, a decker. The other type of pack saddle is a sawbuck. It originated over in Idaho. I liked the sawbuck. My father used it. Those who don't know how to tie packs prefer the decker saddle.

By eight o'clock we were on the trail with two strings of five pack horses each. It was eight miles to the top of Cougar Mountain and those switchbacks were hard on the horses. Cougar Mountain is close to sixty-five hundred feet and you felt on top of the world up there. If you lie on the ground down in the valley, you can look up and see the top of Cougar Mountain because it is that steep!

About 1952 the Forest Service got started raising Morgan horses. They had a lot of unfenced lands and they asked me to pack up the fence posts. I packed as many as sixteen posts on a horse. That country was steep and it was tough on the horses but I took care of them. I felt sorry for them but it had to be done. I had a little mule to carry the fence wire.

I had to go up and back in one day. I had lunch when I got back because it was too much trouble to pack in a lunch. I traveled fifty miles to Cottonwood and sometimes it was a long time between stops, but I didn't mind it. I lived in Entiat and we had to move the horses fifty miles from Entiat to Cottonwood.

I began packing in hunters in 1940, because the right side of the river was a game reserve until 1940. That first year I packed out fifty-nine bucks. Then thirty-seven the next year. Now, thanks to that lousy Game Department, we don't see any bucks. We should have an open season on those Game Department guys. They have to kill the does off to raise more money in fees.

The game wardens won't even get out of their cars. I remember seeing a buck with the lower jaw shot off of him. No one could shoot him because if they got caught at it, they'd get a two hundred fifty dollar fine. I called the game warden and he went up there for about an hour and said, "I couldn't find him."

I don't think he ever got out of his car. They hear of a deer like that and they say, "Oh, the coyotes will take care of him." That's why folks are mad at them.

The Forest Service is the same way. They just ride around in pickup trucks, one person at a time.

The old Forest Service guys had some sense. When I worked with the Forest Service, when the lightning storms struck, all the volunteers went up to the station, waiting to see where the fires would strike next. Now they won't even let us fight the fires.

In 1970 when the Entiat fire began, I heard two Forest Service guys here at the store. They were imported from somewhere and I heard 'em saying, "When it is fifty thousand acres, we'll put it out."

That fire went on for a couple of months!

Horse packing was the best time of my life. But those days are gone forever, as I am seventy-five years old and won't do it anymore.

ROY "PUNK" SHETLER:
WHISTLEPUNK
Deming, WA
Born: 1909

"I whistled for years," says Roy Shetler. "I did a lot of it. I tried to be the best whistlepunk there was!"

Since you first read the title of this book you have probably been wondering what a whistlepunk is. But before I reveal that mystery I should tell you about donkeys. Steam donkeys, that is.

Northwest loggers originally used teams of oxen to skid a log away from its stump. Gargantuan old-growth fir and cedar lengths could be moved that way, but very slowly. Horses were a bit faster, but the introduction of steam engines (called donkeys) into the woods added a new dimension of power and speed, a revolution which continues to this day.

Before the advent of logging roads and logging trucks, the steam donkey[1] crew winched their machine on skids to a site called a cold deck, to which logs could be yarded or collected. As it eventually evolved, the yarder[2] was a steam engine which, through a main drum, haul-back drum, and a straw line (pass line) drum, operated three types of long steel cables. The straw line was a thin cable which the crew pulled manually into the woods and fitted into large, detachable pulleys called snap blocks. The straw line was used to power the haul-back cable out to the blocks, and that line,

---

[1]At the peak of their evolution, steam donkeys took several forms. Yarders pulled logs into a landing and roaders moved huge volumes of timber along skidroads. There were also half-breeds or swing donkeys, somewhat comparable to today's skidders and duplexes, which combined yarding and railroad car loading.
[2]Many of these machines were "duplexes," which could be used simultaneously as railroad car loaders.

in turn, to the main cable. The main line cable was the largest line, used for yarding the logs into the landing (or railroad siding) where they could be loaded onto railway cars. The haul-back line was a less hefty cable used to reposition the main line out at the cutting site again. As it eventually evolved, these cables were likely to use a "high lead" system of pulleys and guy-wired spar trees so that the log could be airlifted as much as possible over obstructions.

No siding crew was like any other siding crew, though the crew's duties and equipment were similar throughout all of the Northwest. But what differentiated one crew from another was the camaraderie of the members, who might number as many as fifteen. In addition to the highrigger[3] and his helper(s), a high lead siding crew usually consisted of: the loader engineer; yarder engineer; duplex fireman; head loader; second loader; third loader, and the choker-setting crew. The head choker man or "rigging slinger" chose the fallen logs to haul in to the siding. He chose sites for the haul-back line blocks (pulleys) and he decided which stumps and trees had to be dynamited out of the way. The second, third, and fourth choker setters placed the chokers or hooks on the downed logs, and hoped that they would be able to work their way up in seniority in the crew. If there were a fifth and sixth choker setter, they kept the haul-back line's location current. In addition, there was a dynamite expert or powder monkey. And last, but definitely not least, there was the whistlepunk.

A typical fifteen-man siding like this would load thirty to sixty carloads of logs a day depending on the difficulty of the terrain. A large camp often had three or four sidings going at once—with resultant rivalry.

Imagine the donkey sitting at the foot of a topped-off one-hundred-fifty-foot-tall high lead tree. From the donkey's main drum the main line extends up the tree to the bullblock[4] and way, way out into the woods to a tailblock. Out there the rigging slinger is directing his crew about which fallen log to take next. All of this is taking place amid much noise and activity. And in the days

---

[3]See pages 34 and 338.
[4]Bullblocks were enormous pulleys which sometimes weighed more than a ton and were from thirty to forty-two inches sheave diameter!

before radio communication there was only one way for the boss to communicate his desires to the donkey engineer ("puncher") about how and when the main line and haul-back should be moved.

That was the whistlepunk. Until replaced by electronic communication, he physically relayed the choker setter's orders to the donkey engineer through a "jerk line" to the steam whistle.[5] At the site of a major "logging show," the woods were alive with the sound of differently pitched steam whistles.

Of course, the logging railways' steam locomotives had their own whistles, too. Roy Shetler spent many years in the cab of those lokies as a fireman fueling the wood-fired furnaces.[6]

From my point of view, the arcane details of steam donkey and steam railroad jobs are much less important than the spirit in which men approached them. This work in the woods was so dangerous that many men were killed and injured every year. Wages and living conditions were more a reflection of the country's depressed economy than of the jobs' dangers. Job security and job benefits were limited to a man's ability to work long hours, six days a week.

At the risk of oversentimentalizing a very tough situation, I like to think of this whistlepunk as a hero. A good woods crew had to have as much precision and grace as today's N.B.A. teams. The whistlepunk's skill with his cumbersome jerk line often made the difference not only in a siding's productivity, but also in the life-and-death safety of its men.

As the primeval forests fell to the axe, the misery whip, and the chainsaw, thousands and thousands of men were caught up in something much bigger than themselves. A big country engendered great pride in people like lokie engineers and firemen (who often stayed together as a team as they moved from camp to camp).

I remember the story of one logging engineer named Charles "Bill" Eckenburg who, whenever he moved to a new camp to drive a new Heisler-geared locomotive, would custom weld that beast almost beyond recognition. He would double the capacity of the

---

[5]The jerk line was usually a number nine metal wire, suspended on pullies. It needed to be relocated often as the choker setting crew moved through the clearcut taking out the logs.
[6]Locomotives were later fired by coal and then by oil.

Roy Shetler (center) on a locomotive.

sand dome atop the boiler so that he'd have as much sand as he wanted for slowing his descents down mountainsides. He added extra water reservoirs and steam braking capacities. And he scrapped the Heisler's oversized puny original whistle and grafted on a godawful steam demon that they could hear way over in China.

That Eckenburg loved steam! He loved its power and lore so much that his personal automobiles were steam, too. The smell and sound and living presence of those steam donkeys and lokies *was* romantic.

And so was the raw spectacle of a 1930 fifteen-man siding crew a true "logging *show.*"

This chapter is about Roy Shetler's experiences with steam donkeys and steam lokies, but I want to end it with the story of how he came out of the woods to get up steam to confront an irate father and marry his daughter.

To show that he isn't just whistling through the top of his hat, Roy's wife will help to tell that tale.

My brother Harry got me my first job in the woods. I looked up to him. He was good at his work and I tried to be as good as he was. He was happy-go-lucky, but he was tough. Loggers had to be, then. That's all there was to it.

Harry didn't take nothing off of anybody. He was the second loader on a crew loading big logs on railroad cars at Baker Lake. It was hard work all day, juggling tongs like he did, giving them a spin, and getting them on a log to load onto the car.[7]

Harry Shetler on the end of a logging car belonging to the Lyman Timber Company.

I was too young. I wasn't skookum enough to do that. It takes a pretty good man to do that job because they were big logs. A lot of logs they take today would have been left in the woods when I was a young logger. Now they take logs whether they are konky or not.

We were working on the Baker River near Concrete where they were making a hydroelectric dam. They were clearing that all out where Baker Lake was going to be. Art Ray was the head loader and my brother Harry was second loading man. They loaded the logs on railroad cars and sent them down to the mill at Anacortes.

---

[7]In order for the second loader to do a good job, the loading engineer needed to have the right "touch," from years of experience.

I went up to Concrete with Harry and they just happened to need a whistlepunk. I told them I was sixteen and they gave me the job.

So I started blowing whistles up there when I was fourteen. The rigging slinger picked out which log for the second and third chokermen to get and yelled instructions for the donkey to me. I would pull on my line to blow the steam whistle. One whistle meant for the engineer to start the rigging if it was stopped and to stop the rigging if it was running. Two, to back the rigging up again. Two and a bunch, to slack it all back. And a bunch of whistles slacked the main line.

When the choker was set, then the rigging slinger would let a yip out of him, I would blow a signal, and the yarder would take the log in. This had to be done exactly right or rigging could be wrecked, and men killed and injured.

I liked whistling and I stayed with it for twenty-five years.

Because I blew whistles, they always called me "Punk." I was good at it. I made good money at it. I wasn't in the road of any danger unless I pulled a tree down on myself. But I could always stop the rig and get out of the road.

Oh gosh, I think I got a dollar a day and board. Pretty good wages for me.

We lived in bunkhouses on railroad cars then. You had a bed in there and a place to wash and everything. You would hang your clothes and stuff when you came in. When you came in you were dirty, and to take a shower you poured a bucket of water on one guy and the other guy would pour the water on you, and you would get washed off that way.[8]

So you got washed up, put on clean clothes, and went to supper. The food was the best you could ask for. In them days, they put the best out on the table. The cook. . . . If the food wasn't good, men got up and kicked everything off the table. Harry did that up in Saxon. He cleaned the table off. He got right up and walked down that table with his caulk shoes and kicked everything off

---

[8]As logging evolved, camps (including railroad car camps) had to provide adequate facilities in order to keep their crews. In addition to hot water and showers, the camps had a "bull cook," who fueled the wood stoves in the shower car, drying room, and bunkhouses.

because they had rotten grub one day. They had a new cook in and he messed the grub up.[9]

A lot of gambling went on in camp. Yeah, when I was starting out in the woods, I won five hundred dollars one night. My brother took it away from me and took it home with him that night. (He give it back to me later on when I decided to buy a four-cylinder Star automobile.) Next morning I had two hundred and fifty more that I had won.

I didn't know nuthin' about gambling. I set in there with a dollar just to have something to do. I started winning but I didn't know how to bet. So a guy that knew how to bet was bettin' for me. I didn't know how to bet; all I did was play the cards.

Blackjack. I could turn up twenty-one or twenty all the time, it seemed like, when they was dealin' them 'round. The dealer would come and deal them around and I would get twenty. Instead of bettin' a nickel, this fella would bet a quarter or fifty cents for me. I bought that Star automobile and drove it home to Bellingham on weekends.

In camp we had homemade bread, homemade pies, baked beans. The fallers, they would take beans out with their lunch because it stayed with them.

Everyone had a square bucket with a lid for his tin lunchbox, and you put your coffee in the top and set that on a fire to warm your coffee up. At lunch time there would be a lot of fires scattered out through the woods with people warming their coffee. When it was wet weather, it was nice to have a fire to come up to to warm your hands and dry 'em before you started eatin'.

I feel all right that they don't need whistlepunks no more. I imagine its safer with a walkie-talkie. When I was way out in the woods with the crews, I would have my jerk wire out there a thousand feet or sometimes more. I had to string it out through the woods carefully over limbs and put in pulleys to make that thing work perfect. So that when I jerked it three times, it blew three times. If I jerked it twice, it blowed twice.

---

[9]Roy's mother Evelyn Lillian Shetler was later hired as a cook at that same camp. Her specialty was packing lunches of beans and homemade bread.

I've had two thousand feet of wire out up here on the hill at Galbraith. We had a slack line up there and they side blocked and you had two whistle lines out. One on the yarder and one on the slack line. You had two wires to work. You better get them down, because. . . .

You get out there in the woods, you got to have good ears, and you got to listen and know what is goin' on. You got to know just about as much as the hooktender and the riggin' slinger to be good at what you are doin'. You can't see them all the time. You just got to keep your ears open. When he hollers, you blow the whistle that he wants. If he wants a little slack, you give it to him. If he wants you to back up, you back up. If he wants to go ahead a little, you go ahead a little. Then the engineer puts the donkey in gear and does whatever whistle you blow.

It's relayed messages. And with the whistle, everybody can hear it. So if you make a mistake, they can get out of the road, too. You don't want to make a mistake or you can kill somebody very easily. I have seen guys get killed in the woods. Snags and trees come down and hit em. I run a speeder at Bloedel and after that I run speeder for Saxon up there. Guys would get killed and I would haul them down to the siding with the speeder and load them out. Some of them were crippled and I would take them down to the ambulance.

I was working up there one time and we was on the big rig, big high lead deal. My brother Harry and Arty Gray were up there loadin' and I was yardin'. This dead snag come down and killed two guys and put three or four in the hospital. They all run down a log and that snag come down and just shattered them.

I've seen a lot of them get killed and hurt in the woods. Up at Saxon, that was a highball outfit up there! Your hide wasn't worth two cents for them. They had a crew acomin', hiring on, and one agoin'. You didn't waste no time on those skidders. When the hooker snapped a button and the rigging slinger hollered, you better get the heck out of there. Skidders would take off. They didn't watch. They had to produce so much or they would get canned. They just highballed 'er through.

You was lucky to get a job in the Depression. I don't think the guys got over two or two and a half a day in the woods. Times were tough and it was hard to get a job.

I blew whistles. . . . Oh, I started in for Puget Sound-Baker River. I blew whistles there. I blew whistles at Lyman Timber Company. I blew whistles for Galbraith's here at Deming. I blew whistles at Saxon. I never had a hard time gettin' a job blowin' whistles. I was always good at it. I just naturally was.

Here's a photograph of me on a saddlebag locomotive. That's Percy Ferris the engineer on the left. I was the fireman until Percy got drunk and didn't show up one day, so they canned him.

That's how come I got to run saddlebag up there at the camp above Acme when Elmer Campbell was bull of the woods. A saddlebag locomotive, her water tanks are on the side. When she goes around the corner, her nose goes way out and a lot of guys got scared because they thought it was goin' off the tracks.

Here's a photo of an old Heisler. It has a big light in the front. An old electric. It run off the generator but it never worked because the generator was haywire.

That's wood in the back there, stacked up. That's an old-timer all right. It was small and it only had a set of drivers on the front. It wasn't a big machine, but it did the work up there. I would burn three cords a day goin' up and back. I put the wood in the firebox, kept the steam up, and when the water got low, I injected water.

When I was on the flat, settin' still, I filled her up with water as much as I could. Then I fired her up and took off up the mountain. She wouldn't hold enough steam to make it all the way up. I would get about halfway up there and I would have to stop and get the steam up again before I could continue.

It was exciting driving her, because you never knew. . . . If it was frosty in the morning, I would have to whistle for the brakeman to set the hand brakes on each car because I couldn't hold it with a lokie. Then I would let it come down slow. You didn't let it get a run on ya. You only had steam brakes on the old lokie itself and no steam brakes on the cars.

You could only bring three cars down at a time. That's all she could hold comin' down.

Sometimes it was a little faster than you liked it and would get to run on you a little bit, so you just kept acomin' and the brakeman would hop off and set 'em. He set them on the run comin' down because you couldn't stop.

Yeah, it was dangerous. He could get hurt there if he didn't watch what he was doin'. He would be on the first carload of logs. When you whistled for brakes, he would set that one, then hop off, and catch the next one.

I was engineer on that Heisler for two years hauling logs down to the snubber, the incline railway which lowered the cars and logs down to the mill at Blanchard, Washington.

That old Heisler had a couple of windows in the side that you could stick your head out of. It was open air. It had a bell in the middle. I rang that when I started up so that nobody would be in the road.

That big stack on there is a spark arrester to keep from settin' fires. Her whistle was just a boop. That's all I can tell ya. They all sound different. You could make a shrill sound that would carry for miles.

This guy here in the photo, he was the brakeman. If I wanted him to set the brakes coming down, I just gave her three short blasts on the whistle, toot, toot, toot, and he would bail off and start setting the brakes. He was a good brakeman and was there for quite a while.

That Heisler was practically wore out when we got it up to that Chuckanut Mountain camp above Blanchard. In fact, one day comin' down, it jumped off the track. We put it back on the track and it would jump off again. We found out it had a broken axle. So they closed the camp down and that's the last time the camp ever run up there. They didn't have the five or six hundred dollars to put a new axle in it.

Yeah. They closed her down then. But that Heisler was run to the bitter end, all right.

I think somebody got it for scrap iron.[10]

[Roy Shetler told me that while he was working as a whistlepunk at Saxon, he met a seventeen-year-old girl named Mary Knight and

---

[10]See page 122 about Monte Holm, logging railroad scrap iron dealer.

eloped with her three months later. I asked Mary Shetler to tell me how they had met.]

Mrs. Setler: I was working for his cousin's wife, takin' care of their two little girls. I was engaged to another fella at the time and one Sunday afternoon I was out for a ride with him in his car. Roy was walkin' down the road. (He was probably going to go see another girl. Rita, I think it was.) I had never met him but I said to the fella I was with, "See that guy down there?"

He said, "Yeah."

I said, "I'm goin' to marry that guy." So Roy was had before he even knew it! Three months later we was married.

Shortly after, I got home and I told my dad about the guy I had seen walking down the road. He said, "That's Roy Shetler. Leave him alone." Dad never should have told me that.

He said it because the Shetler brothers (three of them worked in the woods besides Roy) were raised around our area, north Bellingham. They lived close to my grandparents, and my father said, "It's just a bad bunch to get hold of."

My dad had a mill and my Uncle Ben Knight and Bert Couchman had a mill and skidded logs with a team of horses. My sister was just two years older than I was and she would slop grease on those skids for the logs to be skidded down on.

So my father knew all the young loggers in north Bellingham. He was serious at that time about what he had said about Roy, but Roy proved him wrong. Roy never went to school beyond third grade, but Dad found out that he was a really nice guy. Very, very brilliant, mechanical-minded. He has been very good.[11]

Just from seeing him that one time on the road, I just knew Roy was the guy that I was goin' to marry. Just something about him. I just knew I was going to marry him. Unusual, but that's the way it was.

I met him the next Sunday, ridin' horses down at his cousin's place. Roy's cousin dealt in race track horses. I was only seventeen when I first saw him. He was seven years older than I was.

The next month I was eighteen and I knew that I could get

---

[11]Roy Shetler died September 26, 1987.

married without my parents consent, so we just ran off and got married June 23, 1934. He had an old Studebaker. He didn't have any license on it and we didn't have any money. His sister lived in Centralia. So we get in the old car and quickly used what gas we had. We picked raspberries goin' down and raspberries comin' back to make gas money.

We went down to Centralia and got married. I don't know why Centralia. I know it's a long way. Just decided to do it, I guess.

Anyway, we got married down there and we came home in about a week or so. Roy's logging company was down then because of the hot weather. So Roy went to work for my dad, farming part time.

We were six girls in my family and Dad had already warned me against this Shetler boy. Oh, yeah! If you had six girls, wouldn't you be warning them, too?

DR. ISRAEL SOSS:
ROMANIAN IMMIGRANT
TO THE INLAND EMPIRE
Spokane, WA
Born: 1899

Israel Soss arrived in steerage at Ellis Island in New York harbor at the turn of the century. His family soon moved to Spokane, Washington, where his father opened a downtown clothing shop and was active in the city's small Jewish community.

Israel Soss served in the Navy in World War I and in the Army in World War II. He was a Spokane optometrist for many decades.

My folks were born and raised in Romania. They were Jewish and spoke Romanian at home. They weren't very rich. The whole city, Lionesti, all the land, belonged to the general in the town.

My uncle got out here a little ahead of my father and did very well and liked it here. He told my father that this was a very fine country and that he had a good chance to make a living for the family here. My father was a bricklayer and stonemason.

I was born over there. When I was two or three years of age they came over in a boat to Ellis Island. They came by steerage.

I remember New York City very faintly. Plenty of sidewalks and brick buildings. No trees or grass around, no place. I came to Spokane from New York City when I was about six years old. My sister was three years younger than I was. The train trip took nearly a week coming out here.

My father had had an accident falling off something in New York as a bricklayer. So he had a little clothing store in Spokane. Underwear, socks, and shoes and pants and shirts.

My uncle was already here and my family was accepted in Spokane right away. There was a Jewish butcher and a grocery store catering to Jewish people. They came from all over Europe. Especially after 1905 and 1910. A lot of my relatives came through New York City, but a few came through Canada.

There was not as much Jewish life in Spokane then as there is now. There were a few old-timers who had come over at the end of the last century. At that time there were quite a few Jews, mostly Russians, who came over. My father was very religious. Friday night and Saturday was the big day. We had a little community with a synagogue.

My father was a good, fair man. Very fair. He helped those who were coming from Europe and didn't have much money. After starving when young, he was very charitable.

This is a fine city and a fine country to live in. My family was accepted in Spokane right away. We made friends right away. There was never any discrimination. We got along fine. I grew up like any other kid in the neighborhood, playing games, baseball. We grew up with a kid who went to Catholic school. We never paid any attention, as long as they were good-natured and a good person.

I found out later about discrimination.

ADELINE "TINY" STEFANO STRUBLE

Seattle, WA

Born: 1922

Today, when women work in just about every profession, it is hard to remember that until very recently industrial jobs were the exclusive preserve of men. Wartime patriotism temporarily expanded women's roles when millions of draftees left the workplace for the armed services. A popular World War II song celebrated that bigger-than-life home-front heroine "Rosie the Riveter." I was fortunate to find a true-life Rosie who had not only worked as a riveter on B-17's, but had also grown up within sight of Boeing Field.

Adeline Stefano was only twenty years old when she began to build B-17 tail assemblies at Boeing Plant II in south Seattle. The amazing thing about her is not just that she weighed only eighty-seven pounds (hence her assembly line nickname of "Tiny"), or that she would work at Boeing for forty-five years, but that every member of her enormous Italian clan would be part of the "Boeing family." Parents, aunt, uncles (her Uncle Mike Pavone began as a mechanic in the Red Barn, Plant I, in 1920), sisters, nieces, nephews, husband, children, and grandchildren—a total of twenty-four Boeing-employed relatives. Everyone, in fact, except Uncle Lou, whose Bataan Death March captivity so inspired Tiny to her own heroic efforts to help build B-17's.

Toward the end of the war, when the breakneck pace of warplane production had eased, Boeing was called "the Lazy B." By then Tiny had transferred to secretarial work. In January of 1945 she was asked to replace a secretary who was having an appendectomy. "I said, sure," says Tiny. "I took off my coveralls and my snood [a protective hair covering] and I went into the office. While Edith was gone she married and moved away, so they just kept me in the office—until I retired in June, 1987."

The irony is, as Tiny is quick to point out, that she probably would not be hired today. Boeing employment became the foundation for Puget Sound prosperity, as the Boeing Depression of 1970–1971 proved, and even today a severe retrenchment at "Boeing's" would send the region into an economic tailspin. Increased competition for jobs has meant ever higher requirements for employment. That angers little Tiny Struble, normally the most loyal of Boeingites.

When I retired, I gave them the names of girls who had worked with me at different times and who wanted to get back to office positions. But they wouldn't accept them because they didn't have a college education. I said, "But they have the actual experience!" They don't want that anymore. It is sad. It is really sad.

Throughout the war Tiny lived with her parents. Then as now, she was a peppy, irrepressible person. Through her I can easily imagine the camaraderie of the B-17 assembly lines.

And the working conditions. Tiny has recently had operations on both her ears because of their years of factory din and abuse. "We didn't even think of it as noisy," says Tiny, "but all of us in that tail section had rivet guns and bucking bars and metal booming on top of our heads all day long."

A common Tiny Struble expression is, "Now when I think about it, I don't know how I ever did it."

For Tiny and for probably most of the other women it was not just a job. The B-17 was part of a great cause.

They came home on a wing and a prayer. The wheels were collapsed. A wing was shot off. A nose was shot off. A tail was shot off. But they always managed to come in and land. It held together. This is what Rosie the Riveter did. To think that we put those planes together! It makes you think, "God, I really did something good in my life."

Riveters working on an airplane at the Boeing Plant in Seattle during World War II. (Credit: The Boeing Company Archives)

When I graduated in 1940 from Cleveland High School in south Seattle, it was very hard to get a job. I had lived all my life at 1312 Bennett Street looking down at Boeing Field. My mother still lives there. We could see Boeing Field from our home. All my life I saw airplanes, but when I graduated from high school I thought, "Oh, I'll never get on at Boeing."

Then there was the war. I liked to sew, so I went to the N.Y.A.[1] and they taught me how to use a power sewing machine. That is what I was going to go into when the war came on and Pearl Harbor in 1941 and they were hiring people at Boeing's.

The employment office was in downtown Seattle. I went down there and passed and went through everything until it came time to take the blood out of my arm and it scared me. I said, "Oh, I am really not interested" and I walked out.

By May 1942 I thought, "Well, that was dumb. I better go down there and work."

---

[1] The National Youth Association, which taught trades to young people.

So I went back and did the blood test and I started on the ninth of June 1942. I walked into Plant II down there. A "rivet bucker" is what they called me.

The thing that inspired me to go down there was my Uncle Lou who is the same age as me. He was on the Bataan Death March and was a prisoner of the Japanese for five years. My uncle and I grew up together. I was born in May and he was born in August. He had been on Corregidor and we never heard from him at all during the war. I just had him in my mind all that time and I wanted to help him. "If he is still alive," I thought, "I want these planes to go over there and free him."

He was in that Bataan Death March and saw his buddy Gordon shot by the side of the road when Gordon couldn't continue the march.

My mother has pictures of Uncle Lou coming home on the train and everything. He told us that when he was in the prison camp, he was fed fish but he ate grass to keep alive. They made him work in the mines underground. He came back a broken young man. We are the same age and it was pathetic. He has got scars on him to this day that he won't explain. We knew that somewhere he had been mistreated by the Japanese. He's just recently had extensive surgery on his intestines because of the food that he had to eat when he was in that prison.

I felt sorry for all the kids that were in the service. Way back then we had compassion for people. It seems as though in this modern day that compassion for people is no more. Our family was very close, very loving people.

Both my grandparents knew each other in Boston and migrated out here. My mother still lives in the same house since the day she was married. She has never moved.

My mom and dad were both born in Boston. My four grandparents were all four born in Italy and came over here to Boston. My mother's mother came over here to get married. You know they had young girls that came over here. . . . They had men that came over to get jobs and then they had somebody fix up marriages for them. The girls would land in New York or Boston.

My mother's mother was only about fifteen when she came over.

She was so young and, of course, coming over from Italy, she didn't know how to talk English. She lost contact with her whole family in Italy. She couldn't remember anyone. It was really sad but that's the way it went.

My mother was a year old when she came from Boston and now she is eighty-six. She was born in 1902, so they came over here about 1903.

My dad was eight years older than my mom, so he was goin' on nine when they came from Boston to Seattle. They came over together, both couples with their families.

My Grandpa Pavone sold produce at the Pike Place Market for several years beginning in 1912. My mother was the oldest of his thirteen Pavone children. She had seven children including me.

Uncle Mike Pavone was the next in line. He is eighteen months younger than my mother. Uncle Mike started with Boeing's in 1920.

The rivet buckers like me were on the inside of the tail section. They called it the tail fuselage. We stood on a board about a foot wide, and the section was in what they called jigs to hold them up while we put up the skin.

We had a crew framing it and putting the stringers on. Then a crew came and put the skin on. A crew came around and did all the drilling of the holes and they had what they called "clecos" to hold the skin onto the stringers. Then the riveters came and put the rivets in there with an airpowered rivet gun like an electric drill motor. They had different size rivets. We had to use larger ones when it came to a joint. And then smaller ones when it was just between joints.

Somebody inside had to hold the bucking bar and they were quite heavy. We held them and we had a strap around our wrist which went through a hole in the bucking bar so in case we dropped it, it wouldn't fall and clonk somebody on the head that was working underneath us.

The riveter would put the rivet in and press in on it and I had to be in the tail section holding my bucking bar until the rivets were all perfect along the stringers. When the riveter on the outside took his thumb and pressed down on the trigger, that thing would rat-tat-tat-tat. I was on the inside holding my bar steady with both hands so that the rivet outside would smash right down almost flush with the skin.

And standing on a little board up in the air. I don't know how we ever did it! Our arms really got tired holding them up in the air while we bucked the rivets down.

We did that all day long, ten hours a day. We had to work two hours overtime every day. We worked seven days a week, ten hours a day for sixty-two and a half cents an hour.

For an eight-hour shift, at sixty-two and a half cents an hour, I made five dollars a day. That was big money back then. It amazes me now, these young kids going to work. They gripe about having to start at seven-fifty an hour. I think if they had to start at five dollars a day, there would be very few young people down there today, believe me.

Five dollars a day was a lot of money in 1942, but I wanted to work on the B-17 because I wanted to do my part for the war effort. It made me feel good. I never griped or anything.

There weren't many men down there in 1942 and 1943. Most of them had gone to service. We had men who had some kind of a handicap. My riveter Herman, he wore. . . . I swear he couldn't see without his glasses! And then all of a sudden after I had been there six months he got drafted. I was really surprised that Herman had to go, because he couldn't see very well.

But he had basic training and immediately he was sent overseas. He wasn't gone even a year and the next thing we knew he was killed. Herman was from Sultan. He only saw his baby once when it was a month old.

When Herman went to war, I was promoted to riveter.

The majority of B-17 workers were women. Every place that they could put a woman to work. There were a lot of women doing a lot of things. We had women doing electrical work, putting electrical components together. Then there were women who put fabric on parts. There were women who did structural work like putting the stringers together.

It was like one big happy family. Everybody worked harmoniously together. All that time that I worked in the shop, you never heard any squabbling. Even when we got drilled. Someone would put a drill through the top and it would get caught up in our snoods and twine it all up. Nobody even got mad.

Oh yes, one big happy family. It seemed like we spent more time together down there than we did at home. Really. When you got home it was six o'clock and by the time you ate, you went to bed, because you knew you had to get up early and go to work the next day.

We were working so fast that we would have. . . . I swear that there wasn't that much room between us on the board while we were working inside the tail. They had us really jammed in.

I was in the very narrow part because I was smaller.

One day I was on the board bucking rivets in my little area and I got to the point inside the section that I had to stand up to reach. Somebody was going to move the board and yelled, "Hey, Tiny. We're going to move the board. Hold on." So I held onto the stringers while they moved the board.

That was how the name "Tiny" started back in 1942. And that name stuck with me. If you had gone down there to ask for Adeline, they wouldn't have known who you were talking about.

I weighed eighty-seven pounds and was only five feet tall, so one day the superintendent came to see me when I was riveting. He said, "Come with me." I got down to the floor. We walked down to the wing line. They had this big wing laying on the floor. Somebody had forgotten to put a very important something in one of the stringers inside the wing and they wanted me to climb inside the wing in between all the struts and to put that thing in.

I wouldn't do it. I have a little bit of claustrophobia, I think. No way was I going to climb in there, because I thought I would never get out.

I remembered we had some little midget men at Boeing. They couldn't go into the service. I said, "You've got to be kidding. I'm not going to climb in there. I cannot make myself climb through those zigzag things. I told them to get one of the little people to do that. They did, and he was happy to climb in there.

He did a real good job.

Because I was little they thought they could just put me in any little spot. And I tried as much as I could. Even when the tail fuselage came to a very small spot, I smashed in there sometimes.

But that was open and I could turn and look back to the open end of the section. In that wing I wouldn't have been able to see out.

Anybody can bake a wedding cake, but it is the way that it is decorated that makes it beautiful. I felt that I was decorating the outside, the only part that I ever worked on. I always thought that everybody who worked on an airplane felt that the part they did was the most important. I always felt that the outside of the airplane that held it all together was the most important.

The planes were rolling out the door just as fast as they were being shot down. If I went to the restroom, that was when Herman drilled out holes and put the rivets in. If Herman had to go, then I would put the rivets in for him. That's how we did it, so there was always one of us right there to keep it going constantly. Curly and Cec did the same thing. We really worked hard every day.

We were working fast and furiously. In fact, one day the superintendent and the boss of the shop where I was, and my immediate supervisor, they called Herman and I down from the top deck. They also called another riveter and bucker down and they said, "Tomorrow morning we are going to time the two pairs of you to see how long it takes to do one whole tail fuselage."

The tail fuselage was sixty-eight feet nine inches long on the B-17. At the beginning of the morning shift they started timing us. It was amazing how fast we went! Of course, the skins were on and clecoed at the joints. Herman had to take the rivets out of his apron and put them all in a whole row. Then he would say, "Ready." Boy, we would go right across.

Curly and Cec did the bottom section and Herman and I did the top section. We worked like dogs, let me tell you. It was really fast. You know how it is to work and have people down there timing you. We did one whole tail section by lunchtime, which was really good.

After just a couple hours of working on it, it was gratifying to see that section be picked up by the crane and moved on to the next area over from us and be joined to the aft body section of the plane. When that was done they would pick it up and move it over someplace else until they got the wings on. They pushed seventeen airplanes a day out that door.

I brought my own lunch all the time. We had bomb shelter

tunnels down under the main floor at Boeing. At lunchtime we all went down and we would get together and we would write notes to the airmen. Some of the gals put their addresses and stuff like that. I couldn't do that. I was raised very strict.

I would always say, "Hi, GI Joe. Hope you come home safe." I would put it under a stringer. I don't know if anybody ever saw it because I never had my name on it or anything.

Everybody was GI Joe in the service, just like we were Rosie the Riveter.

It gave us something different, a little break in the day. We had a half hour for lunch and that was it.

I never saw any kind of bickering, ever. All the time I worked on those airplanes, inside, outside, and around them. Never ever saw any bickering. Nobody had time.

Everyone who worked on the airplanes during the war should have a medal. I'm sure that we worked as hard as the people who were flying the airplanes. We really worked hard. I don't know how I ever held together.

Chromate would drop on us when someone above us was putting on the skin, fitting it along. It is a green, smelly something, like a paste. We had to put that on the stringer before we put the skin up on it and it kind of sealed it on there. When we drilled, it would go through the hole and drop all over us. It smelled, but nobody thought anything about it.

Those shavings, you have never felt anything until you. . . . When someone is drilling the skin on the outside and you are on the inside waiting for your riveter to put the rivets in, those hot shavings, if they get down your collar or on your arms, they burn!

We really suffered along with working. But nobody complained. We were doing something to help.

BILL SULLIVAN:

GEODUCK HUNTER

Discovery Bay, WA

Born: 1942

A geoduck hunter like Bill Sullivan can be a very popular man. Not that geoducks themselves are very lovable. Some people like to promote them as the state bird, but three-foot-long neck or no, that thing won't fly.

That neck or siphon is the most amazing feature about this bivalve except its taste. The geoduck is a docile beast. "Keep clam," the late Ivar Haglund's famous motto, applies to this odd fellow who is content to loiter three feet under the sand. That's where Bill Sullivan finds geoducks at low tides along the Strait of Juan de Fuca.

Bill and his brother own and operate the Discovery Bay Grocery along Highway 101. Sport fishermen have left many photos of themselves with trophy-class salmon, but I want to start a new tradition. I want to find a four-pound geoduck and have it immortalized with a wall photo at the Discovery Bay Grocery.

I asked Bill about the best places to find my trophy geoduck.

Everybody has their own "best spot in the world" where they go. But the best places are the harder to reach ones. I have dug a lot of geoducks in the Docewallops area because there is a state park there for easy access. But mainly they are far enough out on the tide flats that it is not real rocky. It's sandy or gravelly where I find most of them. If there were big rocks, you could never dig down three feet to get them.

It's not like digging a steamer or a butter clam where you only need to go down four, five, or six inches. Geoducks have their necks sticking up three feet. So you work your hand down the neck till you can get to the shell and break the suction and pull him up.

A razor clam does dig. These guys do not dig.

The biggest ones are not necessarily the deepest. I've seen one-pound jobbies way down there. It all depends. The largest ones are farther out in the tide where people have had less chance to dig them.

It's a lot of fun and a lot of work. You got to have low tide. You got to plan on a good sweat by the time you pack all your stuff out and dig a few three-foot holes. If you go with a big low tide like at Dungeness out in front of the Three Crabs, that's a half-mile walk, carrying a shovel, a tub, and a little bucket to bail the hole out, and carrying the sack to put them in. You've got to be into it. And you've got to plan on spending a few hours even if you're tired.

I enjoy it. I find nifty things, like a crab now and then. And I see sea cucumbers. I throw incidental steamer clams and butter clams in my bucket, too. And I bring the horse clams in for crab pot bait.

There are all kinds of nifty things that you can do with geoducks. Pound some little steaks. Run them through cubers. But the basic thing is to make a chowder or a nice fritter with a little lemon juice and tartar sauce. Friends come beating at my door for more of them.

I like to take people out who haven't done it before. That's always a thrill. But a lot of people who have tried digging geoducks with me on the beach won't go back out there again.

They won't go to the trouble.

But they will come over and *eat* them every day.

DENNIS SULLIVAN:

MUCKER/MAYOR

Port Townsend, WA

Born: 1897

One constant of life in Washington state is the division between the wet west side of the Cascades and the arid east. Usually these are two different worlds. I like to encounter stories of people who have successfully surmounted that divide.

Dennis Sullivan was a gold miner, the son and grandson of miners in Ferry County. Yet he went on to become mayor (1963–1968) of Port Townsend on the Olympic Peninsula.

Because I have so often visited Republic during the last twenty years, I was fascinated by Dennis Sullivan's descriptions of the town when it had wooden sidewalks and dirt roads. (Recently local businesswoman Denise Zipperer led a campaign to restore Republic's Old West look for tourists.) About 1910, Republic was a place where hapless Chinese miners (cheap labor) would be unceremoniously escorted out of town, and where Dennis Sullivan's father died slowly of black lung disease without any insurance, government or private.

Dennis Sullivan's father, John Francis Sullivan, was a popular man who ran a hand-operated jackhammer in the gold mines and then ran the miners' elevator or hoist until he became too ill to work.

Disease, accidents, entombments, primitive working conditions. Who wouldn't have preferred Port Townsend to the Quilp, Surprise, and Knob Hill mines? But many miners, then as now, thought of doing nothing else. Republic's mines were warm in winter and cool in summer. And there was the glint of gold.

Dennis's mother's father had been killed in a mine in Ironwood,

Michigan. One of Dennis's father's favorite stories was about how he and his wife, Mary O'Brien, had met. One day he had gone with his mother Bridget to see the neighborhood's new baby. John had held the baby Mary in his arms. Later, after Mary's father had been killed, Flurry and Bridget Sullivan adopted that baby. Eventually John Sullivan and Mary O'Brien married. John loved to say that, "Not many men get to hold their wives when they are babies."

The photo shows Dennis Sullivan's uncle at work beside an ore cart. He was Louis Sullivan, a mucker like Dennis himself.

One day a group of miners were in the "Dry" (a room for drying muddy clothes or for changing clothes to go to town) while one of the James boys was in the powder house, a short distance away, preparing blasting powder and fuses. A spark from his carbide light set a box of powder on fire and that heroic brother ran with it to save everyone else's lives. He threw it over the ore dump. Just as he threw it, it went off, killing him.

Dennis Sullivan's family was Irish. Dennis's grandparents Bridget and Flurry Sullivan came to the United States from Ireland in 1865. Flurry Sullivan had been born in County Kerry, Ireland in 1833. In 1865 he married his boyhood sweetheart Bridget Harrington. She had been born in Waterford County in 1839.

Flurry Sullivan worked in mines in Michigan, Butte, Montana, Coeur d'Alene, Idaho, and Republic, Washington. His last underground work was at the Republic Mine, then in its glory.

Whenever the family saw Bridget putting on her special white apron, they knew she was going out to the neighbors, nursing. Either helping someone come into the world or leave it. When Bridget was old and could no longer climb the hill to church, she would sit beside her house when the churchbell rang and look up at the church and say her rosary.

In 1903 Flurry Sullivan located a quarter section of land on O'Brien Creek. He and Bridget had had fourteen children and had adopted seven others. Most of the children were grown before the family moved to Republic. The family's money was in the Bank of Republic, which went broke about 1909, and times became very tough for the Sullivans.

Dennis's father, John, was born in Ireland and came to the United States at the age of two. Eventually he worked in Republic's

Quilp Mine, Surprise Mine, and Knob Hill Mine, usually as a "powder monkey," drilling the holes and preparing the powder and fuse
for a blast.

During the gold rush days of 1900, Dennis arrived in Republic
by stagecoach with his mother, Mary, and brother Johnnie.

Grandfathers, fathers, brothers, and cousins all worked underground. "There wasn't too much work around Republic," says
Dennis, "except the mines."

Dennis's uncle Louis
Sullivan with an ore
cart.

I was born in 1897 in Butte, Montana. My father worked in the
mines there before he came to Republic in 1898. My mother and
my brother and myself came to Republic in 1900.

He was a fine father, I'll tell you that. We never heard him swear.
He drank a little bit.

I looked up to my father. He always provided for us at home.
There were six boys and one girl. The girl died when she was
eleven months old of the measles.

My mother was sick quite a bit and my father would take over.
He'd bake bread and pies. If we weren't in time for the meals, it
was put away. If we put our coats on the floor or on a chair, he'd

throw them outside and we'd have to go outside and pick them up and hang them up. He was very good.

My Father was one of the best drillers in that country. And drilling contests were a big thing in Republic, with a lot of betting. All the boys practiced this, but I didn't. That was too hard a work. They drilled and practiced on big granite boulders about six feet around. You can still see them around Republic.

Every Fourth of July right on Main Street there were horse races, mucking contests, and drilling contests. On the Fourth of July about 1914, Dad and his partner, Horace Mason, who was a very fine blacksmith, competed in Republic against two Swedish champion drillers from Canada. Rocks were hauled in and a platform was built around the rocks for the men to stand on.

Each man in a two-man team had a hammer with a three-foot handle. That is why this was called double jack drilling. A single jackhammer has a smaller head and a foot-long handle. My father won many contests drilling with a single jackhammer.

They start with a steel drill about eight inches and then progressively longer ones as the hole gets deeper. One man holds the drill and the other man swings the double jack. They changed every two minutes.

Mr. Mason had sharpened their drills just right so that they wouldn't stick in the granite. He and my father had practiced so that every move counted. Uncle Lou Sullivan was timekeeper. He also put water in the holes to keep the drills cool.

When those two Canadian champions came, their drills were not sharpened right for our granite rocks. Their drills kept sticking. Dad and his partner drilled twenty-nine inches and the two Swedes drilled twenty-six inches. Their drills stuck, and that's the only way my Dad beat 'em.

I sure hollered a lot that day! A lot of money traded hands. The saloons really did a big business after that. Everyone in town got drunk.

The Knob Hill where I worked was two and a half miles from Republic. I lived in town then. In winter when we walked up to the mine, it was about thirty below and the ice would just pop and the snow would squeak.

As you went up Eureka Gulch, you came first to the Quilp Mine.

Then the Surprise, the Lone Pine, Ben Hur, Knob Hill, Tom Thumb, and Mountain Lion.

The miners would wear their carbide lamps back to town. Sometimes you'd see the miners walking around town at night with their carbide lamps. And you'd hear the music from the saloons. Some had swinging doors. There was one saloonkeeper, Patsy Reardon, owner of the Butte, who'd stand out front and say, "Come on in here, boys, and put your money on the bar and we'll all go broke together."

Ladies were never allowed in the saloons, but there was a little room off to the side, and if they had an escort, then they could go in there for a drink.

There were a lot of fights. In any little mining town there are always fights. At one time Republic had thirteen saloons and there is always someone who is going to fight in a saloon. I don't know if my father was ever in a fight or not.

There were a lot of Irish people in Republic. And a lot of Swedes. Saint Patrick's day was quite a big deal. If you didn't have a green ribbon on, you might as well stay home.

I worked in the Knob Hill Mine for several years as a mucker. To be a mucker you have to be strong in the back. I really didn't care for this work.

It only smelled when they blasted, and we were out of there then. They drilled about twelve or fourteen holes by hand in those early days and it took about half a shift to clear that smoke out. When the smoke had cleared, the muckers would go in and shovel rocks into those little ore cars. And it would be quite a lot of mucking to do!

One day a boy called Harold Townsend and myself were in a little chamber on the eleven hundred level. There was just space enough to crawl in and take out this high grade ore from the room. It was creepy.

To get there from the surface we had gone down in the skip to the seven hundred level. The skip then slanted off to eight hundred, nine hundred, ten and eleven hundred levels. The skip was also called the hoist. Finally Harold and I crawled for a while until the tunnel opened up to the big room where we worked. They had blasted in there but the smoke was all gone.

The blasters had followed the vein of ore and sometimes we could see the little sparks of gold in the black streaks in the rock. Harold and I were shoveling out the high grade ore in little pieces through this hole that we had crawled in through. Outside, they took the ore away in ore carts on their little rails.

We had carbide lights hanging on our caps. The carbide light had a little reflector with something like a wick. You filled its can with carbide lumps and put a little water in there and flicked that little striker wheel on the flint. It lasted the whole shift and put out pretty good light. Much better than the candles miners had used before.

Well, we were working in there and the mouth of the place caved in. When it caved in, it came in quite a rumble, and falling rocks and dirt spread out right next to me. I could smell the dirt in the air. We didn't know how deep it was where it had caved in. Harold Townsend, the other boy, was more scared than I was.

The men on the outside knew we were in there. They dug from the outside. Harold and I dug from the inside out. We had to move some big rocks together.

It was an hour and a half until we got out, but it seemed longer than that. You can think of a lot of things in a short time. Other mines had had cave-ins. I thought of that. I thought of everything. I thought how nice it would be to see the sun shining.

I knew men who had been hurt in the cave-ins. I'll tell you a story about my father and another man. My father was in a vertical shaft about twelve feet down from a horizontal tunnel. He and his partner had completed drilling their holes and had lit the fuse. They had to climb the ladder to get out. My dad was first on the ladder and his partner was next.

Just as Dad got close to the top, the powder went off. There must have been a fast fuse in there. It threw my dad up out of the shaft onto the landing. His partner was blown back into the shaft. Dad went back in to get him out. He took him to the hospital, but he only lived two days.

Dad did not go back to work for four or five days. He was really shook up.

I guess it was about one hour and a half, two hours, that Harold Townsend and I were in there. My father was running the hoist that day and he pulled us up. When we got out on the top I told him that was my last shift down in the mine. It felt like the end of the world to me. It was really scary.

The boss gave us a job sorting ore on top.

I never went back down in the mine.

THE VERY REV. CABELL TENNIS: DEAN, SAINT MARK'S CATHEDRAL

Seattle, WA

Born: 1932

Just before World War I the First Presbyterian Church of Seattle was the largest Presbyterian body in the world. Its leader, the Reverend Mark Mathews, was an influential force statewide on moral/political issues, especially liquor control. Three quarters of a century later it is difficult to think of a Washington cleric of comparable importance. Catholic archbishop Raymond Hunthausen played such a role in the early 1980's because of his anti-nuclear activism, but the Vatican quickly silenced him. Probably more people are influenced statewide and nationwide by Tacoma's J. Z. Knight, a "channeler" of a so-called ancient warrior named Ramtha, than by *all* Washington's mainstream clerics. In fact, a century after its founding, Washington is said to be the state with the lowest per capita church attendance in the nation.

Virginia's Cabby Tennis was dean of Seattle's Saint Mark's Cathedral from 1972 to 1986. To me, the office of dean of an Anglican cathedral has always suggested images of Anthony Trollope novels and certainly not of rough and ready Washington. But Saint Mark's cavernous concrete spaces are home to a truly local color combination of high church ceremony (what Bishop Tennis calls the Episcopal "symbols and myths") and a democratic come-as-you-are congregation.

In 1986 Cabby Tennis was appointed bishop of Delaware. His return to the tidewater haunts of his Hampton, Virginia youth prompted the following reflections about his Seattle years.

My experience in Seattle taught me the profound importance of the religious community. The work of the ministry, how deeply it has impacted people's lives as they reflect back upon it. How often many people who came out Sunday in the Saint Mark's community are struggling through basic issues in their lives.

The symbols and the power of the religious community are often both a stabilizing and transforming influence on people's lives. They don't talk much about it. In fact, in our culture many folks won't talk about it at all because that is just not done. It is a matter of personal style not to have any religious sensibilities.

Meanwhile, I deeply believe that all of us are essentially pilgrims and sojourners, that the great images of the religious search are in every person one way or the other.

When I left Seattle I received an avalanche of reflections from people. Many of them very detailed experiences from their lives about how they had felt strengthened by the church. I really learned how important is the work of the priest in our lives.

Yet it is typical of Seattle that religion is pushed into a small corner page of the *P-I* and that what they print is mostly ridiculous stuff. The last page that I read in the paper is the religion page. I am really not interested in the kind of stuff they put on the religious page. I don't think it has anything to do with what I am about.

I used to think that Saint Mark's was a refugee colony, in the sense that we were seeing a hundred to a hundred and fifty new people a year there. We may have seen more, but these were the folks that identified themselves. These were folks that were coming there from a whole variety of circumstances.

Let me tell you what I mean by refugees. Some of these folks were coming from a sort of fundamental religion. They were burnouts from highly moralistic experiences who had fallen away from their church and had decided to give it another try. Some were refugees from some of the secular/religious fads: diets, gurus, pathways, attempts to find some meaning in their lives. Almost all of them were people in transition, going through some major experience in their life for which they were having to look beneath the surface at what their next goal was going to be. Really looking at fundamental issues of life.

I couldn't divorce myself from that. We were all fairly conscious that we were sojourners and that made a different kind of community.

I think that characterizes the Northwest. It has been a place of mountain men and of pluralism. People wear different clothes and there is a fairly wide range of acceptability in terms of what you can look like, what you can do, how you can be, and what you can think. The Northwest is often an adventurous, restless place. St. Mark's was a ministry right in the middle of all that, which made it fascinating.

Seattle is out there on the frontier. Archbishop Raymond Hunthausen, like others in the religious community, is dealing with this sort of refugee population. In Seattle there is an openness to look at new possibilities. You are also farther away from the centers of power. Most of the folks on the East Coast don't know Seattle is even out there. They are unconscious of the Northwest, and that gives Seattleites a kind of freedom. For instance in the Episcopal church, the church in this country was under the jurisdiction of the church of London for a hundred and fifty years before the American Revolution. That meant that the church in the colonies was free to develop some autonomy because it was so far from the bishop of London. I think Seattle is the same way. I think the Roman church there has been so far away from the hierarchy and the establishment that it has had relatively more freedom than it would have had in Chicago, Baltimore, and other places.

When we first arrived in the Northwest, we noticed a definite absence of lots of social life. People didn't entertain as much, they didn't get together as much, and we wondered, "What is going on here?" It took a while to realize that that was simply the nature of the place and that when people entertain, it is more often in smaller groups. We had been in Buffalo, where in the wintertime the great recreation was either skiing, in which case you went with lots of other folks, or entertaining at home. Buffalo people created a sense of coziness against the harsh winters by gathering together. But entertainment in Seattle is to go off on your own. At first, I felt a lack of a sense of community. Later on I learned that the Seattle community gets built in different kinds of ways.

Probably because of its early history, the religious community in the Northwest is not very well established. A lot of people that moved out there were sort of refugees from religious establishments of one kind or another. So today there is a fairly high degree of anti-clericalism among the folks. A good healthy and also unhealthy sort of pagan enthusiasm, nature worship, sets the climate for the place.

None of the churches has had a really strong hold on the area. As a result, the cults can run rampant. For instance, when I came to Seattle, there was a planeload a week of people that went from Seattle to the Philippines, to these people that were pulling chicken guts out of folks. They called themselves "bloodless surgeons."

The absence of a strong religious tradition leaves people open to all sorts of charlatans and quacks. Such a movement was called

Basic Youth Conflicts, which was kind of a fundamentalist approach to family life. In Akron, Ohio their tent show might get fifty people on a nice night. They would come to Seattle and fill the Coliseum.

Here is something that illustrates the phenomenon of the low profile that religion has in the Northwest. I went out to Ernst Hardware one day. I was looking for some plumbing parts. I was in that section of the store, wearing a clerical collar, wearing a black suit (uncharacteristic for me; I must have been involved in something very priestly that day) and a lady came up to me, not at all identifying the fact that I was clergyman of any kind. Completely oblivious of all the signals that this was a clergy person, she said, thinking that I was an Ernst employee, "Excuse me, will you please direct me to the toilet seats?"

That's an example of the state of organized religion in the Northwest.

Saint Mark's has a *good* sense of community. The ministry there was a ministry to people who were living on the boundary lines and who were searching for some sense of foundation in their lives. They were, and are, looking for a community open enough to allow them to explore the meaning of life.

When I was in my mid-twenties, I found a whole different perspective on *my* life. I was a young lawyer practicing in Hampton, Virginia. My partner's mother sold life insurance for Connecticut Mutual. She came by one day to sell the new guy in the firm a policy. I bought it and I still have it. When she came back with the policy she left a book by Paul Tillich, *The Courage to Be.* I read that and it really rekindled my interest in theology and my whole sense of perspective. He made sense. I had been dealing with people from a legal perspective, dealing with the whole gamut. Some criminal experience, some domestic relations, divorces, business practices, etc. I began pondering what it is about people that makes them do what they do. Asking some of those basic questions about what makes people the way they are.

Paul Tillich made me look at theology to understand what goes on in human life. What human life means. I began to reevaluate myself and decided that I really wanted to spend my life dealing with some of those basic fundamental issues of living. Rather than dealing with how to take marriages apart, I would rather deal with how to put people together.

Here is a story from where I grew up in Virginia. One day, just before I moved from my church at Buffalo, New York to Seattle, I was standing in the churchyard after Sunday morning service in my home town parish. In Hampton, people don't understand that anybody born in Virginia would be crazy enough to live anywhere else. My mother never understood that. Mothers never understand why their sons want to be anywhere else but right next to their mothers. It's a lifelong thing. Anyway, I was standing there in the graveyard and one of my cousins (everybody in a small town is a cousin) she came up and said, "Well, Cabby, I understand that you are moving again." And the *again* was emphasized.

I said, "Yes, ma'am."

She said, "You are in Buffalo now?"

I said, "Yes."

She said, "Where are you going now?"

I said, "I'm going to Seattle."

She sort of muttered and stuttered and she said, "You will go anywhere, won't you?"

I said, "Yes, ma'am. I will."

One of the things that just struck my mind, thinking about the nature of the Northwesterner—the Northwesterner is sort of a solo, individual person. The sense of individualism being so strong. For instance, you notice a lot of the activities are not necessarily corporate or team sport sorts of things. They are hiking and things that are individual pursuits. I can remember people coming in and I would say, "How was your weekend?"

"I went hiking."

"How was it?"

"It was good."

"You sound a little tentative."

"Well, we did see a few other people!"

That kind of individualism makes the work of a priest more difficult, because the church's traditional forms are not as readily accessible as, say, a mountain landscape. Priests are mediators of the conscious and the unconscious. They connect us to the symbols, to the leviathans that come up from the deep. I think the religious enterprise is deeply rooted in all that. One of the troubles with American culture is that it gets too preoccupied with the cutoff, rational side of ourselves. Mormonism is a totally rational but absurd religion as far as I am concerned. It all ends up in practicality and is really an *immoral* system. It ends up in a code of behavior, to the neglect of the deeper undercurrents of things. Mormons take everything literally, but symbols exist to be *broken up.* If you begin to take a symbol literally, it hardens and loses its power to communicate the underlying reality.

I think that fundamentalism is driven by anxiety. We are at this point, I think, at the end of an era and so there is a great deal of anxiety. Not only are people searching, but they also have a sense of dis-ease. And that can draw people to apocalyptic and fundamentalist answers. The work of a priest is to somehow keep before us our anchors, the real things that connect us to our origins. Our genuine origins.

The unavoidable religious issue is, "Am I connected to anything that gives me a sense of meaning over against the void?" In the Northwest I was touched by the loss of an anchor that many Native Americans had earlier brought to that question. I saw a lot of them suffering from alcoholism. Sad business! Anybody who's at a church sees people come for help all the time. When we lived in the Deanery, we put people up in the living room at night. A lot of Native Americans showed up on the doorstep. Some drunk. Some lost. Some women needing help.

I think their native culture in the Pacific Northwest gives them a sense that they are people of the land. Their whole mythology is deeply rooted in the natural order of things. All that marvelous art, the cult of the salmon and of the beaver and all. To our eyes their art looks like strange and exotic stuff. To their eyes their art contains icons of the natural world.

So, in a sense, Native Americans represent what is so apparent in the Pacific Northwest. Namely, that it is the natural world that was there before we came and which will remain there after we are gone. The Northwest's natural world dominates its reality. Even Seattle, a magnificent city, is a secondary reality in relationship to the Cascades and the Olympics that surround it.

New York is the reality of Manhattan Island and of anything near a hundred miles of it. That is not true of Seattle. Seattle is the second reality. The first reality is Mount Rainier and the surrounding mountains.

I think the Native American people understood, and understand, and are a part of that primary reality. Only recently the whites came in with civilization and in some sense they are still at war with the dominant reality of the natural order.

That is the continuing issue in the Northwest.

LAUGI THORSTENSON:

ICELANDIC WATERMAN

Point Roberts, WA

Born: 1897

America is full of immigrant communities that have become ethnic ghost towns. Traditions, especially the use of the immigrant's native language, die out amazingly fast, except where a conscious preservation effort is made, such as in the Scandinavian enclaves of Poulsbo and Ballard. Laugi Thorstenson was born in the fledgling Icelandic community of Point Roberts, Washington and began life speaking only Icelandic. Today neither he nor anyone else on that isolated peninsula speaks Icelandic regularly.

Helgi Thorsteinson (1859–1945) was a Canadian citizen of Icelandic birth who brought his young family north from the provincial capital of Victoria to the tiny American outpost of Point Roberts, beside Boundary Bay and the Strait of Georgia. Laugi Thorstenson (actually Gunnlauger Thorsteinson, but shortened for ease of pronunciation) was born on his father's squatter's rights stump ranch in 1897.

By 1904 there were ninety-three Icelanders at Point Roberts, half the peninsula's squatter population. Point Roberts might have maintained its Icelandic character if the economy had not shifted so decisively away from the Icelanders' original pursuits. Their cannery and fish trap employment had foundered by the mid-1930s, when the traps were outlawed. Fishing and stump ranching faded, too, as times changed. By the 1980s Point Roberts had become a second home community for metropolitan Vancouver, B.C.

Does anyone there still speak Laugi's mother tongue? He says, "My wife and I and our next door neighbor are about the only people that can speak it yet. And we only speak it when we don't want anybody to understand us."

"We have made three trips to Iceland and *they* marvel at how well we speak Icelandic. We speak an old-fashioned Icelandic, so I think we speak the language better than they do!"

This chapter is a remarkable family saga of Laugi's father, Helgi, and Helgi's foster brother Paul Thorsteinson. Helgi and Paul were raised on the same coastal farm, South Vik, in Iceland. Across the creek which divided that valley, Helgi's future wife and her mother worked on the North Vik estate. There, too, were Paul's future wife Oddny and their lifelong friend Siggi Scheving. Years later at Point Roberts, Washington Helgi and Paul and their large families all homesteaded and lived together. They shared the same barn and cleared land until Paul could build a barn of his own. Siggi Scheving, a bachelor, was like a part of Helgi's family, working and living there unless he was doing carpentry work in Victoria. As Laugi Thorstenson says, "Christmas was always celebrated at our house when both families got together on Christmas Eve. Me and my one brother and three sisters, and the five in Paul's family made quite a gang of kids for Christmas. Then everyone would spend New Year's Day with Paul and Oddny."

That custom continued until well after the two families had grown to over forty members.

The friendship between Helgi and Paul, and Dagbjort, Oddny, and Siggi that began when they were children at Vik in Iceland continued as long as they lived. The grandchildren are still friends and neighbors.

About 1871 my father's father was so poor and the famine was so bad in Iceland that they were almost like serfs. So my grandfather sent Helgi away to work. My dad when he was twelve years old was practically raised by this big estate where he was sent to be a shepherd boy.

My grandmother Groa Magnusdottir and her daughter Dagbjort Dagbjartsdottir came to work on this same estate. Dad said he fell in love with Dagbjort just as soon as he saw her brown eyes. They were raised together and came together to Canada.

My mother had never gone to school in her life. In those days

women weren't supposed to learn to write, but she learned from an old man who taught her with a homemade quill pen and a bottle of sheep's blood. She wrote a diary from the time they left Iceland until she settled here. She and Helgi were very fond of books, and much later here at Point Roberts she was the secretary of the Icelandic literary society, a sort of neighbors' lending library which shared old books and ordered new ones from Iceland.

A lot of Icelanders settled first at New Iceland on Lake Winnipeg in Manitoba and then moved from there to Victoria. But my folks came directly from Quebec to Vancouver on one of the first through-trains, arriving in August 1887.

On New Year's Day 1888 my father wrote home to his parents and brothers[1]:

---

[1]Translation by Laugi's sister, Runa Thordarson.

Last night, New Year's Eve, the Icelanders here all got together. Sigurdur Myrdal read scripture and we all sang hymns and other songs. It was a very enjoyable evening for both of us. They did the same thing on Christmas Eve, and plan to meet each Sunday evening. I feel well but am still very homesick. I think I would get over it if I could get steady work. Last summer I worked in a lumber mill. This winter only off and on with Sigurdur Myrdal at construction work. Daga is a maid in a large house. The weather is very good here, no snow and very little frost. My pay was raised twenty-five cents a day.

My parents didn't get married until December 22, 1888, a year and a half after they got to Victoria. It was quite common in those days, like it is now, that a couple lived together without getting married. They were up-to-date way back then.

By 1892, there were two hundred Icelanders in Victoria. They even had their own literary society and their own church, probably the first Lutheran church on the west coast of Canada.

My father could not find steady work as a carpenter and had to do dangerous work as a sewer ditchdigger. My mother worked in the hospital and did housework. By 1893 Canada was in a depression.

In 1894 my parents and some other Icelanders moved to Point Roberts, because of British Columbia's unemployment and because Victoria had an epidemic of infant cholera. My parents lost a boy and they almost lost their oldest girl. Kids were dying like flies. So parents wanted to get out of the city of Victoria.

At that time there was a saltery at Point Roberts where they salted down salmon in barrels. An Icelander working for that saltery told the Victoria Icelanders that a cannery would soon be starting up at Point Roberts and that they would need people to help build it. He told them that squatters could get free land over here on a military preserve.

So my dad and his foster brother Paul Thorsteinson, they bought eighty acres with a log cabin and a little clearing. They paid the squatter for his log cabin and for his squatter's rights. I was born in that same log cabin in 1897.

When my parents came here to Point Roberts in 1894, my father went to work for the new cannery, building a big warehouse. That Alaska Packers Association was the biggest employer here at Point Roberts, but Dad was always determined to be a self-supporting farmer. He kept on clearing land and building up his squatter's rights farm. He had chickens, sheep, and about twelve cows he was milking. That was considered a pretty middle-classed farmer in those days.

My father wrote home to his parents on March 14, 1895.

We live a quiet life here, which is a relief after all the noise of the city. I didn't mind the noise much when I had steady work. I guess we left Victoria just in time, as unemployment is getting worse instead of better. Many Icelandic families have moved here from Victoria which makes it nice for us.

We built a small skiff and bought twine and made our own little beach seine. We have been able to catch fish both for ourselves and other neighbors who have no beach or boat. The families gather on the beach on warm summer evenings and visit while the men "fish."

Paul and I have cleared, fenced, and seeded about three acres and are now clearing for pasture in hopes that some day the land will be ours. We plan to plant a big garden next month, then work at the new cannery during the summer.

On December 22, 1895 Helgi wrote home again.

Our first winter here was exceptionally mild and the summer warm and dry. The pasture dried up, but the vegetable garden did real well, especially the potatoes. I am going to tell you, just for fun, what our first garden produced. We raised sixty pounds of beans, fifty pounds of onions, some corn and other small vegetables, nine big sacks of potatoes and four sacks of rutabagas. There is no market for anything, but we were able to sell one sack of potatoes and some butter. We used the surplus vegetables to feed the pigs. We also raised five tons of hay from the old clearing and from around the stumps. We have cleared two additional acres which we will seed, so we should have more hay next year. Paul and I work together. We own thirty chickens and seven pigs. We butchered one this fall and also a steer we bought from Brewster for seventeen dollars. He dressed at five hundred fifty pounds and the pig at one hundred sixty pounds. I own two cows and two calves and Paul owned two, but unfortunately one of his cows fell over the bank and was killed.

We built a barn thirty by sixteen feet and a storehouse sixteen by twelve. We also built a small chicken house, pig house, and a smoke house. We are real pleased and proud that we can now have smoked meat for Christmas just like we always had back home in Vik. Our buildings are made from driftwood salvaged from the beach and split cedar from the woods. Mostly we have worked at home, but we each made nineteen dollars working at a nearby fish cannery. We also worked in the hay for an Englishman and got one and a half tons of hay for our work. Last summer we worked two weeks at road building and were paid one fifty a day. We have no taxes to pay, but each man has to build roads for two and a half days without pay. This is done in the spring and summer.

We decided to try our luck at salmon fishing. We bought a net for two hundred dollars. It is one hundred fathoms long and seven fathoms wide. We had intended making it ourselves, but through some misunderstanding it was sent all made up. Therefore costing more than we had expected. There are three of us in partnership, Siggi Scheving, Paul, and myself. We hope to do well. There is an abundance of salmon here and the cannery last year paid sixteen cents apiece for them and we hear the price will be twenty cents next summer.

We had quite a scare the other day when someone read in a newspaper that all the settlers on Point Roberts were to be driven off without receiving any compensation for their homes or their work. It happened in a place not far from here and the place was taken for a fort. We settlers on Point Roberts got together and signed a petition which was sent to Washington, D.C., asking that Point Roberts be opened for homesteads. I would feel terrible if we had to leave this place. I feel so well here, better than anywhere since I came to America. Our children are healthy and I have never been homesick since I left Victoria. We look forward to a good future here. I have no idea where we would go if we have to leave. I am sending a picture of your two granddaughters. Daga took them to Victoria last summer. Groa had tonsillitis for quite some time, but the doctor said she was too young to have them removed before we left Victoria. All went well and Daga was real happy to have this over with. Groa is five years old and the picture is good of her, but your namesake Gudrun (Runa) is a little too happy. She is five months old.

Greet all my brothers for me.

Your loving son, Helgi.

On March 22, 1898 my father wrote to his brother Einar in Iceland:

We now have three children living. Groa will be eight in August. She is now going to school. Gudrun was three in March and Gunnlaugur was five months old on the ninth of this month. They are all in good health which we are very thankful for.

Paul built a house nearby but we still share the barn, garden, and hayfield and work together. They have two boys, seven and three years old.

Siggi Scheving lives with us and works for his board and room. He also does carpenter work in the community and in Victoria. He owns a share in our boat. We now have a post office in Point Roberts. I am sending you our new address which I hope will not have to be changed. I will not leave here unless I have to. When we first came here, our mail came to Ladner, B.C. in Canada. We men here took turns walking the ten miles to bring the mail and buy much needed supplies. Later one of our Icelandic friends bought a horse and made deliveries.

There is a store here now and the post office is in it. They buy from us butter at twenty cents a pound and eggs, fifteen to twenty-five cents a dozen.

Like I told you in my last letter, we three, Paul, Siggi, and I built a boat. We used it last summer and were very pleased with it. We bought canvas and Daga sewed sails for us on her little hand-sewing machine. We added eighty fathoms to our net. Bought the twine and made it ourselves so we now have two hundred eighty fathoms. We caught twelve hundred salmon but due to the low price, ten cents, later eight cents apiece, we only shared thirty-three dollars each. Then we had to quit in the mid-

dle of the season because the cannery had more fish than they could handle.

We also built a shed thirty-two by thirteen on a ledge at the beach to keep our boat in. We have a padlock on the door and hope it will be safe. Our little skiff was stolen.

I now own four cows and two heifers and a steer and pig to butcher this fall. I find it better to have just one pig at a time and buy a young one when I butcher the old one.

We raised a lot of potatoes and as there is very little sale for them, we feed them to the pigs and cows. With lots of milk it does not cost much to raise a pig.

We built a new barn fifty-three by forty-two feet. Hay storage in the middle and room for thirteen stalls on each side.

Last fall three men were sent here to appraise all the homes and farms on Point Roberts. Then they were to be sold to the highest bidder. This was a big worry to all of us here on the Point. We hired a lawyer for the second time. This time to contact the State Legislature which was in session and try to get them to allow each settler to buy his land for the assessed valuation. We also sent a petition to Washington, D.C. We are waiting to hear.

Our land, mine and Paul's, was valued at six dollars an acre for the front forty acres but three dollars for the back. If it ever becomes ours, we'll divide it so that each of us has twenty acres in front next to the beach and twenty at the back. It will come hard on us to pay it, but harder still if we have to leave.

Greetings to all my relatives.

Your loving brother, Helgi.

By 1899 the Point Roberts fish canneries stopped buying fish from us because they could get all the fish they needed from their own fish traps. So Dad and Uncle Paul sold their fishing boat and gear and went to work in the A.P.A. cannery.

In 1900 we all became American citizens. In 1906 my parents sold their Victoria house for three hundred dollars.

In 1908 Theodore Roosevelt opened up Point Roberts to homesteading and my parents were able to obtain title to their land. My father sent the president a gift, the hide from his largest sheep, that Mr. Elsner had tanned and made into a rug. Teddy Roosevelt wrote that he was using that rug in his bedroom in the White House.

My parents never got very fluent in English. All the neighbors spoke Icelandic. Even the grocery store would always hire Icelandic girls to clerk because they would have to be able to talk to the newcomer Icelandic farmers.

I didn't understand a word of English until my second sister, Runa, started to go to school. My oldest sister, Groa, would go to school and come home and speak Icelandic at home like everybody did. When Runa started going to school, the two of them would come home and talk this foreign language that I couldn't understand at all. It didn't take long for a little kid to learn that language. In a couple of months I was talking English as well as Icelandic!

About 1903 they built a better school near the west side of Point Roberts. I started walking three miles to school there in 1905. The trail was marked by blazes. In the fall when the ground was covered with dry leaves, it was very easy to lose the way. Us kids went to school here and learned the American ways right away.

We always kept busy. I would help my dad clear land. There was always continuous land clearing, making a pasture out of the woods. This was all solid woods. It was all practically done by hand. We blasted stumps with dynamite and we drug a little bit of stuff around with horses, but mostly land clearing was done with burning and by hand.

Roads were made the same way. I remember going everywhere by trails. For instance, there was a trail diagonally up through this way across our farm up to a road that went north and south from Boundary Bay to South Beach. That's where they came in from Canada. When my Uncle Thordur came from Iceland in 1903, my father had to meet him to show him the trail from Ladner to our house through the stumps.

Work at Point Roberts was seasonal. You worked about seven months in the canneries and then you picked up odd jobs through the winter. The summer of 1909 was a big salmon year and the canneries were so short of help that they hired all the kids that wanted work, even nine-year-olds. Jonas, Arni, and I were like three brothers. We got a job at the A.P.A. cannery. The pay was ten cents per hour. The work was light but very boring. My first job was watching the machine that put the lids on the cans and shutting it off if a can jammed. We were hired by the Chinese labor contractor and were paid off in gold coin after he added up our hours on an abacus. I remember how scared I was of the Chinese in their Oriental-smelling bunkhouse where this boss had his office.

In the summer of 1911 we kids all worked in the George and Barker cannery and then in the A.P.A. cannery. My job at the A.P.A. was moving cooling racks. Wages were thirty-five cents an hour and I made sixty dollars. I was fifteen that fall and was allowed to buy a twelve-gauge Remington pump shotgun for twenty-two dollars and fifty cents. I also got my first dog. The night watchman at the cannery gave me a six-month-old cocker spaniel named Bennie. The next few years we supplied the family with pheasant, grouse, and ducks all fall and winter.

I eventually spent many years working on or around the fish traps until they were outlawed in 1934. I've worked on a scow that got twenty thousand salmon in an hour's time.

Fish traps were made of pilings and wire net. They were constructed by a ninety-foot derrick on a barge. A steam donkey hammered in those pilings. They were up to a hundred and ten feet long. It took a big derrick to get them up.

They were capped from piling to piling by planks so that the wire net could be hung to guide the fish into the trap on incoming tides. In the fall, traps had to be dismantled. The company just hooked a cable on these planks and yanked them out and set them adrift. Planks washed up on the beach, where settlers would salvage them. Most all the barns and the oldest houses on the Point were built out of those planks. Beautiful lumber. Two by tens. Two by twelves.

Dad built his house that way in 1900. He and his partner had their own thirty-foot sailboat. We sailed to Blaine to get the shingles, windows, and tar paper. The rest of the materials in that house all came off the beach.

In those days the only means of transportation was by boat. From Point Roberts we always used to see sailing ships being towed into Vancouver because all the shipping went by here.

By the end of 1910 I was losing interest in school and thinking only of getting through the eighth grade. I had no desire for higher education. My ambition was to be a steamboat man! They always wore gold braid on their uniforms. They had kind of a lordly manner and I thought that was for me.

I quit school in 1912 after the eighth grade. By the time I got my tugboat captain's license, steam was on the way out. But I became a lifelong fisherman and spent many years salmon fishing in Alaska.

When the first canneries opened in the mid-1890s, a lot of shipping came directly to Point Roberts. The canned salmon was shipped out and cans were shipped in. Freight and mail for the whole community was by boat. A paddlewheel steamer came all the way from Seattle and stopped at all the ports clear up to here. This was their last stop.

But I had actually learned about boats from an Icelandic fisherman named Larson. One day Jonas and Arni had gone to the beach. It was low tide and there on the sandbar was a thirty-two foot sailboat high and dry. They walked up to it and a man crawled out of the forepeak where he had been sleeping and greeted them in Icelandic. They came home and told Dad and he went down and met the man and found out that Dad had known the man's brother in Victoria. Dad invited Captain Larson up to the house and they became good friends.

Captain Larson taught us kids how to sail. He really took us over like we were his grandkids. He worked alone on his sailboat, fishing at night when the fish couldn't see his net. One of the big hazards for a gillnetter was to drift into these fish traps at night. Captain Larson told us that one night he was drifting, sound asleep, with his gillnet set. What woke him up was a salmon that jumped out of the water and landed on the deck and was kicking around. He woke up and saw that he was almost into a fish trap. He figured that it was an act of God to wake him up with this salmon.

So he threw that salmon back overboard.

One night Larson took me and Jonas and Arni fishing. He was to have brought us home the next morning, but it didn't work out that way. He put out his net on the west side of the Point and drifted south when all of a sudden a westerly gale came up and a tide rip bunched and tangled up his net badly. He managed to get the net on board and then he sailed into a bay on Sucia Island and there he spent the day untangling the net.

By sunset the wind had changed to the southeast and he sailed for east Point Roberts and set his net and had a real good catch of sockeye.

Larson taught us kids how to tie knots and splice rope and he told us many stories of his adventures. He had sailed deep sea and had fished in Bristol Bay. We boys idolized him. He had also smuggled opium, which he didn't seem to think had been a crime. He was an expert boatbuilder and had built his boat and his floating house at Mount Vernon on the Skagit River.

Larson was a real Puget Sound sourdough. I remember several other old-timers who made their living from the salmon.

The fact is that salmon has been our heritage. It was the livelihood of all, from the lowly siwash to the pot-bellied cannery owners. It was either salmon fishing or related work, combined with logging or farming, that was the Puget Sounder's way of life.

GEORGE UCHIDA: FROM INTERNMENT CAMP TO CAMPING OUT

Seattle, WA

Born: 1924

When I first visited Seattle in 1968 as a summer backpacker from the East Coast, I was extremely impressed with the area's interest in hiking and mountaineering. In Washington, D.C., where I was from, the newspapers were not likely to put missing hikers or ongoing expedition news on the front page. In Seattle they were. I even remember when my Spokane hiking partner Chris Kounkel's photo was spread across the front page of *The Seattle Times* in the late '70s because he had waited in line three nights to be the first person in the door at R.E.I.'s winter sale.

Scouting had had a lot to do with that community interest in the outdoors. George Uchida is a perfect example.

George's parents were too traditionally Japanese to participate in such a thing as Scouting. Also they were locked up in a "camp" during all of World War II with much of the rest of Seattle's Japanese community. That was almost the only camping young George did until he put in two years in the Army in World War II, mostly in the Pacific in military intelligence.

But because of his son, George became a Scouting dad in 1958. In fact, it became almost a second career for him during the '50s and '60s. Seattle Scouting had something that places like Philadelphia or Atlanta did not have. Under the right leadership, nearby wilderness camps put the outdoors in the souls of a lot of kids. George Uchida began to work closely with an outstanding motivator of boys, Max Eckenburg, originally a Boeing engineer and then the chief ranger at Camp Sheppard on Mount Rainier. Max's High Adventure climbing program on the fourteen-thousand-foot volcano was a national model for outdoor leadership. Max Eckenburg, George Uchida, and Ome Daiber also pushed Scouting in the direction of search and rescue.

As someone who moved here from across the continent of my own free will, I always like to believe that Seattle is not just another megalopolis. I also like to think that life is not just what you can take, but also what you can create.

George Uchida had every excuse to be bitter about life. During the war, his country had treated him and his family in a despicable way. But George went on to help create a legacy of pride in many, many boys.

I was born and raised in "Garlic Gulch," which was predominantly immigrant or second generation Italians. We were only one of a couple of Japanese families there. All our neighbors were Italians, including our landlord. It was all Italian and broken English. Mostly swear words. I probably learned how to swear in Italian before I learned how to swear in English. I spoke Japanese at home and outside I spoke broken English and some Italian. Once I started school, it was all English and I forgot everything else. Dad worked for an automobile wrecking yard, salvaging parts off of automobiles, and my mother worked a local glove factory sewing gloves. My family and the Italians all got along just great because we were all poor. Poverty is a good common denominator. If you're poor and somebody else is poor, you make good friends no matter who you are!

In 1933 my Scout troop was on the fringe of Garlic Gulch, right there by the Buddhist temple. My brother Jack was our Scoutmaster and he emphasized a lot of hiking for us kids. Of course, fifty years ago it was a lot easier because nearby areas were all woods. Everything was in the boonies then. A big outing was to take the ferryboat out to Mercer Island, which was all woods. Mercer Island is very well developed now, but there was no bridge then and very few houses.

The traditional Japanese thing was all based on the family. But

George
Uchida (left)
talking with
Max
Eckenburg.

when you pooled that many people together with no privacy, it was
hard on family cohesiveness. Young kids would all get together in
gangs and their folks were in no position to tell them what to do.
In town the father had been able to say, "Be in by ten," because
he had put bread on the table. But kids were no longer dependent
on the head of the family in that camp.

I was nineteen. As soon as I could, I left. Because although I got
fed three times a day, I still had to have the other necessities. I went
to work on the farms picking potatoes and onions. We were working cheap, because the guys in the shipyards were making one
twenty-five, one fifty an hour. When I worked my way down to
Nevada doing tough construction work, I was the highest paid guy
on the crew because I was shoveling cement all day. It was seventy-
five cents an hour for me and forty for the rest of them!

The people in the camps had no idea what was going to happen
to them. The people who were very optimistic had left their homes
with friends who could look after them. The people who were
rather pessimistic had just walked away or had gotten ten cents on
the dollar. My parents were fortunate. They had an iddy-biddy
apartment which they left with an agent. All during the war they
never made any money, but at least we had a place to come home
to.

My dad and mother and sister spent the whole war in the camp.

It wasn't a physical strain, but my parents had worked their whole lives for nothing. They were retirement age when they came back and they had to start all over again. My mother passed on in 1950 and my father only lived another half year after that.

My brother and I were both in the service.

When I first came back from the war, I gave an application to Boeing. I waited three days and decided that I had given them a chance and I started my own company. Since then Boeing has sent me four Western Union telegrams to work in their tool and die department. But I started a contracting firm rebuilding and redecorating homes.

I got into Scouting when my little boy was eight years old in 1958. I took him to get him inducted into the Cub Scouts and I came home as a Cubmaster. I should have remembered what I had learned in the Army, "Don't volunteer for nothing."

We had three Boy Scout troops, and Max Eckenburg had one of them. And Bill Pitts had another one. And Don Wilson had another. They were all very active troops. At about the same time they decided individually to take advantage of the outdoor training that their kids had gotten and form a Scout search and rescue group as a community service. After a few years this was incorporated into the exploring division of the Boy Scouts here locally and eventually nationwide.

For a long time our search and rescue kids were not accepted by the law enforcement people. But about 1966 we were called by the sheriff over there in Renton. Two little kids had wandered off. So our search and rescue Scouts went out there and we searched all day and eventually found them under a bunch of leaves out in the woods. They had been stabbed and killed.

The sheriff called us the next morning. He wanted to come up with a weapon in this big patch of woods. We came up with a hunting knife, all bloodied. That knife had had three owners. One had purchased it from the store and had given it to another. And the third one, a young guy, when he saw that knife, he broke down and confessed.

Ever since we aided that one search, we have often been called upon to look for lost people, bodies, and evidence.

It is just great working with those young fellows in the Explorers.

To know that we can leave this country in their hands. Like Max's climbing program at Camp Sheppard. Quite a few of them are now deputy sheriffs, detectives, or park rangers. Many are in mountain rescue.

I volunteered with Scouting a lot of years. It wasn't for the sake of the Scout Council. It was because of Max Eckenburg. He's that kind of guy. There wasn't a week that went by that I didn't fight with the Council people. But because Max was at Camp Sheppard, he got me involved with the Sheppard program.

Max ran the program. Me and Tom McCartney, we were Max's support team. I went out and recruited fourteen- to nineteen-year-old kids for staff. Each one was just top-notch. We would train them and put them in charge of a climbing group and send them out for a week. We never had a serious accident or fatality.

Once or twice they actually got into rescues as they were climbing around Mount Rainier's glaciers. That was the finest young people's program in the country during the 1960s. We had people from all over the United States come for that program and for glacier mountaineering and for summit climbs of Mount Rainier.

The High Adventure program was self-supporting, but the Seattle area Scout Council objected because climbing was "too dangerous." They canceled it and had Max design a hiking program for the Cub Scouts. Then they kiboshed that because they didn't want the Cubs to go more than seven-tenths of a mile from camp, because they claimed that young kids could not hike that far. All these things forced Max out and when he retired, I quit too, in 1981.

Some of my best Scouting memories are of the Order of the Arrow, an elite group of older Boy Scouts. I had this little Chinese kid who came into our Arrow chapter and became our chapter chief. I was his advisor. He was fifteen years old and so wet behind the ears that I had to advise him how to do everything about leading his chapter. His family was not the outdoors type. His father and mother had a little grocery store.

Most of the people in Scouting are followers. You get one strong guy and everybody follows him. The Order of the Arrow includes probably the smartest of all the Scouts, because the only way to join it is by election. Only one kid per year gets elected from each

Scout troop to join the Order of the Arrow. All the kids vote for the guy they think is most qualified. Then, among that group of kids who have been elected, there is an election and one kid gets to be the chief of that chapter. Gary Locke happened to be elected chief. He was a smart kid with a lot of initiative and he took very willingly to whatever advice I gave him.

I was his advisor and we would meet once a week. I would never tell him what to do. He had to come up with it. Half the time the meetings would be in my car at Dag's Drive-in, over a hamburger and a malt. The meetings at my house downtown, we always had cookies because I figured that the best way to a young Scout's heart was through his stomach.

For two years Gary ran the best Arrow chapter in Seattle. I could just see this kid's confidence build up. Of course, he was asking me for advice on everything. Finally he asked me, "What'll I do in college?"

"Going into Liberal Arts is good," I said, "but if you get into law, it will help you in whatever you do."

He got a full scholarship to Yale and went to Boston College for law school. Then all of a sudden here he is, deputy prosecutor for King County.

Now Gary is a state representative and probably one of the most astute congressmen in Olympia.

BILL VAN WEIRINGEN:
WHEAT SACK SEWER
Sedro-Woolley, WA
Born: 1893

Bill Van Weiringen immigrated from Holland early in this century when Whidbey Island had a growing Dutch population. But Bill decided to work for English-speaking farmers in order to assimilate as rapidly as possible. Even so, he worked sixteen years in Island and Skagit counties before he could speak English very well.

Bill worked for a succession of Whidbey Island farmers at a time when the island was considered Washington's richest wheat land. Those record crops were horse-power harvested by what today look like Rube Goldberg combines. The business end of the contraption was a grain chute which fed wheat into burlap sacks. After each sack was full someone sewed its top shut and then other men hauled it away. The whole operation was efficient except for the sewing shut of these sacks. That's where Bill Van Weiringen became an American. I didn't have a Depression," he says. "I had more work than I could throw a stick at."

Bill was Whidbey Island's champion sack sewer. But inevitably sack sewing, like so many other forestry, fishing, mining, ranching, dairying, and aerospace jobs in Washington, was mechanized out of existence.

Bill Van Weiringen bought a farm near Mount Vernon in 1937. He stopped speaking Dutch, and went on to raise a large American family.

He has never forgotten the excitement of those Whidbey wheat harvests.

I was a sack sewer before I was twenty years old. The farmers hired their own people, but it took a skilled person to be a sack sewer. Sack sewers were awfully hard to get and they had to pay them well.

Everyone else was getting two bits an hour and I was getting forty cents an hour!

The sewer is the most important thing in the whole thrashing outfit. He has to get the grain sewn so that they can haul it away. If you had fifty bundles to put in the machine, you could get it done in five minutes with a good sewer. Otherwise, you might have to wait ten minutes while the sewer catches up to the output of the thrashing machine.

I sewed them up and took them over to the pile of finished ones. I'd sew up the next one.

If I sat around, the men would be standing around waiting for me!

EVERETT WHEALDON:

CASCARA BARK PEELER

Port Townsend, WA

Born: 1910

Cascara trees are a characteristic coastal species which have entered into our folklore like the Bunyanesque firs and the dugout canoe cedars. But the cascara, prized for its "shittim bark," has gone out of fashion in recent decades because its laxative benefits have been surpassed by man-made chemicals.

Some people still peel cascara bark but it is a dying tradition.

Everett Whealdon was a twelve-year-old in rainy Pacific County during the Great Depression, when a poor boy had to work hard for his dream of a bicycle or of a .22 rifle.

Driving along the Clearwater River in northern Idaho, I spotted a thicket of small trees growing in a fencerow. The dark, shiny leaves looked familiar. I stopped. Could it be? This far from the Pacific Ocean?

With my pocket knife I peeled a sliver of bark from the side of a slender bole and took a good strong sniff. No doubt about it—for a moment I was a twelve-year-old boy again, peeling cascara bark on the old homestead in Pacific County, Washington.

Loggers, fishermen, and homesteaders of the Northwest have always had, and still have, a large place in song and story. But who remembers the bark peelers?

Are there any left?

Call it cascara, barberry, or shittim bark, the stuff was in the early part of the century the raw material for the active ingredient in many kinds of commercial laxatives.

I'm not familiar with the pharmacopoeia, but my druggist friend tells me that they don't use cascara much anymore. "We've got better things now," he says.

Used to be, you could find a place to sell your bark in most any little burg from Eureka, California to Juneau, Alaska. And about the time the boys came home from World War I, dried and chopped cascara bark would bring you (the peeler) somewhere in the neighborhood of twenty cents a pound.

But by 1935, looking over the market prices listed in newspapers for such items as hides, wool, mohair, and butterfat, you might, just might, see: "cascara bark, lb., .03."

Cascara *(cascara sagrada)* trees range in size from fencerow thickets of slender sprouts to large branching oldsters up to two feet or more in diameter at the base of the trunk.

You never find "groves" of cascara trees. You may find a fair sprinkling of them scattered among alders and evergreens, or they may be few and far between, and they always grow in areas of fairly heavy rainfall.

Cascara trees are found mostly in the valleys of the Coast Range, the western slopes of the Cascades, and in many places in the broader valleys between. The thicket I noted in Idaho made me guess that they may grow in rainy climates farther east.

Of course, you were supposed to get permission from the landowner to peel on his property. Big timber companies set rates for "stumpage," and required that the trees be felled and stumps at least a foot high be left with the bark on so that new growth could start. But there was always a good deal of "pirating," the wasteful practice of skinning standing trees only as high as could be reached from the ground. Those trees died with much bark left on and unsalvageable.

Most peelers went into the woods with only an axe and the favorite tool for the job, a "spud," a knife-like blade with a curved point at one end. I carried a gunnysack or a skeleton sort of backpack on which I could rick up the sections to carry out of the woods.

Model-T pickups or, along rivers, rowboats might transport the cargo the rest of the way to where you could spread the bark out to dry in the sun and later chop it into small pieces.

On older, bigger trees, the bark might be up to a half inch thick, and when the sap was up, felled trunks and branches could be "unwrapped" freely.

Once the job began, there was always that distinct, pervasive odor. I can't describe it but I know it, just as everyone remembers the smells of childhood. An old familiar smell will stir the memory in ways that no amount of conversation or reading can.

Peeling cascara was the stump rancher's salvation, a summer job for the trapper, and a means of financing many a boy's dream of a .22 rifle or a new bicycle. I recall one "bootleg" expedition two other boys and I made into a stand of cascara located in a draw between the hills up along the South Fork. One of the boys had located it. He said it was good peeling and he invited two of us to go along. We worked half a day and lugged out several sackfuls.

I don't know who owned the property. (I hope it was Weyerhaeuser.) Anyway, we got away with it. We didn't meet anybody coming, going, or while we were there.

Cascara bark peeling was pretty common in our neck of the woods just after World War I, when the price was high. In fact, a pro had bought some of the "stumpage" on our woodlots a couple of years before I got inspired. So I just took the old butcher knife and went after the leavings. Then I spread the bark out to dry in the pasture.

Sometimes the calves chewed on it and got the scours!

ADOLPH "BIG DOBBY" WIEGARDT:

BEAR DANCER AND STEAM LOCOMOTIVE FIREMAN

Nahcotta, WA

Born: 1897

Now that Washington statehood is a century old there is a temptation to think of the state's distant past as a static period. Nothing could be further from the truth. Adolph Wiegardt's story is a good example.

Big Dobby (the name used to differentiate him from his son Dobby) began life in Bruceport, Washington. But Bruceport soon faded away with the oyster harvests on which it had been dependent. Another town, Cranberry, is mentioned by Big Dobby, but it, too, is gone. So is the railroad on which he worked as a bear dancer (gandy dancer) and fireman. Before Big Dobby's time that same railroad had doomed the economy of Oysterville (now revived as a tourist center).

Less apparent than dried-up towns and railroads has been the change in social attitudes in the last hundred years. Adolph Wiegardt's views about other social groups—blacks, Jews, Indians—in his corner of early 1900s Washington reflect a strong sense not necessarily of prejudice but of apartness. (Perhaps the most recent example of such attitudes came out of Judge Boldt's Indian fishing rights decision, when Indian treaty fishermen were widely castigated by people who knew little about the issue or about Northwest Indian history.)

Social theorist Michael Harrington has written that one reason the United States has never developed a viable Socialist Party is because early in this century when such parties were developing in Europe, American working people's self-identity was primarily of race and ethnicity rather than of class. Often the melting pot melted slowly.

Big Dobby's father's eagerness for himself and his family to become real Americans is striking. As often happened (then and now), the parents prevented the second generation from learning their language of origin.

The logic of assimilation, however, is that eventually it will no longer be us versus them, but simply us.

School integration and housing and job desegregation have succeeded more than people realize in changing the social climate of Washington. Rural areas probably still have the furthest to go in this regard, but even there a steady influx of newcomers, often retirees in search of cheap land, will greatly alter outmoded attitudes.

The first hundred years of Washington state have been anything but static. And I predict that the pace of social change in the second hundred will be even greater.

My name is Adolph Wiegardt. I was born in 1897. I happened to do railroad work because it was just a case of making an existence. I was born in Bruceport about fifteen miles from here. The name of Bruceport is still there but that is about all. We were the last family in Bruceport when we left there in 1897. But there were about twenty homes or so at one time there. A couple of hotels, stores, and things. Bruceport was founded by the crew of the Robert Bruce in about 1851. I think it was a lumber schooner, or it could have been an oyster schooner from San Francisco. Bruceport turned into an oyster village.

My father had just come to this country and needed work. He was in Astoria and he would fish in the Columbia River when the fishing season was on. And when there was no fishing season, then they would come over here onto Willapa Bay and work in the oysters. In 1870, my father bought an old hotel in Bruceport and fixed it up as a residence.

Dad came from Denmark. Tonder, Denmark. My mother was

born in Denmark too, in Horsens. I didn't speak Danish myself.
When Dad and Mother were married, and we kids were getting to
be born, Dad said, "We are speaking English. We are not speaking
any foreign language." Mother wanted to teach us Danish but he
said, "No, we are Americans."

I was four months old when we left Bruceport. We came up here
because of educating the older children. There was no school or
anything anymore in Bruceport. So Mother was having to educate
the children herself. So we came up here.

Dad had oyster beds right out in front here.

Oysterville had been the big oyster center around here. It had
been founded in 1854. Up until about 1903, there were one hundred and three children in school in Oysterville. And then twenty
or more years later they had to import children to keep the school
going. Oysterville just disintegrated all at once when the railroad
came into Nahcotta about 1887, making it the shipping point for
oysters to California.

I went to school in Nahcotta.

In 1914 at the age of seventeen I went to work for the O.W.R.N railroad. I went bear dancing to start in with. Bear dancing is what was called working on the ties, laying and putting in new track. I suppose that would be the same thing as a gandy dancer. But we always called it bear dancing.

We didn't sing as we worked. We had a boss that made us work. J.L. Spring was our boss. He was a good fellow to work for, but he insisted on getting a day's work out of you. He was the superintendent of the construction, and stuff.

I was putting in ties.

In the wintertime, if there would be a storm or something, we would have to go along and shore up the track down by McGowan and in through there where there was a washout with the tides. The winter storms would sweep in off the Columbia River and the waves would wash out underneath the tracks, which were built out on a rockway. It was along the edge of the land, but it was all reinforced with rocks. And these rocks would wash away and then we would have to shore up the roadbed before the trains could travel over it.

We had what they called a work train that would take us out, and then it would probably lay on the siding all day and wait for us to get our jobs done, and then bring us home at night. We were part of the section crew. At one time at the start of World War I there were only four of us on the job. Then in the spring or summer a lot of the college kids would come down from Portland and get jobs working on the section crews.

I put in ten years on the railroad along the edge of the Columbia river. Then I did a lot of sports fishing on the Columbia, too.

I worked for ten years on the railroad. In 1924 the automobiles came in, roads were built, and they took over and railroad business dropped. Finally we were laid off.

I had worked on the section crew for maybe a year and a half. Then I went night watching in the roundhouse up in Nahcotta. From there I got promoted to fireman on a passenger train and sometimes on a work train.

I miss the railroad days. In 1930 to 1935 if I would go to Portland for a day or two, I would hear the steam trains coming in. I would go in to the city and at night I could hear these engines whistling their signals. Of course, I knew what the signals were for and it just kind of made me homesick.

I haven't been into town now for a long time.

The best thing about the railroad was the wages we got out of it. We had a little nigger that used to work with us on the section crew. He was Benny and he was kind of a character. He was a singer and whatnot. His main headquarters was down at the Breakers Hotel, where he was a bellhop. Then he moved up to Cranberry and bought a little cranberry bog. Then the Breakers went haywire and he got a job on the railroad.

There was a town called Cranberry. It was eight miles down the peninsula, about half way between here and Longbeach. All that is there now is the name. Cranberry.

The train went through Cranberry. There was nothing to firing the train. You just sat there in the locomotive by the engine and you had a valve that you pushed back and forth. That was all there was to it!

We didn't put wood in. We had oil when I was working there. I would put a little more oil in, watch the steam gauge, and keep an eye on the track and on the crew behind.

There was an engineer running the train and I was called the fireman. We sat in the locomotive right across the gangway from each other, side by side. And the engineer always said, "I don't care if I see it. You tell me if you see anything, because I want to know. I might not see it."

He wanted to be sure because he couldn't see everything from his side.

All the engineers were interesting. They were all nice fellows to work for. I always got along nicely with all of them. There was an old gentleman whose name was Henry Rudolph. He was kind of a character. I don't know where he came from. He was imported in here to run the engine from the outside world. People considered someplace else "the outside world" because the railroad was the only way we had of getting them out of here, except by boat to South Bend.

In the summertime we would have about four passenger trains a day back and forth between here and Megler. I would jump on the engine here and go to Megler on the Columbia River and then we would turn right around and come back again to Nahcotta. Then there would be another train just as soon as we got into Nahcotta and we'd put off for Megler again.

On Saturday nights there was always a big load of people that came down from Portland on the old J.T. Potter, and the Harvest Queen, and those boats there. We would leave Megler about five o'clock in the evening and come through to Nahcotta with about seven to eight hundred people on board fourteen cars. They would get off all along the railway.

The railroad was really active from about 1887 until 1930 when the roads began to open up, and they got a ferry across the Columbia River, and cars began coming in.

In the old days, automobile drivers would bring their cars down from Portland to Astoria on the highway there and then transfer them across the Columbia river on the mail boat. And then we would pick them up and load them onto flat cars and bring them as far as Ilwaco and dump them off again.

Ilwaco was about half way down the line. When they first built the Nahcotta railroad, Ilwaco was the end of the line because it connected to the boats. Then about 1904 or 1905 they extended the road from Ilwaco on to Megler.

Mother was really the one, I guess, who was an inspiration to me. When I was night watching, I couldn't sleep at night. We would sleep in the daytime. We had to sit up all night with the engines and keep them warm. Every so often you had to get steam back up in the engines again because once they cooled, why then they were dead. So we kept steam up at night and I would sleep in the daytime, and I would have nightmares all the time.

I was going to quit and mother kept telling me, "No, keep on, keep on. You have to give them a thirty days notice and maybe something will change in that time." So I stayed with it, and it wasn't very long before I got a job firing. So everything turned out OK.

I don't know why I had nightmares. I guess I was worried about the engines losing their fire power. Sometimes I would just jump out of bed and run to the door and wake up.

It was really, really lonely at night in the roundhouse. And kind of spooky, too. You would hear these strange noises and things.

Every so often an engine would seem to settle on its springs, or something. There would be a loud crash and you would wonder what it was.

Longbeach was a big resort. And the Breakers Hotel was a very nice hotel. It would fill up with what we called white people. And then as time went on, the Jews got into Portland and they began to come to the Breakers. They took over everything and the white people just disintegrated and never came back again. Then Seaside came into prominence and the Jews all moved to Seaside, and then the Breakers Hotel went busted.

The people on the train were of the well-dressed type. They were mostly Portland men that would be coming in on Saturday night trains. Their families would come down here the first of June when school closed, and then stay all summer. They would camp out along the beach. The fathers would come in on Saturday nights and then on Sunday night we would run the "Papa Special." That was the train that would take them back out again to Portland.

The Seattle people didn't come down this way. Too far out. There were no roads, no way that they could get in here. There was no boat to Seattle. If you went to Seattle, you would have to go over to South Bend on the boat. That would be an all day trip to South Bend. And then from South Bend you would go to Seattle by train, which would take another day.

We saw very few hoboes because it was not on their regular route. They had to get on a railroad where they could keep on going. But when they got here, then they were stuck.

Ilwaco was quite a flourishing town around 1914. But when my mother came to this part of the country in 1883, there was only one house in Ilwaco. The town was known as Unity then but there was only one house in it. I'll be darned to know why it was called Unity.

My mother came to this country to take care of the lighthouse keeper's baby at Fort Canby. She came right direct from Denmark to Fort Canby, which was then known as Fort Hancock. That was 1883 and she was married in 1884 and moved to Bruceport from there. I don't know how she met my father. They met some way or other. It seemed like somebody made a match for them.

There were some other Danish people around. The lighthouse

keeper, Jacobs, I think was his name, he was Danish and he would get these girls from Denmark to come out and take care of his children as a governess or housekeeper.

Dad was involved in the oyster business when he came to this part of the country. By 1870 he was in business. When the old sailboats used to come in from San Francisco and pick up oysters at Tokeland, he used to ship oysters on those boats. He had a big crew of about fifteen Indians working for him. About every five days he would ship around two hundred fifty sacks of native oysters to California. The Indian men got two bits a bushel for them. You would need to have a pocketful of rocks, because every time an Indian would pick a bushel of oysters, he got a rock. And that meant two bits. When he cashed those rocks in, he would get two bits for each rock he had.

My father was only eleven years older than my mother. She was born in 1858 and he was born in 1847. When Dad came and was going to start in the oyster business, you couldn't buy any oyster land. I think they didn't even have to lease it. They just marked out a piece of ground and that was theirs. Then eventually we had to buy the land and he owned quite extensive oyster beds down at Bruceport. Then in later years he sold it out and moved up here to Ocean Park and Nahcotta so that we kids could go to school. Bruceport went to nothing then.

The native oysters, they petered out. In 1914 there was nothing in the oyster business. We had to do something else. In 1920 the hard times began to come and there was nothing to do here. So we started digging razor clams for the market. You could only dig about so many razor clams and then you would flood the market. Then you would be shut off. So we started a cannery to take care of our own clams. And then from there we took more clams and more clams, and then finally we bought a clam cannery down at North Cove that we broke, and moved up here. Built the cannery and got into business that way.

And then the eastern oysters came in here about that time. They got diseased and then finally they brought the Japanese oysters in. They just took over everything.

My two brothers moved the cannery from North Cove to Nahcotta while I worked on the railroad. They hired a man to go with them down there. My wages paid for his wages, so we weren't really out any money.

That is the way we got started. We started on nothing. We borrowed, I think, about five to six hundred dollars from mother to get started.

My father died in 1920.

When I was railroading, I would get three months off in the spring when the clam season was on and work in the clams. I did any clam work that came along. I would go out on the beach and buy clams. But I generally had to scald the clams. A scalder had a tank of boiling water and he would take a box of clams and dump them into this boiling water until the shells came off. Then he took them up and put them on a conveyor. Then there would be men standing on the sides to take the shells off. From there the clams went to the openers (who were white). We had at one time about forty-eight people that would clean clams.

Master Clams was our label, but if a wholesaler sent in an order for clams, maybe he would want them under his own label. They all came out of the same plot, but he got them under his own label.

I like to eat anything that comes along. Oysters are pretty good, but you can't eat too many of them. But you can go quite a few clams. They are tougher.

They are all good.

During the Depression a lot of people would exist on clams. We had plenty of clams. The beach used to be loaded with crabs, too, in those days, and you could go out and get a whole wagonload of crabs if you wanted them. Or a washtub full. Or whatever you wanted.

The crabs would be maybe eight to ten inches across the backs. They were really good ones. Big male crabs on the beach in what we called crab holes or pot holes. When the tide would go out, there would be a sand ridge on the outside of these pot holes and the crabs would settle down in there. And then you would wade through those pot holes with a rake or a shovel and pick up the crabs.

The Indians used to say, "When the tide is out, the table is set." We used to feel that way. I remember when I was a kid, we would go out to the beach early in the morning with bare feet, a swimming suit, and a rake and go out to the crab holes, especially on a foggy low tide. We would bring back crabs and a lot of clams, too.

Dad had a big garden. We had cattle and pigs and all that stuff, so we didn't fare too bad. The hard times didn't affect us too much.

The razor clams are going. There is something wrong someplace. They say that there is a disease that gets into them now. Of course, the weather has a lot to do with whether you get clams or not. If you get an east wind, you might as well stay at home. None of the clams will show. And a southwest wind, the clams will show. Northwest, they do fairly well.

I don't know why the clams don't like an east wind. You will have to ask them.

JACK WIEGARDT:
"OYSTERMAN PROPHET"
Nahcotta, WA
Born: 1930

Paradoxically, Washington, the state with probably the lowest per capita church attendance, is also a hotbed of religious experimentation. Recently J. Z. Knight of Tacoma gained international attention and great prosperity by "channeling" messages from an ancient warrior named Ramtha. In a different sphere, so to speak, Washington's Republican Party has recently become a fortress of evangelical Christians while New Age tides have been sweeping in from California.

Jack Wiegardt studied at Stanford University but he was as local as, well, a Willapa Bay oyster. In fact, he was a self-proclaimed "oysterman prophet," a guru of the integration of mind and being, of word and deed.

Jack grew up as a precocious lad in Ocean Park. Strained relations with his father led to an early tendency toward introspection. Jack's cousin Dobby recalls,

Jack would work all day with his father out in the garden, or whatever, and his father would never talk to him. He had a tough time growing up. I think that influenced my cousin's life, that he didn't feel close to his father.

Though the Wiegardts had long been oystering leaders, Jack's fresh oyster business failed in 1972, probably from too little attention to the bottom line and too much attention to philosophical fine lines. But that left Jack free to concentrate on metaphysical matters. Not so much about whether oysters have souls, but about whether the questions posed by their lives are answerable.

Jack began to grow oysters on long lines in Willapa Bay, a far better vantage point, he said, from which to study life than graduate school at the U-Dub had ever been.

Jack and I stood near a huge pile of sun-bleached oyster shells. I asked him if he thought that that tremendous bier of dead bivalves possessed ongoing life.

No. But if you look out in the bay at low tide, you are going to see live oysters. You will not be able to look into the future and see living oysters. You have the oysters that are relics of the past. But in the present there are living oysters. Life is going on as a response to ongoing conditions. Life is a present response: whether to man and his efforts to control the present and the future, or whether to God's drawing the present into being through the power of His love and desire to reveal Himself.

What is life? That is the essential message of this pile of corpses.

This New Age stuff is kinda rolling like a tide across the country. There are New Agers in every town. By thinking through things, you can think your way to a new level of being. It's everywhere.

There's a lot of refugees from California. One of the Ark Restaurant gals, Nanci Main, is from the Bay Area. We got to know Jimella Lucas when we had a community co-op when we closed down our oyster business. She was involved with the co-op then before she went up to Portland to chef for a restaurant there. Then she came back and associated with Nanci.

My grandfather was a sailor who came up here to Willapa Bay in the 1870s. My grandfather was in the native oyster business by the 1900s. Not long after that the natives went out of production and Eastern oysters were introduced to Willapa Bay. After World War I, my father and his brother got into the Eastern oyster business. That went gunny sack and left them in the clam canning and fish processing business until the Pacific oysters came in and they got into that.

My parents were brought up in the pioneer way. They didn't come here as seekers after truth. They were more involved in establishing a foothold in the country and working through the

Wiegardt's Clam Station, Ocean Park, Washington.

economic requirements of getting by. They were ambitious and saw the opportunities in the razor clams and the chub salmon. By the time the Pacific oysters came in, they had the experience to take advantage of the situation. My dad said once, "A lot of guys have been in the oyster business, but I doubt that many have taken out more money than we have."

They were hard-working, disciplined. Once when I was getting a fishing license renewed, there was an older guy sitting there. He heard them call my name when the license was ready and he introduced himself. He told me about how he had come down here in the middle '30s as a kid, just eighteen years old. The county dock used to run out here into the channel. He went out on the dock and there was a ramp and a big float where there was a guy loading stakes into a skiff. There were a bunch of guys standing around while this man did the loading all by himself. The kid went up and said, "Sure looks like you could use a hand." The loader turned out to be Uncle Fred, who soon offered him a job. That kid worked there for years and he told me that many people in the area had only been able to stick there because of our oyster jobs. He made a comment that stuck with me. He said, "The Wiegardts were always willing to give a job to anyone who was willing to work."

When I was a little boy, we went to the community Methodist church in Ocean Park. I was involved with ushering and taking up the collections, but Methodism was a pretty sterile ground as far as I was concerned. There wasn't much relevance as far as I could see with growing up. I happened to be a bright kid with an I.Q. of one hundred and eighty-six and I was kind of a misfit in school. They kicked me ahead two grades in grade school in Ocean Park. So when I got to high school, I was way behind the other kids physically and emotionally. There were a lot of problems with parents and their own hang-ups which I had to work through the best I could.

After high school I stayed out a year and still started Stanford in 1946 at sixteen, which is really too young to start that stuff. It really wasn't an easy way starting out, but I survived.

Actually I dropped out of Stanford when I had to declare a Philosophy major. About midyear I ran into this Emmanuel Kant thing. At that time I was really searching anyway and the emptiness became mind-blowing and shattering.

I came back here and worked in the oysters that spring and came over to Whitman College in the fall and turned out for football there. When football season was over and I was in a Philosophy class, the emptiness was back. I volunteered for Army Officer Candidate School.

After I had been in the Army and had finished Stanford in Philosophy and Sociology, I had started to challenge the Western university approach to life and reality. I had started Stanford in 1946 and I finally finished up in 1955. The New Age in California was on the horizon. The academic world there was sorta leading the way.

The leading sociologist on the West Coast was Dr. George Lundberg (1895–1966) and I went to study with him at the University of Washington. He was a real character. He was staffing the department with scientific people who would build up Sociology as science. He brought over Stuart Dodd (1900–1975) from Beirut. I used to say that, "There is no Dodd but Dodd and Lundberg is his prophet."

I was there from the fall of '55 to the middle of '57. No, I didn't get my M.A. The questions that I developed about the meaning of life were more meaningful than the academic work that the chairman wanted me to do. I got to the point where it was time to move on. I got back down here and got involved in 1960 in trying to develop a fresh oyster business. It later went Chapter 11, but after twenty years of struggle I paid the government off and I am now involved in oyster aquaculture.

Some years ago I started attending a Baptist church in Seaview, Washington. One thing about the Baptists, they believe in a lot of Bible study. It may be mediated by their own ideological propositions, but they do believe in an open Bible. So by the time that I got into the study of aquaculture, I had that Bible knowledge behind me. I could put those two together to see if there was any relation between oysters as living structures and the truths of Christ.

It seemed to me that there had to be some relationship between technology and the mind and meaning. If you look at the world and cities and the great works of man, and the way that man has taken over the environment, there has to be some explanation about what is going on that is relevant to the *process* of life. That is why I came down here. To find my answers by *doing* life.

An oyster is, of course, a low form of life. It's one of the early developments of evolution. The oyster grows its shell to protect itself. All it needs is a good supply of nutrients and a way to get rid of its waste materials so that it will grow to its genetic potential. As you try to culture oysters, you end up serving in life-serving ways.

Essentially, we are either here to destroy life on this planet or to work in a way that is going to see life continue. An integration of life with mind with understanding and meaning. That's where it is at.

In his classes Dr. Lundberg was wielding the crusading sword. He was welding the scientific method to Sociology. He was shooting down the theoretical approaches that others were taking.

He had a Swedish accent and he didn't like what he called "Huu-uuuuumanists." He'd say, "There is no such thing as a psyche, so how can you base a science upon that?" He chopped through any existing structures of meaning that I had. He really chopped through them all!

It was a very valuable experience. Where it began to come apart was when you've chopped away everything else and what you've got left is a scientific approach to life. What about the life that is supposed to be lived in the meantime? Where is the relevance and meaning?

Lundberg's life was a crusade but eventually I realized that it was not my crusade. Essentially, I was looking for answers relevant to a meaningful life. To incorporate the head with the heart, to live life in a meaningful way. . . . Any encounter with life is always meaningful. No matter how you do it. You can totally "fail" and it still will be a meaningful encounter.

But there ought to be some way to keep it on track.

The concrete question that we faced in developing this oyster system is the need for a provision for a nursery for the cultureless seed. It wasn't abstraction. It was a "real life situation" where I needed oyster seed from the standpoint of my business. It was all from my living context here rather than from some abstract kind of formula.

Walk out here on a nice clear morning and look over the staked oysters growing in clusters and rows and it looks just like those amber fields of grain that were celebrated in the song. It's a beautiful sight out here with the oysters doing so well and obviously enjoying the surroundings. So yeah, I enjoy participating with this. I am not a mystic. I just work hard and keep plugging away most of the time.

But my life has been redirected. Obviously, the academic world is hostile to the idea of the real presence of God on earth. Not in the pile of oyster shells but in the real oysters that are growing out there as a real witness of what is going on.

Let's say that you got something like this laid on you out of your experience. And all your academic training doesn't deal with this sort of thing and is essentially hostile to it. You are not going to start out as a crusader for what you have seen or heard without some very serious soul searching. I've done a lot of soul searching and have tried to reach out and contact others. Each contact that I've made has been a story in itself.

I was building this aquaculture system that held together masses of oysters in this population. Once you can see the underlying living process out in the oyster, you can see it in anything. All life is proceeding to build manifested channels of this energy, interchanging or converting it into living structure.

What is that binding force? Like the oyster shell, it is the manifestation of what held together the oyster.

What is the form? The form disappears or disintegrates until this pile of shells is only a memory where only a few of the elements are left. The drawing power of God is holding those materials together just as He manifests Himself in the channel or heavenly form of Jesus Christ.

An oyster is a living being. The husbandry or the stewardship of man has a directing role in the process. My aquaculture system is a form of organizing the lower level life into a form that is serving the higher level of life which is man.

I am serving as God to the oysters to the point that I desire them to produce for me as vassals to my will. But if you've worked out here in Nature where you have storms that come on without your willing it, then you find that your will is less than almighty. And you learn that oysters are not perfect servants to that will.

The process is humbling.[1]

---

[1]Jack Wiegardt committed suicide July 9, 1987, nine months after this interview. I was totally surprised and shocked by his death and by the news that he left a wife and six children.

HOD WOOD:
HIGHRIGGER
Hamilton, WA
Born: 1923

The North Carolina tarheels of Skagit County are famous for their music, moonshine, and logging. Hod Wood of Hamilton was a highrigger and a gyppo logger. A highrigger, or treetopper in the days before portable steel spars, was the foolhardy soul who spurred his way up a one-hundred-fifty-foot fir tree and transformed it into a giant post for a block and tackle through which steel cables would haul logs into a loading "landing" (or railroad siding).[1]

Climbing the tree, cutting its branches as you go, lopping the top (originally with an axe), and attaching the blocks, guylines, and other rigging—it sounds like a job description for a major insurance claim. The most dramatic of the many dangers was the uncertainty about what the falling treetop might do to you.

Hod Wood (pictured with his favorite hound Bo Bo) relaxed from highrigging by going after bears and mountain lions with guns, knives, and dogs. That's tarheel, too.

The funny thing is that this Carolina backwoodsman learned treetopping from "one of the finest old Indian guys you'd ever want to meet." Well, Bow Hill was after all almost an honorary tarheel, he worked with so many of them in the woods. (See the chapter about Bow Hill.)

Hod lost his treetopping career after Dave McIntyre (of Skagit Steel and Iron Works in Sedro Woolley) introduced the steel spar

---

[1]Oscar Wirkkala (1881–1959) invented the spar tree, overhead line (high lead) logging method in 1914. See page 257 about whistlepunk Roy Shetler.

tree in 1963. "He saved me!" says Hod gratefully, knowing that his luck was certain to have run out.

In 1977 Hod Wood became a gyppo, an independent logging contractor bidding for acreages of standing trees to sell as logs to a sawmill. Hod says that he had had a lot of good teachers in the woods about how to "get the logs out" but that it was a different story when the time came for him to negotiate contracts "with some of these Ph.D. people." He says that as a graduate of the eleventh grade, he used the "dog food method" of negotiating. He figured that he needed so many sacks of dog food for his hunting hounds. "We never discussed dollars," he says, "but more dog food."

Recently Hod sold his gyppo outfit. The cougars are feeling pretty sassy now that Hod is not on their trail much anymore. And, well, most of the big old growth spar trees were cut long ago anyway.

Does he miss highrigging's many thrills?

"Hell," he says, "I'd like to go back some day and rig one just for the heck of it!"

I've had some real tough times hunting for cougar. One time Pete Silvia and I were all day about eight or nine miles back in the mountains and we got three mountain lions. But the last one I shot out of a tree wasn't dead. I hollered at Pete to let one dog loose, but he let all the dogs loose. When they caught up with it, it was in a small tree. It fell out just as the dogs got there.

Then a dog had the cougar by the throat and I couldn't shoot. So I grabbed the cougar with my left arm and I shoved my knife in his rib cage. When I did that, he lunged at me. And the dog, still holding the cougar, hit me in the face.

As I fell back from the cougar down an incline, the cat kicked me in the right arm and ripped it open. And the blood was just pouring out. The cougar had died from the knife thrust but I was scared.

When Pete got up to me, he asked which dog was bleeding. I said, "Pete, it's not the dog. It's me! Get your shirt sleeve off and make a tourniquet."

He did and damn near twisted my arm off. He stopped most of the blood but we couldn't get it all stopped. I had to walk out in

Highrigger at work.
(Credit: Special
Collections Division,
University of
Washington Libraries)

the snow after dark. I was losing the feeling in all my toes. My fingers were numb but my arm didn't hurt too much until later. About twelve or one o'clock at night we got back to the truck. I was just about done in.

The next day I was all right except for a sore arm and a few bruises!

I've hunted in Idaho, Montana, British Columbia. I've been around a lot of cougar. I've been in it for years and years. It's bred in ya. Either you like it or not. My son, earlier on in life, used to go out with me. But he didn't quite take it up. It was bred out of him on his mother's side. He's like his mother. He likes to work all the time.

I realize you've got to work a little for necessities. I was a highrigger. That's where, before the steel towers came into operation, you had to climb those tall trees, and cut the limbs, and cut the tops off, and hang the guylines and your pulleys up in there to get the logs out of the woods.

There was one old Indian that always went up with me, Bow Hill. He lives over there at Bow Hill, over by Alger. At the Alger tavern, go in there and ask for Bow Hill.

You talk to him and you'll meet one of the finest old Indian guys you'd ever want to meet. One of the smartest men that ever logged. Skagit Indian. Tarheel.

He's worked with every Tarheel that ever came out here. He was one of the nicest guys you ever could log with. He could get more work out of a crew. He did it the easiest way. He was just an artist at communicating with people of all different lives. Buy him one beer and charge it to me.

He was the one that used to go with me to top the spar trees. When I was a young guy coming up, he was an older guy. He was the one that did all the thinking and I just watched him, more or less. He took care of me.

If there was a guyline to be moved or something, he would never tell me, but he'd walk down the hill and put it on the stump where it needed to be. We'd go and eat, and then I knew to go back and notch the stump and attach the guyline, see.

He was an old hooktender and a rigger. The hooktender is the boss of all the men out in the brush except the yarder operator and the log truck drivers. I hired on at an early age to hooktend, and I had old guys, old hands like him around. The ones who got in trouble were the ones that didn't pay attention to older guys like him.

You'll never meet a more remarkable man.

He taught me a lot of things. Since I had hired on at a young age, when things went bad I did a lot of cussing and throwing down my hat. Bow Hill came and said, "You don't want to do that no more. All you're doing is drawing their attention to you and the fact that you don't know what to do."

So that stopped me and made me realize that I should always stop and think and talk to Bow Hill.

You'd use half a two-man falling saw to cut the top off the tree. It was work! Sometimes you'd hit a knot and, man, it was tough sawing. Or maybe you'd bang the saw on a rock or while coming up, and it wasn't sharp.

I would be up in the tree about six or seven hours, with a lot of climbing to get up there. You've got to cut all the limbs off the tree as you go up. It would take about an hour to saw off the top. I done highrigging for years. There aren't too many of us left. It was real hard work. You had to have a weak mind and a strong back for that.

There's a number of dangers. One of the worst dangers is that one of the trees sways over while you're tied on it and it goes and splits. Here's the tree. You climb up to the top of the tree. Like more than three-quarters of the way up. I always measured around the tree with my arms. When I could touch my fingers, then I cut it off. I always like to have a lot of wood there at the top because when a tree was rigged with huge blocks and cables, the yarder could break the top off!

The only way to get those logs out of the woods is to pull them out. You can't talk them out. And making the spar tree is the first part of the job. You get up there and you think, "This tree is leaning in this direction and maybe the guylines will straighten it up. So you make an undercut here where you are going to cut off the top. Then you got to go on each side. When you cut on the back side, one lick might pop her off.

When the top goes, you want it to break clean and not split down. You have to be real cautious. A lot of times you have to be across from where you are cutting and when that top goes down, that tree bounces right back and you don't want to be hanging on the side there and get thrown out. You want to brace yourself so you go with the tree and not be dangling up there flopping.

I've had 'em kick back so much that if I had an ax on me, it popped right out and went aflying. A tree with a little go like that, they are worse than the ones that are straight.

The part that was cut off and falling was usually fifty to seventy-five feet long. Even more. And the bigger they were, the bigger the ride. The bigger the thrill.

I had to climb close to one hundred and twenty feet off the ground. I had climbing spurs and I'd have a rope around the tree. You have to carry a lot of gear. Your gear would just eat up your back, because you'd get sweaty and blistered and the blisters would break open. And the belt would rub your waist. And my legs would get raw sores from the spurs.

To get your rigging up to the top, you start out with a little ball of twine. I'd tie a loop on it and put it around my thumb so I wouldn't lose it. When I'd get to the top and want to bring up a cable, I'd throw that ball of twine down. The guy on the ground would send up a little bitty pencil rope—three-quarter-inch sea-grass rope. Then I pulled a block up with that and hung it on the top of the tree.

When the yarder came to rig up, they'd send up the cable, a three-eighth to one-half-inch wire rope. They called it a passline. And that went on the yarder and pulled all the rigging up. These guylines were very heavy one and three-eighths-inch steel cables. Sometimes as many as eight. They had to reach from the top of the tree out to anchoring stumps.

Sometimes spar trees were cut higher because the higher in the tree that that rigging was installed, the greater the lift for pulling logs up over stumps and brush to the landing. The rigger was instructed to cut off the top where the diameter was smaller. But that's when they had trouble. That's when you'd pull your spar tree over onto the guys who were working under it.

You just had so many days to work in the woods before being froze or snowed out. So I went for the most money, and treetop-ping was where the money was.

Oftentimes I'd get off of one crew truck and get on another and go top more trees and work Saturday and Sunday. I'd get twenty-five, thirty, forty dollars a tree. On a toughie, they'd get real generous and I'd get a hundred dollars for a tree.

But when the snow was coming down in another month, I didn't want to hear about logging. I wanted to be snowed out, so I could go bobcat and cougar hunting.

PHOEBE YEO: FLUMING LOGS TO THE COLUMBIA RIVER
Stevenson, WA
Born: 1898

Phoebe Yeo had not held a pickaroon for many decades when we paid a visit to the Northwest's last operating timber flume near Bingen, Washington. The Broughton mill was shipping cants (unfinished lumber) down its nine-mile-long flume to be transported on the Columbia River to a resaw mill in Oregon. It was so natural for Phoebe to stand at that wooden waterway with pickaroon in hand that I was afraid that she would apply for a job there and not get around to telling me the story of how she had helped her father and brother ship out cordwood.

I feel privileged now to have seen that flume, because it shut down forever shortly after our visit. Of course, many related activities had already passed into history long before I ever came along. Mills, scows, railroads, flumes, donkeys, and steamboats.

The temptation is to feel nostalgia for a Washington that we never knew personally. That's why Phoebe Yeo and her pickaroon are so important. She grew up with no electricity and no fuel for cooking or heating except wood. She, unlike today's kids, cut her own fuel with a two-man saw, the famed misery whip.

Although Phoebe Yeo, as a child, was relatively polite to her father when he pretended to goof off and drag his feet while sawing, the adult loggers' words defy any feelings of nascent nostalgia we may have now for that world. "I don't mind your riding on the saw," they would say, "but don't drag your goddamned feet."

When we began, I was nine and Bruce was eleven.

Do you know what a cordwood stick is? It's a piece of wood cut out of a fir log that is four foot long. Now a cord of wood is a pile of sticks that long and eight feet wide and four feet high. My brother Bruce and I handled those cordwood sticks that weighed more than we did. They were sawed out of logs eight feet long and then split into sticks. Sometimes those sticks were kinda big.

We put them in a boxcar, but before the railroad went through, Dad had flumed his cordwood down to the Columbia River, where it went onto sailing scows to The Dalles. The scows would hold five hundred to six hundred and fifty cords of woods. They were big and had a big mast in the center. One mast, but it had big, big sails that went clear across it. So when they went up the river, they always had to wait for the west wind to take them up to The Dalles, which was as far up the river as they could go. There was no canal or dam up there then.

When I was ten and Bruce was twelve we moved to Stevenson. Dad had his timber cut out for cordwood sticks then and we didn't have to handle the sticks except to keep them running in the water down to the river where the scow crew loaded them.

It meant a lot of running up and down the flume, as sometimes the sticks would jam up and we would have to break up the jams. Otherwise the men on the scow would have to leave the scow to see what had happened to the wood. So you see, we had a real important job.

We did not mind that work at all, even though sometimes we got soaking wet working out a jam when we were tending the flume.

We started at the flume over at Home Valley. It's gone now. It was from Colter's mill down to the river. When that mill was operating, it had cut the logs into cants, pieces of wood measuring eight-by-ten, ten-by-twelve, six-by-eight, and four-by-four inches. And they had flumed the cants down to scows on the river. Then took them across the river in a log boom with a little tug to the Cascade locks where there was a huge resaw mill. There they had cut those cants into all sizes of finished lumber.

After Colter's mill had cut all its timber and was gone, Dad used that flume to float his cordwood.

Oh, there were flumes all over this country. At Colter's mill they logged with steam donkeys, but at Porter's mill at Home Valley they used horses to pull the logs to the mill to be sawed into cants. They had a plank road from their mill down to the railroad. Although they didn't have a flume, they could have had one, because there was enough water, but they used the horses to draw the cants down to the river.

We cut our own firewood. Where we lived we had to have four stoves. We didn't sell the firewood to other people. We had to use it!

I helped my dad fall the trees for wood for the stoves. I was awfully strong in my arms and I could pull a crosscut saw as well as Bruce or my dad could. Oh, he used to have me pull on that old saw until I was blue in the face.

Often one person in a two-man crosscut saw team did not pull the way he should. I was always stronger than my brother Bruce. So Dad and I would be falling a four-foot tree with a crosscut saw. He would drag his feet just to kid me. Well, it wasn't funny to me. I'd flip the handle away and I'd say, "Go to hell. Do your own tree."

And he'd say, "Oh, honey, I was only fooling. Daddy won't do that anymore. Come on back and help Daddy fall the tree."

So I'd go on back and help Dad fall the tree. Then after it was down, Bruce and I sawed it into sixteen-inch wood for our heating stoves and cookstoves.

Dad did sell firewood to steamboats. And I don't know how many hundreds and hundreds of ties for the SP&S (Spokane, Portland & Seattle) railroad when it went through in 1908.

Bruce and I cut the firewood for our own use with our father. But when Dad was selling four-foot lengths of cordwood, he had woodcutters come and cut that and stack it in cords. The four-foot wood went down the flume. After the railroad went through and Dad was selling the wood to Spokane and Walla Walla, Bruce and I loaded it into the boxcars.

Dad hauled the wood with a team and wagon from the bottom of the flume to an empty boxcar. The big boxcars would hold twenty-two cords of wood. Dad and his helper would throw the wood off the wagon onto the platform. Bruce and I would carry it into the boxcar and stack it in there.

Some of these four-foot lengths were big and some were small. Some of those sticks came from trees that were four feet through. When they cut them into the four foot lengths and then into smaller pieces, sometimes there were knots where they couldn't make smaller pieces out of them. I know that Bruce and I sometimes handled sticks that weighed more than we did.

Bruce would carry one and I would carry one. Sometimes we'd have to double up and carry one stick in.

You'd go to the far end and start your load. A boxcar is forty foot long. You start at one end and you put in your row. You go as high as you can. You can't put a big stick up eight feet high, so you'd have to start another little pile to step up on.

Well, Dad and Jake would have to fill in way up high because Bruce and I could not reach. We were too small.

GLOSSARY

BANNOCK: biscuit dough fried in a frying pan.

BARBED WIRE TELEPHONES: battery-powered farm phones that used a single line of fence wire, grounded through the earth.

BARBER CHAIR: a stump which has split while being cut, leaving a piece of wood standing up.

BEER: a fermented mash used to make moonshine.

BINDLE: a bundle carrying a wanderer's possessions.

BLINDS: the platform immediately behind a train engine's tender.

BOAT PULLER: a man on shore who pulled his Columbia River gillnetter upstream with a rope on windless days.

BOONDOG: to drift down a river while fishing.

BOW AND ARROW HORSE: a mustang or Indian pony.

BRAIL: to hoist fish out of a fish trap with a net.

BULL BLOCK: a large wide-throated pulley for yarding logs.

CAMP IRONS: homemade andirons used as a platform for campfire pots.

CANT HOOK: a sturdy lever with a blunt end and a movable hook used in logging.

CAT FACE: a tree with burnt-in black spots.

CAULKS: spike-soled logging boots (pronounced "corks").

CAYUSE: a mustang or Indian pony.

CLEARCUT: a forest area in which all the trees have been removed.

CUTTYHUNK LINE: a braided cotton fishing line made in Japan.

DALLY: to wind the rope around the saddle horn before roping an animal.

DOG: a metal hook for holding a log.

DRY SQUAD: a popular term for revenuers during Prohibition.

FALL: to cut down trees.

FISH TRAP: a pilings and net device for catching migrating fish.

FLUME: a water-filled chute used for transporting wood or water.

FOOTBURNER PLOUGH: a simple plough guided by a person on foot and pulled by horses.

FOUR-HORSE SPRING TOOTH: a horse-pulled harrow with flexible, curved teeth.

GARLIC GULCH: the Rainier Valley multi-ethnic neighborhood of south Seattle.

GEODUCK: (pronounced, "gooeyduck") a large bivalve (Hiatellidae) averaging two or three pounds and weighing as much as sixteen pounds, much prized for chowders along the Northwest coast. Geoducks are distinguished by their long necks or siphons and by reportedly living, if lucky, to over one hundred years old. In recent years vast beds of them have been discovered in Puget Sound, thus leading to a new crime, geoduck rustling.

GILLNETTER: a fishing boat equipped with a vertically suspended mesh net that entraps the heads of fish.

GRUBHOE: a heavy hoe.

GRUBSTAKE: a loan or gift to finance a prospecting trip or other enterprise.

HACKAMORE: a halter used especially for breaking horses.

HARDY: a blacksmith's chisel with a square shank that fits into a hole in the anvil.

HEADBOAT: the boat that controls all the water operations of a horse-powered fishing seine or horse seine.

HOOF RASP: a hand file for grinding down and shaping a horse's hoof.

JACKPOT: a large logjam on a stream; a difficult situation.

JAMMER: a mechanical hoist for loading logs.

KLOOTCHMAN: Chinook jargon for woman.

KONKY: rotten (as in a konky log).

LATIGO: a strap for tightening and fastening a saddle cinch.

MACKINAW: a heavy wool coat.

MALONE PANTS: heavy wool pants.

MERCANTILE: general store.

MOLLY HOGAN: a knot in a logger's steel cable.

OYSTER MONEY: A Depression-era scrip used in Raymond, Washington.

PEAVEY: a lever similar to the cant hook except for its sharp spike on the end.

PLACER MINING: mining by washing sand and gravel for minerals.

PIKE POLE: used by river pigs for handling floating logs.

PULASKI: a single-bit axe with an adze-shaped grubhoe; named for its inventor, Edward Pulaski.

PURSE SEINE: a weighted net which closes on the bottom, entrapping a school of fish.

REVENOOER: a revenue officer, especially one who searched for illegal liquor during Prohibition.

RIVER PIG: a lumberjack who controls the logs as they float downriver to the sawmill.

ROD: the metal framework beneath a railway car.

SACK: to patrol a stream for stray logs at the end of a log drive.

SALTCHUCK: salt water.

SARVICEBERRY: juneberry or serviceberry (genus *Amelanchier*).

SCHOOLMARM: a tree with a fork.

SCOW: a large, flat-bottomed transport boat.

SET CHOKER: to attach a noose-like wire rope to a log so that it can be skidded.

SHINGLE WEAVERS: men who assembled and bound bundles of shingles at a shingle mill.

SHOTY: tool for cutting hot steel.

SIWASH: a derogatory term for an Indian.

SKAG: cormorant.

SKID: to drag a log from its stump; a skidder is a log-moving tractor.

SKIDROAD: a haulway for skidding cut logs out of the woods. By extension, skid row became known as a part of town inhabited by the down and out (historically, such as unemployed loggers).

SKINNER: an animal driver.

SLUE: to turn or twist something around.

SLUICE BOX: a box for washing minerals out of sand and gravel (see placer mining).

SNITCH: to knot; a snitch is a woven knot.

SOAK: to pawn something.

SOUGAN: a logger's cotton-filled comforter.

SPEEDER: a small vehicle used on logging railroads.

SPILLER: a fish trap's business end, from which trapped fish are brailed onto a scow.

SPORTING WOMAN: a prostitute.

SQUAWMAN: a white man with one or more Indian paramours.

STAKE HAPPY: a miner's sudden desire to take his earnings and bolt for town from the backcountry.

STEAM DONKEY: a movable steam engine used for skidding logs by cable.

STEAMBOAT PROW ("THE PROW"): a volcanic formation at 9,600 feet on Mount Rainier.

STRAWBERRY: fish bait made of salmon eggs in a tiny cheesecloth bag.

STUMP RANCH: a roughly-cleared homestead where the stumps of the primeval forest still dot the acreage.

SWAMP: to cut limbs off felled trees in preparation for skidding.

SWEDISH FIDDLE: two-man "misery whip" saw for felling large trees.

TAMARACK: the larch (genus *Larix*).

THRASHER: a migrant worker who threshes grain.

TIE HACKER: a woodsman who makes and hauls railroad ties from standing timber.

TIMBER CRUISER: a forester who estimates types and quantities of trees in a given area.

TINHORN: a boastful gambler with little money.

TOTE ROAD: a lumber camp's supply road.

TRAPPER NELSON: a Yukon pack frame, originally made from a washboard.

TURKEY BELL: a small bell used by steelhead fishermen as an alarm when a fish strikes.

WANIGAN: the company store in a logging camp.

WHISTLEPUNK: a logging crewman who, with a jerkline, signals the steam donkey engineer as to how the machine's cables should be deployed.

WOBBLIES: International Workers of the World, a radical labor union of lumber industry men.

INDEX

ABOUT THE AUTHOR

Ron Strickland is portraying America through the voices of its citizens in a series of regional self-portraits. For more than a dozen years he has been traveling back roads and byways in search of the "real America." After receiving his Ph.D. from Georgetown University in 1976 Dr. Strickland set out to create an 1100-mile foot and horse trail from Glacier National Park in Montana to the Pacific Ocean. An oral history book called *River Pigs And Cayuses* (1984) grew out of his encounters along the Pacific Northwest Trail. Subsequent interviewing tours in New England, the Southwest, and California finally led him back to his home state of Washington for another look at Northwest lore and lifestyles.

Ron Strickland is currently at work on an oral history portrait of *Alaskans.* He lives in Seattle.